Break Up.
Break In.
Breakthrough!

A Formula to Dramatically Change

Your Career Trajectory

JENNIFER LANDIS

For more information, email inquiry@jennlandis.com

ISBN: 979-8-89694-235-1 - eBook
ISBN: 979-8-89694-236-8 - Paperback
ISBN: 979-8-89694-237-5 - Hardcover

Please Note:

- Names of individuals mentioned in the stories told throughout the book have been changed to respect privacy.

- Generative AI tools are discussed throughout the book and encouraged for efficiency but reader discretion is strongly advised. Responsible use of AI tools is the sole responsibility of the reader. Readers are cautioned not to share information online that is not fully theirs to share. The author takes no responsibility for readers' actions.

Discover Your Personalized Breakthrough Formula!

This free tool leads you through an exercise based on Jenn's three-step Breakthrough Formula. You will receive a report that shares your personalized breakthrough formula and a guide to the content of this book that is tailored specifically to your interests and desires.

JennLandis.com/book

Here's how it works:

1) Go to www.jennlandis.com/book (or scan the QR code) and click on The Breakthrough Formula Generator.

2) Respond to the prompts. It should take you about 10 minutes to complete.

3) The generator will calculate your personalized report.

4) Use the report to guide you to the most relevant content within the book.

5) Connect with Jenn on social media to join The Breakthrough Formula community, share your wins, and receive ongoing motivation and support.

Want to work directly with Jenn?
She would love to visit with you!
Jenn offers individual and group coaching,
keynotes, and workshops.

See her speaker's reel and coaching packages by visiting
www.jennlandis.com

Social Media:
LinkedIn.com/jennlandis or on
or on Instagram, X.com, Facebook,
and YouTube: @AskJennLandis

Dedication

To James: Thank you for reminding me I'm strong and can do anything. I'm so grateful for your love and partnership.

To Melissa: Thank you for believing in me and quoting me to myself. You are the best Chief Extraction Officer!

To Mom and Dad: Thank you for listening to random thoughts, unfinished chapters, and wild ideas and supporting ALL of them. You encouraged us to chase our dreams, showed us how to work hard to achieve them, and taught us to believe in, accept, and serve a God who loves us. I wish everyone had parents like you.

To my mentors: Thank you for sharing your time, wisdom, and experience. The lessons you taught me will inspire, guide, and help countless others as your advice and counsel shine through the stories in this book (even when I didn't do the best job executing your advice!).

To the fabulous, strong women in my community: You continually inspire me, challenge me, encourage me, hold me accountable, and cheer me on. I love the world-changing journey we are on together. Here's to breaking up, breaking in, and *breaking through*!

Contents

Section 1
Foundation

<u>Chapters in this section:</u>

1. Walmart to Wall Street
2. The Breakthrough Formula
3. Ignite Your "What" and "Why"

Chapter 1

From Walmart to Wall Street

I'll never forget my first significant breakthrough moment. I was walking down an unfamiliar hallway. The smell of burnt coffee hung in the air, and the sound of a hundred keyboards competed for attention with my pounding heart.

'I did it', I thought to myself. 'It actually happened! I can't believe it! Am I dreaming?'

The job offer I had just received stunned me. I was being hired as a full-time trainer, a job I didn't think existed just a few weeks prior. At the time, I was working three jobs to make ends meet: I was a full-time loan processor making just above minimum wage, I was a part-time stocker at Walmart in the women's clothing section, and I was a part-time computer trainer at a community training center—which was my "fun" job and paid the best by far.

I didn't think there were full-time jobs for computer trainers with no degrees or experience like me. It was a hobby that I got paid for at the community training center, where I just had to know a bit more than those I taught. When I found out it was an actual full-time job with a premier local employer and that I had been recommended for it by my supervisor at the community center, I didn't think there was a remote chance that I'd actually get the job. But here I was!

The offer I had just received was for more money than I thought I'd ever make. It was over *twice* what my three other jobs *combined* were paying me. I'd be able to quit my other jobs—and work full-time in a job that I would probably have done for free.

I fully expected to pinch myself and wake up disappointed that it wasn't real.

'Almost there,' I thought, 'just hold it together a bit longer.' I focused on my breathing and struggled to gather my scrambled thoughts.

As I approached the end of the hallway, I saw the late afternoon sun casting light on the entryway carpet through the glass exit doors. I stopped beside the exit, schooled my features, and turned with a smile as I extended my sweat-dampened hand to my new boss.

"It was such a pleasure meeting with you today. Thank you for offering me the job. I can't wait to get started."

She responded with a smile of her own and a firm handshake.

I reached for the door and stepped out, my gaze searching for our car—an old silver Ford Taurus. My husband, James, drove me to the meeting and waited patiently for me.

As I scanned the parking lot, I saw his head snap up. His eyes met mine in the rearview mirror, and our gazes locked. His eyes were assessing and curious. Mine were alight with excitement.

As I walked to the car, I could no longer contain myself. I gave him a huge smile as relief, gratitude, and pure joy showed on my face. I did an awkward happy dance visible only to him as I tried to walk calmly to the car in case my new manager was watching from the window. I reached the car and slid into the passenger seat. I turned to James with the biggest smile of my life. "I got the job!"

That day I learned what it felt like to achieve a fist-pumping, adrenaline-flooding breakthrough moment. That job offer and the experiences that followed changed our lives and the trajectory of our future. I didn't know it at the time, but that job put me on a path of discovery that would become my life's calling—a calling to support others and cheer them on as they surpassed their expectations and achieved new levels of success—a calling to help others that would one day carry me from Walmart to the bell ringing ceremony at the New York Stock Exchange as a C-Suite member of a $4.5 billion publicly traded company.

The day of my job offer was my first significant breakthrough moment, and it led to many more. That day, I began a journey that would teach me all about breakthroughs. I learned to understand them, create them, and harness them. I'll share what I've learned with you so you can achieve your own string of breakthrough moments.

What is a Breakthrough?

Let's begin the journey toward your next career breakthrough by first establishing a working definition. Breakthrough moments aren't something you stumble into. They are transformative moments of career advancement fueled by purpose and achieved through dedicated effort.

Breakthroughs have four distinct attributes. They are pursued, pivotal, pinnacle, and precious. Here's a brief explanation of each attribute.

1) **Pursued**: Breakthroughs begin with a compelling vision that spurs you into action with intentional and sustained effort.

2) **Pivotal**: Pursuing a breakthrough causes you to change in ways that forever shift your perspective and reveal potential futures you didn't know existed.

3) **Pinnacle**: Breakthrough moments are mountaintop experiences of triumph. They are invigorating and inspiring, giving you an unobstructed view of what might be possible.

4) **Precious**: Breakthroughs are rare, treasured, and unforgettable. They are life-altering experiences made possible through your personal growth and the support of those around you.

I can't wait for you to experience the wide range of emotions, experiences, and successes that come from achieving career breakthroughs. My career journey can be mapped by simply looking at my breakthrough moments. I'll share several of those moments with you as we navigate your career breakthrough in this book.

Before we dive into the structure of the book and what you can expect from it, please allow me to introduce myself. I'll serve as your guide, mentor, and breakthrough coach. If you'd like to get to know me better, let's connect on social media. I can be found on LinkedIn at www.linkedin.com/in/jennlandis and on Instagram and YouTube at @ AskJennLandis.

Fabulous and Fumbling

Hi. I'm Jenn. I've spent my career experimenting with and learning to harness the power of career breakthroughs, which has led to many fabulous and fumbling moments. I've learned from incredible mentors, coaches, and sponsors, and also from the school of hard knocks. The road hasn't been easy or smooth, but it has been interesting! My career philosophy involves aggressive collaboration with others in an attempt to slingshot others forward to help them succeed. I believe success is a team sport.

To better understand my roots and motivations, let me rewind a bit and share a little about myself and my journey.

- I'm from a solidly middle-class family that has a unique mix of Italian and Hispanic heritage. I'm the oldest of five children.

- My mom was an elementary school teacher, and my dad was a manufacturing executive, turned commercial contractor.
- I was raised in church and have held onto my faith. I spent two years after high school serving in a Christian version of the Peace Corps before joining the workforce as a clerk in a cable company.
- I began my career working three entry-level jobs to make ends meet. One of them was at Walmart in the women's clothing department.
- I put myself through two college degrees (BS in Business and MS in Global HR Development) while working more than full-time.
- I didn't have C-Suite ambitions until a mentor encouraged me to consider that path, and I signed up for the rocky road of development that it required.
- I eventually made it to the C-Suite as the Senior Vice President and Chief HR Officer for a $4.5 billion dollar publicly traded energy company. I was the youngest and only female member of the senior executive team at that time. I proudly served in that capacity for six years.
- I've coached leaders at all levels for twenty-five years—from high-potential future leaders to C-Suite executives, individually and through strategic leadership development programs.
- In 2023, I pivoted out of corporate life and began pursuing my dream and mission to help you overcome the obstacles that are holding you back from achieving your dream career.
- Today, I spend my time as a leadership strategist, keynote speaker, author, and coach who provides breakthrough solutions to individuals, communities, and organizations.

I am a testament to the power of breakthroughs. If I can do it, so can you! I've mentored, coached, and cheered countless leaders as they achieved breakthrough moments that created greater income, impact, and joy at work. Let me introduce you to a few of them:

- Melanie overcame political adversity at work, was nominated and awarded her company's highest leadership award and landed her first VP position.
- Jimmy learned to believe in himself and stopped self-sabotaging—finally accepting that the fantastic opportunities offered to him came because he earned them.
- Julie found the courage to go for it and got her dream job in the C-Suite when she thought it would never happen.
- Talia is on the rise and has made the courageous decision to make a bid for CEO. I know she will get there.

So, what about you? Will this book help you achieve your career breakthroughs? Let's find out.

Is This Book For You?

This book was written to help rising leaders who are hard-chargers, high-achievers, and relentless learners—and for those who mentor them. If any of the statements below resonate with you, this book is for you:

- You are frustrated by a lack of professional and/or career growth and can't seem to unlock your next level of success.
- You are hungry for your promotion, an executive role, or perhaps you want to break into a new industry or profession.
- You like process frameworks that contain practical strategies, tools, tips, and techniques.

- You want shortcuts to success that lean heavily on your strengths and leverage creative problem-solving.
- You are willing to work hard, dig deep, accept feedback, and keep going when setbacks happen.
- You want greater levels of impact, income, and joy at work.
- You learn through storytelling and are willing to engage in inner reflection and self-assessment.
- You are ready to move from stuck to unstoppable and have made a *commitment* to attain your next breakthrough and the new level of leadership success it requires.

A note for mentors: If you are short on time but want a ready-made program to help you mentor others, this book is also for you. Instead of creating or purchasing another mentoring program, you can use The Breakthrough Formula Generator, and the activities in this book to guide your discussions and work with your mentees. Just replace my stories and experiences with yours. We need more mentors who are willing to invest their time, energy, and knowledge in others. I hope this book helps you do so more efficiently.

If you are still reading, chances are good that this book will help you. So, let's take a brief look at what you can expect from your breakthrough journey.

Snapshot of the Breakthrough Formula

The next chapter covers the Breakthrough Formula in depth, but I want to give you a quick snapshot of what to expect from your personal breakthrough journey. Together, we will take stock, commit to the journey, build a custom plan, and get to work.

Take Stock

The first item of business is to get real and take stock. You can't achieve your goals if you are cloudy about what you want, where you are now, and what it will take to bridge the gap. So, we're going to examine your thoughts, behaviors, habits, relationships, and commitments in relation to your breakthrough goals and career aspirations.

Commit to the Journey

Based on your insights, you will determine what you need to "break up" with and what you need to "break in" to achieve your breakthrough. Your reflections will be supported by The Breakthrough Formula Generator that is discussed later in this chapter.

Build a Custom Plan

Once you know what you want relative to where you are today, we'll turn your personalized formula report into an action plan using my straightforward three-step Breakthrough Formula:

Strategize + Energize + Mobilize = Your Breakthrough

You will Strategize by performing four PLAN actions, then you will Energize by performing four FUEL actions, and finally, you will Mobilize by performing four MOVE actions. When you've done all three and done them well, you will be primed and ready for your breakthrough moment.

Get to Work

All that's left to do is the work. You *can* overcome your career challenges and *achieve* breakthroughs.

I can't wait to help you succeed. Wildly. Beyond your current belief in yourself. Beyond the limitations you may feel from others. You will create a string of wins and breakthroughs that unlock opportunities and create a career of deeper meaning and impact. So, roll up your sleeves. It's time to get to work. Our first stop is orienting you to how this book is structured and how you can use it most effectively.

How the Book is Structured

I've organized this book to give you a front-row seat to years of coaching sessions and lessons I've learned and shared with countless leaders just like you—from top executives to front-line leaders to those who aspire to be leaders in the future.

I've tried to make this book conversational, engaging, and informal, just as if you were sitting across from me in a coffee shop as we map out a personalized strategy to help you quickly achieve your next breakthrough. To do that, we will follow the three steps in the Breakthrough Formula, which is how the book is structured. Here are the major sections in the book and what they contain.

- *Section 1: Foundation* provides an overview of the complete Breakthrough Formula and focuses on identifying your motivations, or "spark."
- *Section 2: Strategize* helps you clarify your unique characteristics and development gaps, identify opportunities where you can leverage them to create value for your organization, map out an action plan, and then locate sponsors to support your efforts.
- *Section 3: Energize* focuses on your mindset and rallying a team of supporters to engage with you.

- *Section 4: Mobilize* is all about execution, feedback, and verifying that you are getting the results you need and actually positioning yourself for career advancement.

Starting in chapter 3, each chapter begins with an installment of a story about a pivotal time of growth and learning in my career. The story starts with the job I accepted at the beginning of the book and ends with a call that led to my eventual C-suite opportunity. The evolving story shares my successes and failures, with all the twists, turns, ups and downs of a true story.

The opening story installment is followed by the lessons I learned and a series of related exercises, reflection questions, tactics, and implementation ideas you can adopt. When taken as a whole, the Breakthrough Formula steps and their underlying action plans will guide your efforts as you build your career and achieve breakthroughs.

Recommendation for Engaging with the Content

To support your efforts and to make your time and investment in this book worthwhile, here is my suggestion for getting the most out of the book:

1) Create your Personalized Breakthrough Formula by using The Breakthrough Formula Generator at www.jennlandis.com/book.

2) Consider inviting friends to join you on the journey. Your journey through the book will be different from theirs, but having support and companionship can be a game-changer when you are working to advance your career.

3) With your Personalized Breakthrough Formula report in hand, return here and begin your journey by reading chapters 2 and 3. They provide foundational information to help you better understand the chapters that follow.

4) Continue by reading the story installment at the beginning of each chapter. The story unfolds and builds chapter by chapter. You don't want to miss any of the installments. Each installment illustrates the points made in that chapter, so it also serves as a preview of the content covered in the chapter.

5) Consult your Personalized Breakthrough Formula as you work through the book. If the chapter is recommended, dig deeper into the chapter to look for strategies, tips, tools, and actions to add to your personalized formula. Consider whether you should apply a strength, lean into growing a new skill, or take a shortcut by finding a hack to bypass it. The end-of-chapter summary provides additional implementation ideas you can incorporate into your formula.

6) Share your journey with me via social media. I'd love to encourage you along the way. I can be found on most social platforms as @askjennlandis.

Ok. It's time to accelerate your breakthrough journey. In the next chapter, we'll dive into the three-part Breakthrough Formula. The chapter will introduce you to the formula steps and their supporting PLAN, FUEL, and MOVE actions. I'll explain why you need all three steps of the formula to achieve your breakthrough. I'll also introduce you to three fictional leaders who are facing challenges in achieving breakthroughs. Let's start with the story of how the Breakthrough Formula came to be.

Chapter 2

The Breakthrough Formula

I sat in my office staring at my computer screen as two of my professional friends talked about their personal mission statements and the three verbs that define them. As I sat quietly listening to my friends' discussion, I started thinking about how my conversations with these two women always make me feel a bit out of my depth—in the best way possible.

I sincerely enjoy the conversations and the exercise my brain gets when we talk about intriguing things or attempt to analyze or describe things we are seeing and experiencing in our professional work. I could listen to them talk for hours. I always walk away from our casual visits thinking more deeply, and often meditate on our conversations for days after our chats.

"So, Jenn. What are the three verbs that best describe you and the way you show up professionally?"

I was startled when I heard Malorie say my name.

Uhhhhh. I stared at the screen, dumbfounded. I had no idea how to respond.

My friend Malorie is sneaky that way. She has a supreme talent for seeing straight to the heart of an issue and then whops you with a profound question that seems innocuous. I always walk away from our interactions, shaking my head and wondering what just happened. I deeply respect her, and I never want to feel like I've given less than my best during our interactions. She is like that teacher you had in school whom you loved and didn't want to disappoint. Malorie is a Ph.D., executive coach, strategist, ocean swimmer, mom, incredible cook, and all-around amazing woman.

I answered quickly and immediately knew what I said was wrong... or perhaps, just not fully accurate. Malorie didn't correct me; she just gave me 'the look.' I don't think she even realized she did so, but I felt it and knew I needed to do better.

It took me three weeks and pages of journaling to process, consider, discard, and eventually settle on my three verbs. What were they? The answer is: Strategize, energize, and mobilize. Before I tell you more about my three action verbs, here's what you can expect to get from this chapter.

Our Goals:

In this chapter, we will take a quick tour of the Breakthrough Formula. We'll walk through the three main steps, how they work together, and how you can best think about and leverage them as you begin your breakthrough journey. Here are our goals:

1) Take a tour of the three Breakthrough Formula steps to understand how each works separately and together. I'll also introduce the action plan components associated with each step.

2) Discuss why all three steps are essential and what happens when one step is missing.

3) Meet three talented fictional leaders who are struggling to achieve breakthrough promotions. These three leaders will journey with us through the pages of the book.

We have much to cover in this chapter, so let's get started!

Introduction to the Breakthrough Formula

Through the process of deep thinking and journaling, I realized that my entire career has been built on my ability to: 1) recognize unmet needs within my organization and their implications if they remain unresolved, 2) develop a plan to address them in a way that also pushes me to grow in new ways, 3) energize the people around me to catch the vision and contribute to the solution, and 4) leverage that momentum to build teams that execute the ideas and deliver value to the organization. Every opportunity I can recall over the last 25 years has these three markers: Strategize. Energize. Mobilize.

I further analyzed my coaching interactions with others, the growth plans I've written, the leadership development courses I've designed, and even how I evaluate proposals as an executive, sponsor, committee member, and board member. I again found the three markers everywhere. I think, advise, assess opportunities and performance, and am innately pulled toward the Breakthrough Formula anytime I need to solve a problem, write a keynote, coach a client, or sell my husband on a big purchase I want to make. It's in my DNA.

In essence, the Breakthrough Formula is a way of organizing information, building support, and planning action that leads to execution. The beauty of the Breakthrough Formula is that it is versatile, scalable, and straightforward. It can be used as a mental model to perform a quick evaluation in seconds, or it can be used to build a detailed multi-layered action plan. The degree of simplicity or complexity ratchets up or down based on your application and need. You can apply it to projects for just yourself, a team of people, or an organization. And it has *worked*. So, as I share my formula with you, I offer it up as something you can adopt or incorporate into the tools you are already using.

The Three Steps of the Breakthrough Formula: Strategize, Energize, and Mobilize

1) Strategize

In the context of your personal and professional performance, I think of the verb strategize as the process by which you identify opportunities that work together to create value and growth for yourself and your organization. This holistic approach creates a win/win scenario for you and your organization.

Once you learn to look for them, win/win opportunities are everywhere and represent incredible possibilities for value creation. Let me share how this approach played out for me following the job opportunity I received in the opening story of this book.

I was hired as the sole technical trainer in the IT department of an energy utility company. I knew my work was important, but was also considered an expense that could easily be cut if times were hard. I wanted to be seen as integral to the success of my department and company—not as expendable because I provided an "optional" service. So, I instinctively began closely aligning my work with the organization's highest priorities to ensure I wouldn't miss the bus and be left behind. I studied what was happening in the business, in the industry (even when I didn't fully understand it), and what was happening in my department (IT) and profession (training) that would provide opportunities to create value. I constantly asked myself and others where the business was headed and what it would need next. This helped me attach my efforts so tightly to the organization's needs that I couldn't help but create value.

Relentlessly chasing value is also how I led my training department in a healthcare organization off the chopping block when budgets got tight. It's how I landed major project assignments during business acquisitions that provided opportunities to build a brand as someone who could deliver and lead others. It's how I built trust, gained influence, and earned sponsorships that created opportunities to lead several company-wide culture change initiatives. Creating a string of value-creating successes gave my managers and sponsors confidence that I could succeed in first-time situations. And that led to new opportunities.

In all of these cases, I didn't wave my hands and plead for attention. I got to work by first getting good at spotting organizational needs and figuring out how to fill them. I had faith that the right people would notice my work and reward it. Then, I built up my skill sets to support the knowledge, skills, and abilities I needed to be prepared to act on the organization's needs when I found them. And it worked.

I never had to ask for opportunities, increases in pay, or special work assignments—but I got all of them because of the credibility I built from doing good work and closing organizational gaps that created value for the business. If you haven't yet developed a sensitivity to spotting organizational needs, I encourage you to do so. It is a powerful tool that will serve you in almost every situation.

2) Energize

In the Energize step of the Breakthrough Formula, we need to build energy and momentum to carry ourselves out of thinking and planning and into execution. We also need to energize those around us who may be interested in participating or perhaps impacted by the breakthrough plan we are working to achieve.

The act of energizing others often gets a bad reputation. It can be viewed as party-planning, cheerleading, and fluffy stuff. If we are energizing ourselves or others without grounding our activities in actions that move us toward execution, we deserve this kind of criticism. When done correctly, the Energize step creates a necessary bridge between planning and action that connects us deeply and authentically to our mission and community.

Further, it provides emotional fuel that pushes us and our teams into action. The Energize step depends heavily on our ability to lead ourselves. If we aren't able to produce fuel for our plans, we can't expect others to do so. Yet, accomplishing any project requires a community of supporters to promote, engage with, and aid our efforts, whether directly or indirectly. Energizing well is an art form. Without it, plans can stall, energy fades, attention wanes, and we lose the momentum and motivation to sustain us during the execution phase.

3) Mobilize

The word "mobilize" is often used to describe a state of readiness for action, and that's exactly what we're going to do. Once we've energized ourselves and our community to build momentum, we must move quickly into action to accumulate small wins to begin turning our plans into reality. James and I learned that lesson twenty years ago while listening to Dave Ramsey's radio talk show, and it's a lesson that has stayed with me.

When you quickly capture a win, you can leverage the momentum of that win to tackle something a bit larger. When starting something unfamiliar— something that could be overwhelming or that you fear will fail—start small and accumulate wins. Nothing proves your fears wrong faster than evidence you can succeed!

Assessing Your Progress

Once you've completed all three Breakthrough Formula steps, I will ask you to evaluate if you've achieved your breakthrough. If not, we'll take stock and determine if you need to cycle through any of the steps again based on your circumstances and outcome.

When you can confidently say you've accomplished your plan and achieved your breakthrough, you will move on to your next opportunity and start the process over again. Over time, you will experience a string of breakthrough successes and repeatedly attain new levels of leadership and greater impact, income, and joy.

S + E + M: The Need for All Three

Now that we've looked at the three Breakthrough Formula steps, let's discuss why all three are essential to achieve your next breakthrough. If you take only one or two of the three steps, you will likely become frustrated, and your results will not be achieved, or you will underperform and not meet your expectations. Given the amount of work that goes into any goal pursuit, you want maximum performance in exchange for your time, effort, and sacrifice!

I learn most efficiently from examples of failure rather than success. So, let's walk through six examples showing why all three steps are essential and what happens when one or two are missing from the equation.

There are two traps people fall into. The first trap is over-emphasizing one of the three steps. We can think of this as *one-hit wonders*. The second trap is the trap of settling for *limited success*. Limited success often occurs when two of the three Breakthrough Formula steps are taken, and you enjoy some level of success but fall short of achieving the breakthrough success you could have if all three were present and executed well.

The prevalence of these patterns can vary based on an organization's culture (e.g., passive-aggressive versus direct), industry (e.g., engineering firm versus marketing firm), type of work (e.g., computer programmer versus client relations manager), and an individual's personality or work style. Let's explore both patterns: One-hit wonders and limited success.

One-Hit Wonders

When one of the Breakthrough Formula steps is present, but the other two are missing, classic patterns emerge that we've all experienced and seen. It's rare for someone to exhibit only one of the three steps. When it does occur, it is usually during times of stress and extreme pressure.

The 'Over-Thinker' Pattern:
When Strategize is present but Energize and Mobilize are missing.

I've led projects that were so mired in detailed and elaborate project plans that they never got off the ground. In one such situation, a team I inherited had struggled for two years to implement an online training system. When I asked for the project plan, they told me it was over 100 pages long and they didn't have it with them. This is a classic example of the 'over-thinker' pattern. The project didn't need that level of excruciating precision. Granted, the project plan was beautifully detailed and had all the markings of a brilliant plan—but the team had gotten so stuck on the planning they couldn't move into energizing or mobilizing. Further, the sheer weight and overwhelming size of the plan prevented forward action and actively suffocated any momentum the team tried to generate.

The 'Social Butterfly' Pattern:
When Energize is present but Strategize and Mobilize are missing.

Have you ever been part of a project or team with a ton of fun and chaotic energy, but the plan was vague, direction was missing, and no one knew what they should do other than "support the project"? That is the 'social butterfly' pattern at work. Incredible amounts of energy are expended, but people are left wondering what exactly they should be doing and are unable to anticipate what the project needs, where they should contribute, who is in charge, and what the overarching goals are. The team is engaged, the meetings are fun, but not much work gets done. These are the stereotypical 'flavor-of-the-month' projects that leave behind custom project t-shirts but not much else.

The 'Taskmaster' Pattern:
When Mobilize is present but Strategize and Energize are missing.

I think we all know someone who is fantastic at executing a plan but doesn't fully count the cost or understand their impact on others. Meet the 'taskmaster' pattern. In HR circles, this is sometimes referred to as "leaving a trail of bodies." It's not a pleasant image, but it paints a picture of someone so focused on charging ahead that they lose sight of the people they trample (purposely or unintentionally). No one will argue that they get results, but the cost of those results can be at the expense of others and may prioritize short-term results over long-term gains. It's hard to overcome a reputation as a taskmaster. No one wants to give them another chance by working with or for them again. That, in turn, can cause them to push even harder and become even more focused on the tasks to be completed at the expense of the people around them.

Settling for Limited Success

Ok, so I've made my point about being a one-hit wonder by tapping into only one of the Breakthrough Formula steps. In reality, we rarely only hit one of the three steps.

But what about when two of the three steps are present? Do you *really* need all three? Excelling in two Breakthrough Formula steps certainly helps your performance outcomes, but I contend that it still falls short of complete, breakthrough success.

Let's review a few examples of talented people who are frustrated with their limited success and haven't yet achieved breakthroughs. Meet Shawn, Emily, and Magda.

Meet Shawn:
Talented in Energize and Mobilize but struggles with Strategize

Shawn is a bright, enthusiastic, extremely likable person who draws people with an innate charisma few possess. He is the first person to celebrate a team member's birthday. He arranges team bowling events, and he knows the names of everyone's family members and pets. He regularly volunteers for the company picnic, and the planning team breathes a sigh of relief when he's working on the project. He will make it fun and execute it incredibly well.

Shawn's issue is that he is a great executor of other people's plans. He wants to lead a team, and the team loves him, but when given the chance to lead projects that require planning and forecasting, he stumbles and misses the mark. He is overlooked for bigger management roles because of his lack of long-range thinking and planning. He is viewed as a great team member and is well-regarded, but he isn't trusted with additional management responsibility.

Shawn is currently an HR Director, working in the corporate services division of his company. He aspires to become a VP of HR. We will walk through his breakthrough efforts in the Strategize section.

Meet Emily:
Talented in Mobilize and Strategize but struggles with Energize

Emily is a hard-charging, get-it-done professional who is technically brilliant and rarely (if ever) wrong. She knows her subject matter deeply.

If Emily gives an answer, it is right. She is trusted to do the most complicated work and delivers it on time and with the highest quality. She is extremely valued for the consistency of her results and her unquestionable accuracy.

Emily's issue is that she can be rude, impatient, and unintentionally unkind to others who do what she considers to be inferior work. People have quit after being assigned a project under her leadership. She has stated quite clearly that she expects to be promoted and has CEO aspirations. Because of her inability to effectively engage others, she is overlooked for executive positions, and her bid for CEO isn't treated seriously. She doesn't get the feedback she needs about her people skills because even her managers are unwilling to deal with the backlash they fear the feedback would produce.

Emily is currently a senior operations manager and has a background in finance. Her ultimate goal is to become a CEO. We will walk through her breakthrough efforts in the Energize section.

Meet Magda:
Talented in Energize and Strategize but struggles with Mobilize

Magda is an extremely talented and ambitious director with a strong desire for an executive role. She is universally liked, easy to talk with, and strategic. Her ideas are great. She is tuned into what is happening in the company and current events. People flock to her when they have problems and she always makes time to visit with them.

Magda's issue is that while she always delivers for her external clients, she cuts corners, procrastinates, and frustrates her colleagues with unmet promises. Because she is so well-liked, no one wants to tell her that she drives them crazy by promising and either not delivering or delivering sub-par work because she waited until the last minute to do the work. Because of this, she is overlooked for executive opportunities and key projects that would provide visibility despite her strengths and performance with external clients. She has so many great qualities but can't be counted on to deliver quality work consistently nor on time.

Magda is currently a Sales Director. Her ultimate goal is to become a Regional VP of Sales. We will walk through her breakthrough efforts in the Mobilize section.

In each of these cases, the person is incredibly talented in some way. They are hard workers with valuable skills, but lack the complete package for various reasons. Because of that, they don't receive the breakthroughs they desire.

It's worth noting they may need to achieve several breakthroughs as they steadily work their way toward achieving their aspirational roles. For instance, Emily will not jump from being a senior manager to a CEO in a single leap. And that's ok. It's a great thing to have an aspiration that stretches you and requires multiple breakthroughs. It keeps you going and can serve as a North Star when evaluating career decisions.

Alternately, not everyone has aspirations that take them repeatedly up the promotion ladder, as we briefly discussed in the opening chapter. Some professionals want to change paths and pivot their careers by changing their industry, profession, role, function, or something else. Emily did this in the example above when she moved from finance to operations. The Breakthrough Formula will help you with these kinds of aspirations, as well.

If that resonates with you, please don't let Shawn, Emily, and Madga's upward aspirations throw you off. While the primary purpose of this book is to help rising leaders attain breakthroughs like promotions, ascension into the executive ranks, and roles with larger scopes of responsibility, I want to acknowledge that there is more than one path to greater income, impact, and joy than continually ascending the management ladder.

Returning to Magda, Emily, and Shawn's situation, we see that they are all capable of closing the gaps we identified if they get honest feedback, are open to the coaching they receive, are willing to work hard to overcome their obstacles, and leverage all three steps of the Breakthrough Formula.

If you are tempted to judge any of them, beware. We have all likely been one version of these stories at some point or another. And if I'm not diligent, I can still show up as one of them. I share these illustrations not to judge but to shed light on how we can get in our own way if we lack awareness, knowledge, or skill. None of us are perfect, and most of us are working to improve, so the Breakthrough Formula can be helpful by highlighting *how* we can improve.

Enhance Your Personalized Breakthrough Formula with PLAN, FUEL, MOVE Action Plans

Based on our discussion so far, you know my firm belief that all three steps are needed, but the degree to which you apply the components within each step will depend on your experience, skills, and the nature and size of the breakthrough you are seeking.

Let's dig a bit deeper into the Breakthrough Formula by walking through a set of four action plan components within each step to help you build out your plan, shore up any Breakthrough Formula steps that aren't in your area of genius, and customize it to your own situation.

The components in each action plan are covered by an acronym to help you recall them. The Strategize action plan is represented by the acronym PLAN, Energize is FUEL, and Mobilize is MOVE. The diagram below shares the individual action steps associated with each letter of these three acronyms.

The Breakthrough Formula:

STRATEGIZE **+** **E**NERGIZE **+** **M**OBILIZE **=** **Y**OUR **B**REAKTHROUGH **M**OMENT

PLAN Actions:
P: Pick Your Opportunity
L: Lay Out Your Plan
A: Add Specific Actions
N: Network for Assistance

FUEL Actions:
F: Fan Your Flame
U: Unleash Your Community
E: Embrace Input
L: Lighten Your Load

MOVE Actions:
M: Move Into Action
O: Obtain Regular Feedback
V: Verify Your Results
E: Enjoy the Moment

Now that you have an overview of the Breakthrough Formula and its associated action plans, I want to pause briefly to discuss where you should start your journey.

Everyone has strengths that come naturally and effortlessly. Everyone has areas they can improve on with knowledge and practice, and everyone has areas they will likely struggle with for the rest of their days. That unique mix of talents, skills, and abilities is your differentiator and what makes you stand out from everyone else.

The point of this book and the Breakthrough Formula isn't to create perfection in each of the Breakthrough Formula areas. Instead, our goal is to build knowledge and awareness that is needed in each of these areas. Growth will naturally result as you exert yourself to attain your breakthrough. But I also want to acknowledge that some of these items may not be worth your time to develop. You may be better served by outsourcing them to friends, colleagues, or processes and tools that shore up areas you are less skilled in and allow you to lean more heavily into your strengths. I want you to be the best and most effective version of *you*.

Strengthen, Grow, or Hack?

One of my mentors used to tell me, "Be you, but better." I love that. He didn't ask me to be someone else. Honestly, I'm terrible at being anyone other than who God made me to be. I'm talented and flawed, curious and geeky, confident and insecure, fabulous and fumbling. My only job is to become a better me. I can do that. And so can you.

Don't let the list we just walked through overwhelm you. Instead, I want you to work through each chapter, thinking about how you can put the lessons to work. For each topic discussed, should you strengthen it, grow it, or hack it? Let me explain:

Strengthen It

If the Breakthrough Formula topic you are reading about is a natural strength, read through the material to explore potential ideas, concepts, or practices you could use to enhance your natural strength. This kind of reading should be easy, entertaining, and validating. You already do this!

Dig into the material with *confidence* and *curiosity*.

Grow It

In some cases, the Breakthrough Formula topic may be an undiscovered or underdeveloped strength. I believe we all have both. This can happen when you have a strength that could be applied more broadly than you realize or that your current work doesn't use, so it goes unnoticed.

If you think that may be the case, read with an investigative and assessing eye. Look for hidden gems that won't take much work to implement or improve. I think of "Where's Waldo" type games when I'm reading this way.

This reading should be *exhilarating* and *informative*. These are quick wins.

<u>Hack It</u>

If the Breakthrough Formula topic you are reading about makes your skin crawl, then finding a hack for it may be appropriate. We all have areas of work that we want absolutely nothing to do with because we naturally dislike the work, have had a bad experience with it in the past, or know we have no natural affinity for it.

Don't try to force yourself to build these areas into strengths. Instead, use your other strengths to determine possible alternatives or workarounds. Is the area something you can ask a friend to help you with? Is there a strategy you could substitute that would work better for you? Could you hire someone to help you with it or do it for you? Could you use an AI tool to automate portions of it or to help you think through it?

When we read passages that contain information about topics we shy away from, our natural tendency can be to put the book down, walk away, and say, "That's not for me." I want to challenge you not to do that. Remember: Our goal is to make *you* a better *you*. Not a *different* you!

So when you come to these passages (and everyone will), read with a mindset of *exploration* and *cunning*. How could you do this differently, work around it, find a hack for it, or hire it out? Make it fun as you challenge the ideas and find a hack that will work for you.

Keep an eye out as you work through the book. I've highlighted some "hack it tips" to provide additional alternatives for some of the proposed activities and action items. I encourage you to find your own ways to strengthen, grow, and hack your way to success, as well.

Ok. Now that we've toured the entire Breakthrough Formula and its PLAN, FUEL, MOVE action plans, grab your personalized formula, and let's continue our journey by igniting your "what" and "why."

In the next chapter, I'll share the first full installment of my break-through journey, which you will read at the start of each chapter. We will also dive into your specific motivations and desires. After all, you can't map your route until you know where you are headed and why you are taking the trip!

Let's Review

1) In this chapter, we walked through the three-step Breakthrough Formula (Strategize plus Energize plus Mobilize) for creating plans that move us toward greater income, impact, and joy at work. Each of the three Breakthrough Formula steps is supported by a four-part action plan that delivers the full potential of that step, represented by the acronyms PLAN, FUEL, and MOVE.

2) We discussed that all three Breakthrough Formula steps are required for optimal success. When only one is present, we risk falling into the trap of a one-hit wonder. When two of the three are present, we can be tempted to accept limited success that falls short of a complete breakthrough.

3) As you read through the book, consider how you can approach the topics through the lens of strengthening it, growing it, or hacking it.

Think About It

1) Think about projects you are currently working on or involved in (either personally or professionally). Are all three steps of the Breakthrough Formula present? How so?

2) What components of the Breakthrough Formula are you naturally gifted in? Which components tend to be a struggle for you?

3) What is one thing you know you would be happier and more effective doing if you could find a hack around it? Brainstorm possible ways you can outsource it, work around it, or approach it differently.

Take Action

1) Complete the 'Think About It' questions to prepare your brain to engage with the Breakthrough Formula.
2) Decide how you will commit to spending time reading, thinking about, and taking actions associated with this book.
3) Share your commitment with a friend or accountability partner.

Chapter 3

Ignite Your "What" and "Why"

My Real-Life Breakthrough Journey: *Installment 1*

In the introduction chapter, I shared my first big breakthrough opportunity. At the time, I had been working three jobs: one at a bank in the loan department, one at Walmart stocking women's clothes, and one at a local community center where I taught computer classes.

My dream at that time was to teach computer classes full-time. I didn't think it would even be possible. I had no college degree, no real experience, and I didn't meet the qualifications of the jobs I longed for. Two people helped turn my dream into a reality: my husband, James, who pushed me to explore what might be possible and who has always had unwavering faith in my ability to do hard things, and Debby, the community center director who believed in me and advocated for me without my knowledge. Between the opportunity created by Debby's advocacy and the courage I borrowed from James' faith in me, I was able to prepare for and land the full-time training job.

Two years into the full-time training job, I started taking college classes and used my day job as a living laboratory to implement the lessons I was learning in night school. I started paying closer attention to what was happening around me at work, and I began to see holes in our service offerings. Our training programs and support services weren't matching well with the needs of our internal clients. I started asking questions of people who attended my training classes, and I began conversations with trainers in the other departments about what I was observing. As I dug deeper into the idea, I became convinced there was an opportunity to make a difference by meeting needs that were not being met. I found my first real organizational gap. Doing so ignited a spark of inspiration and hope that triggered my imagination, allowing me to see a different potential future.

Assessing the gap between what was needed and what was offered led me to an idea that had breakthrough potential for the next step in my career. My big idea was to create a consolidated training offering. It would be a one-stop-shop where our clients could go to see *all* the training available, regardless of the department that delivered it. We would still serve our individual departments, but we would brand ourselves as one corporate training center.

I knew I had a good idea that would benefit employees who needed training, the company, and all the trainers providing the service. But I had to get the other trainers on board.

I invited the department trainers to a meeting. My plan was to outline the idea and ask for their thoughts and feedback. After all, we had been talking informally about our shared frustrations for some time.

I arrived early, got everything set up, and waited expectantly with extreme optimism for the meeting to start. I just knew it was going to be great. What did we have to lose?

Everyone arrived, and we settled on the topic of the meeting. As soon as I got the first few sentences out, trouble hit.

Charles, one of the safety trainers, took exception to the idea and pounced. He rose out of his chair, his face purpled, and in a booming voice, he gestured wildly while demanding, "Who do you think you are? I'm not going to listen to this. This is a waste of time!"

Whoa… What? I tried to respond, but he cut me off.

Charles continued talking loudly over me with insults and sneers. He pummeled me with rapid-fire questions that he clearly didn't want responses to. He never let me finish a sentence before going at me again. Honestly, I don't remember exactly what he said. What I remember was his physical presence, the threatening stance he took, and the tone and volume of his voice while the rest of the room sat back in shock.

His verbal attack totally blindsided me. It never occurred to me that someone might feel threatened by my idea or that the meeting would turn into a debacle. After about five minutes, I couldn't take it any longer, and I fled the room in tears.

I didn't make it far. I found a side hallway and crumpled to the floor, tightly hugging my knees. I buried my head and sobbed. I was so shocked, scared, and baffled. How had this gone so terribly wrong? I just didn't get it. I was trying to improve things and create an opportunity for all of us. I knew the other trainers felt the same way I did. This was my first experience with corporate politics and ego. Sadly, it would not be my last.

One of the trainers found me in the hallway and helped me pull myself back together. I really wanted to stay hidden and badly wanted to leave. But I couldn't. I had a training class to teach immediately after the ill-fated meeting.

That was almost the end of my big idea and the spark that fueled it—a spark that would grow in size and scope in the years that followed. And I can tell you that it took me some time to get over the experience.

The safety trainer was reprimanded and sent to anger management classes. It turned out that he was dealing with issues far bigger than me. I was in the wrong place at the wrong time and became the outlet for his misdirected emotions. Still, I was never in the same room with him again.

I was traumatized, but I held to my idea. I just knew it would work.

So I made the decision to gather my courage, lean into my conviction, and do it scared. I reminded myself that just a few years earlier, I had been working three jobs. I thought about all the hard work I'd invested and considered that I was actually working in my dream job. I thought about the faith and belief that James and the community center director had in me. I thought about the future of my job and my career if I did nothing versus the future I might have if I took a chance to pursue my idea further. And I remembered that I could do hard things.

Reconnecting with my "why"—the underlying reasons that drove me to tackle something bigger than me—gave me the will to dust myself off, dry my eyes, wash my face, and march back into the meeting room. My dream of pursuing my big idea and the future it could bring almost died that day. Looking back, I can say what a travesty that would have been. I would have missed out on so many wonderful opportunities, experiences, and people. Instead of smothering my spark and deciding that it wasn't meant to be, I used my unique "why" to drive me forward and got back to work.

I'll continue the story in the next chapter. For now, let's pause here and dig into your unique "what" and "why." Together, they support the spark that triggers your imagination, produces energy for your journey, and propels you toward your breakthrough goals. Keep reading!

Our Goals:

To set yourself up for success, we're going to spend time in this chapter uncovering your "why" and using it as sustainable fuel to continually provide motivation and focus. This is important because regardless of the friend group and family support system you have in place, there is no substitute for self-motivation and accountability, digging deep for that extra ounce of effort and the decision you make that "I can and *I will!*"

Lasting motivation just isn't something you can outsource to someone else. No one else on this earth is responsible for your thoughts, choices, actions, and emotions but you. No one can grow for you. You must do it for yourself.

If I sound harsh, it's because I've lived this. I've visited Pity City and thought about moving there. I've looked to others to show up and do hard things for me, even when I didn't realize that's what I was doing. It took my faith and a swift kick in the backside from my husband to remind me that only I get to make the choice. And I must do the work. So, my straight-shooting message comes from a place of compassion, love, and the school of hard knocks.

Now that we've gotten that out of the way, let's set up a system that will help you stick to your goals and live your why with purpose and clarity. We're going to transform your "what" and "why" into sustainable fuel by focusing on three activities:

1) Clearly articulating your "what" and "why."
2) Tapping into the power of journaling.
3) Understanding how your brain's motivation engine works so you can leverage it to achieve your goals.

Even if you believe your "what" and "why" are clear, don't skip the activities included in this chapter. The things we want to pursue and our reasons for doing so change over time. As we grow and mature, so do our dreams, aspirations, and ambitions. Use this time to check in with yourself and be brutally honest about your reasons for growth and achievement.

The Importance of "Why"

Have you experienced your own version of the story that opens this chapter? I bet you have. If you look back, can you identify your "why" for sticking with it?

What about right this minute? If I asked you to clearly articulate exactly what you want to achieve (your "what") and your reason (your "why") for wanting it so badly that you picked up this book, could you tell me with no hesitation? Most people can't.

And yet, we begin our lifelong quest to understand "why?" as a preschooler. Around the age of three, "Why?" becomes one of our favorite questions. (Chouinard 2007; Bryner 2009) Before we can write our names or tie our shoes, we want to know "why?."

Our insatiable curiosity to understand ourselves and the world around us consumes our attention and becomes a favorite game. If you've ever dealt with a toddler, you know how curious they are. You can ask them to pick up their toys from the ground, and they ask you, "Why"? Ask them not to put the remote control in their mouth, and they ask, "Why"? They'll keep asking until you get frustrated and come back with, "Because I said so."

We learn at an early age to question those around us and argue for things we don't like or that don't make sense to us. Arguing about "why" still consumes us in adulthood. It's no surprise that when we begin any new venture, are asked to swallow a big change, or are put in a position to commit to something, we start by asking why-based questions.

To set yourself up for breakthrough success, you must uncover your unique "why." I don't mean the surface "why" that is generic and applies to almost anyone in any situation. I mean the deeper, authentic "why" that drives you to make specific decisions, push yourself harder than you think you can, and sacrifice to make it happen. The "why" you are willing to fight tooth and nail to achieve. The "why" that is visceral and remains when no one is looking.

You must be able to clearly articulate your "why" so you can access it more easily as a source of fuel when hard times hit. Without a strong and resounding "why," what will compel you to do the hard work and make the sacrifices that growth will require?

In my own life, I can clearly recall times when I told myself or someone else that I would do something, only to realize that I didn't have a strong enough "why" to follow through. Granted, there are times when my weak "why" is overruled by an obligation I've made, but if I have a choice in whether I'll do something, I can guarantee you I won't do it if my "why" isn't strong enough to withstand the obstacles standing between me and achievement of the task.

Another reason we start with "why" is that the most obvious "what" (as in "what you aspire to do, be, or achieve") may not connect closely enough to your deeper, authentic "why." Have you ever chased something that you thought would make you feel one way, only to achieve it and realize you chased the wrong thing? Again, I have. If you aren't super clear and brutally honest with your "why," you can waste time chasing the wrong "what."

If you were sitting down with me at the beginning of a coaching engagement, the first three questions I would ask are:

1) What are you broadly trying to achieve? What is on the other side of your next breakthrough?
2) Why do you want to achieve it?
3) How much work (and sacrifice) are you willing to put into achieving your goal?

I ask these questions so I can gauge where you are now, understand your aspirations, and assess how strong your foundational motivations are in relation to your desired end state. In my experience, if your "why" isn't strong enough to support your "what," you'll either need to bolster your "why" or scale back your "what." If they are relatively balanced, your odds of success in achieving your next breakthrough increases significantly.

Articulating Your "What" and "Why"

The best way to get to the heart of your "what" and "why" is to interview yourself as if you were an investigative reporter. Imagine a hard-hitting, no-holds-barred interview with direct and rapid-fire questions that probe deeply to get to the heart of the matter. If this sounds uncomfortable, I agree. I also think there are times when we need to practice brutal honesty with ourselves, and that sometimes requires discomfort to break through the barriers that protect us and yet hold us back. There is a time to be gentle with ourselves, and there is a time to shoot straight. If we don't, we won't get to the heart of what we're willing to fight for. So, I'm asking you to dig deep and be willing to look at things that you've either not examined before or perhaps avoided. I'll even do the work with you.

Side note: I realize not everyone is comfortable with the idea of journaling. If that is you, skip down to the next section, "The Power of Journaling," and then return here to complete the activity below in whatever manner you prefer.

I'm going to stop my writing now to complete this exercise with you. Ready… let's do this.

Activity: Ignite Your "What" and "Why"

Grab your journal, a scrap of paper, or your phone to record a voice note. Settle into your favorite thinking spot with your favorite thinking beverage and spend some time really reflecting on your responses to the following questions. Then, write them down. We'll use these questions to tap into our motivations and convert them into fuel to support our spark. If other questions occur to you during this process, ask and answer them. Rabbit trails can be a good thing when you are digging deep and challenging yourself to be honest.

1) What do you want? What is the outcome you want to attain that caused you to pick up this book? Allow yourself to dream and your thoughts to wander. We'll gain clarity and specificity later on.

2) Do your values and beliefs align or support what you want to achieve?

3) Why do you want it? Be honest and thorough. Dig deep to get to the root of your "why."

4) What work are you willing to put into obtaining it?

5) What sacrifices will be required? Are you willing to make them?

6) Have you attempted going after what you want before but failed to achieve it? If so, why do you think the attempt failed? What did you learn from the attempt that you can do differently this time?

7) What will happen if you don't put in the work and sacrifice to get what you want?

8) What evidence do you have that you will actually put in the work and sacrifice to achieve it?

9) If your best friend scoffed at your dream and made fun of your efforts, what would you do in response? What does your response reveal about your "why"?

10) Assess the strength and authenticity of your "what" and "why":
    a. Review your "what" statement in question 1. After thinking about your "why," will your "what" deliver

what you are really seeking? Are you chasing the right "what"? If so, proceed on. If not, revise your "what" accordingly.

b.   Review your "why" statement in question 3. Is your "why" truly strong enough to support the weight of the work, sacrifice, and potential scrutiny from others? If not, what will you do about it? Will you bolster your "why" or revise your "what"?

Note: There is no shame in either response. This is about being honest with yourself about the strength of your "why" and its ability to support your aspirations. It is about the balance in the relationship between your "why" and your "what," not a value judgment about either. Remember, we're doing this to set you up for success. And that success starts here.

The Power of Journaling

Throughout this book, I encourage you to journal, self-reflect, and deeply consider a variety of topics. Gaining insights requires time and space. Journaling gives you both.

Spending time to reflect on what you are mentally processing, insights you are gaining, ideas and inspirations that come to you as you work on achieving your goals, and even using that time to clean up your headspace is crucial to making change. And change is what this book is about at its core. You don't seek out a book like this one and put time and effort into it without expecting to see positive change in your life and work.

I realize that people often have a love-or-hate relationship with journaling. If you are already someone who journals, that's great! If you aren't someone who journals, I encourage you to try journaling or some form of it. You can start small with a scrap of paper and no expectations. I've achieved major insights after journaling. I want you to experience the same.

HACK IT TIP:

If you try it and decide journaling just isn't for you, try stepping into a reflection practice with recorded spoken notes on your cell phone or coffee with a trusted friend who will listen without judgment as you work through what is happening in your head. The point is to get stuff out of your head so you can review and examine it.

Journaling has been proven to have numerous emotional and health benefits, including a reduction in stress, breaking the cycle of obsessively thinking and ruminating, regulating emotions, and even improving working memory. Journaling creates distance between you and the topic of your thoughts, which enables you to gain space and perspective. Recording your thoughts allows you to examine them differently and gives you a chance to gain new insights and awareness. (Smyth et al. 2018; Yang and Li 2020; Thoele et al. 2020; Ullrich and Lutgendorf 2002)

The act of writing out your thoughts on paper releases you from holding onto the details in your head. It enables you to release your grip and look at it from different angles. I've found that releasing the stranglehold your mind has on the journaling topic can bring relief and a lightness that is freeing and helps regulate emotions. Journaling also lets you practice opening up about topics that may be sensitive or tender in a completely safe space, which can lead to eventually opening up to others about the topic as well. (Smyth et al. 2018; Yang and Li 2020; Thoele et al. 2020; Ullrich and Lutgendorf 2002)

The biggest hurdle to journaling is often just starting. That moment of you, a pen, and a blank page can be intimidating and can set your inner critic off with self-doubt and fear. To overcome that, I've found that using a journaling prompt helps, and I write it on my page immediately. That does a couple of things for me:

1) It messes up the page. Silly, I know—but it works. Once the page is blemished, I'm more likely to keep going. My inner perfectionist is silenced because it's too late, and I've already messed up the page.

2) By writing the journal prompt out on my paper, I've released the pressure of what to write first and overcome the blank page syndrome that keeps my mind reeling.

3) Responding to a question is a social expectation that we've lived with all of our lives. When someone asks you a question, you are prone to answer it—even if you don't want to.

Once I've started answering the journaling prompt question, I can let my mind wander, and my pen will fly across the page. Soon, my writing shifts from the journal prompt to whatever my mind needs to process, release, relive, or simply ponder.

Lastly, journaling gives you a chance to purge old thoughts and adopt new ones. (Cascio et al. 2016) Journaling positive affirmations, for instance, forces you to focus on what you are writing. It's more powerful than just reciting something positive and affirming—though that is a wonderful exercise as well. Your focus can't stray as easily when you are writing. It's hard to write while you are zoned out mentally thinking about your task list, email inbox, or what you will fix for dinner.

Journaling slows you down, helps your mind calm, and centers your thoughts. It's like a beach day for your brain. And who doesn't enjoy a relaxing day at the beach?!

Fire Up Your Motivation Engine

Now that your "what" and "why" have been articulated, we need to take a quick trip into your brain to understand how it is wired for work. Specifically, we're going to review some research findings that may be counterintuitive and different than you've heard before. The first one we'll tackle is visualization. *Spoiler alert*: Vision boards and other vision-casting tools may not work well as a way of sustaining ongoing motivation to reach a goal. Huh?! Yep, let's dig in.

Vision tools are fantastic for gaining clarity about what you want. They help you articulate and decide exactly what your goals should include, and they inspire you to start the goal-setting process. Heck, I even think they are fun to create.

I can't tell you the number of vision boards I've made. Or the number of film reels I've mentally constructed of me walking through my desired future. Or the number of sticky notes I've put on my bathroom mirror, car dashboard, and the inside cover of my planner. I can tell you that they were beautifully crafted, exquisitely detailed, deeply contemplated, and seldom used after I made them.

To be clear, I'm not saying that you shouldn't make or use vision-casting tools. In fact, I asked you to do a mini version of just that by answering question #1 in the Ignite Your "What" & "Why" Exercise. I said vision boards don't work to *sustain ongoing* motivation. And behavioral science research has proven it.

Dr. Gabrielle Oettingen from the Social Perception Action and Motivation (SPAM) Lab at New York University has conducted a series of experiments about positive thinking and future fantasies for over twenty years. Her work has found that positive thinking about the future can backfire when it comes to taking action to achieve those goals. (DLD Conference 2014; Kappes, Stephens, and Oettingen 2011; Oettingen et al. 2005; Oettingen and Wadden 1991; Kappes and Oettingen 2011; Clips 2022) Spending too much time fantasizing about the future can trick your brain into thinking the work has already been done, which makes tools like vision boards counterproductive. Instead of arousing your circulatory system for action, it can instead signal a period of rest to your circulatory system. So when you finish creating your vision tool, your brain thinks, "Hey! We did it! Let's party and then take a nap." Does anyone else have faded sticky notes with coffee stains and curling corners that are bleached by the sun and get moved around but never acted on? Now we know why!

So what do we do then? We still want to achieve the things on our vision board, and we really like the film reel we've created in our minds about our futures.

Dr. Emily Balcetis, director of the SPAM Lab, and Dr. Andrew Huberman, Associate Professor at Stanford University School of Medicine and principle of the Huberman Lab, discuss several actions we can take to counteract this effect in a video interview recorded in 2022. (Clips 2022) Let's look at two of their recommendations based on Dr. Oettingen's research:

1) The first is to create moderately difficult goals that are specific and detailed, regularly track our progress, and give ourselves mental rewards for the progress we make on a frequent and consistent basis. Working toward a goal in which the outcome isn't guaranteed and rewarding ourselves for our progress keeps us motivated.

2) The second is to plan for failure. Dr. Oettingen's research found that planning for failure is far more effective in motivating goal effort than focusing on positive thoughts. While this may sound grim, it makes sense. If we think deeply about the things that could get in our way, then we are better positioned to respond when those possibilities turn into realities.

It feels counterintuitive and downright pessimistic but if we look closely at our lives, we can see it at work all around us as my next example illustrates.

I was recently talking with a friend who is a functional medicine doctor. She shared an inspirational story of personal and professional transformation with me. In one portion of her story, she told me she has always been a planner and shared how that helped her maneuver through the many challenges caused by COVID-19 in 2020.

At that time, she had a thriving brick-and-mortar clinic practice. Once she began hearing about the COVID-19 virus, she took immediate action to stock up on items she knew her clinic would need if the virus spread. She was thinking through the potential consequences of failure if she was unable to get the supplies she needed for her medical practice. Sure enough, when COVID and the restrictions associated with it hit, she was prepared and had no issues with her supplies or the smooth running of her clinic.

If only we were all so prepared and ready for when unexpected challenges strike. And that's the point. If we prepare for situations that could cause us to fail in reaching our goals, we can be prepared—just like my friend was.

Next Up: Launch Your Visibility Project with Strategize PLAN Actions

The odds are good that you already have a set of beautifully detailed, color-coded, and categorized goals, daily habit trackers, and accountability plans. If that's the case, fantastic! Pull them out and compare them to the approach I'm about to share with you in the Strategize section. You may want to tweak them, scale them back, or perhaps reorganize them to better align your goals with what we just reviewed about the brain's motivation system.

If you don't have goals written, are starting to pursue a new "what," or are in a period of change and want to refocus your goal efforts, I have you covered. In the next chapter, we'll dig into the first step in the Breakthrough Formula: Strategize.

As we move into the Strategize section, I want you to think of a road trip. When you are planning a vacation, you have to make a series of decisions: where you want to go, how you will get there, how much time and money you will spend, and even who you know that has visited your destination that you could reach out to for information, ideas, and advice. That's exactly what we'll do in the Strategize section. We're planning our trip from where we are today to where we ultimately want to be. Before we grab our suitcases and hit the road, we need to do some planning and preparation.

The Strategize Step is going to walk you through the four PLAN actions:

- Pick Your Opportunity
- Layout Your Plan
- Add Specific Actions
- Network for Assistance

We'll pick the opportunity we'll work on first, build a simplified plan to address it, and identify a mentor and/or sponsor who can support our plan. Let's go!

Let's Review

1) In this chapter, we walked through the necessity of clearly articulating exactly what you want to achieve (your "what") and your reason for wanting it (your "why").

2) We discussed the power of journaling to get thoughts and ideas out of your head so you can examine them, gain new perspectives and awareness.

3) We discussed how your brain's motivation engine works so you can leverage it to achieve your goals. Your brain is more adept at preparing for potential threats by moving you away from failure than it is at moving you toward something you desire. So, use that by spending time reflecting on what could go wrong and working to avoid it. We also learned that writing moderately difficult goals primes your mind and body for action.

Think About It

1) Have you created vision boards in the past? Did they work for you? In what ways did they work for you? How did your experience agree or disagree with the content of this chapter?

2) Reflect on a time when you used a list to regularly track goal progress or a list of tasks that needed to be completed. Can you recall how you felt when you completed the goals/task list? How did your experience agree or disagree with the content of this chapter?

3) Look back on the goals that you had the most success in achieving. What characteristics did they have in common? Does anything in this chapter help explain why they worked particularly well for you?

Take Action

1) Complete the Ignite Your "What" and "Why" journaling exercise.

2) In light of your responses, write or voice/video record a short pep talk to yourself that you can return to later when you need a boost. Be candid, honest about potential obstacles, encouraging, and rooted in your why.

3) Consider digging more deeply into the science of motivation. Watch some YouTube videos or Ted Talks, or check out reference websites and books. Learning about how your brain works to process information can give you many advantages in your journey to learn, do, and become more.

Section 2

Strategize!

Chapters in this section:

Chapter 4

Pick Your Opportunity

My Real-Life Promotion Journey: *Installment 2*

We ended installment 1 of this story with me drying my tears, recommitting to my unique "what" and "why," and getting back to work. That work resulted in the creation of a corporate training program that mimicked a corporate training university. All the trainers across the organization were included, and we accomplished what we had set out to do.

Over the next few years, and thanks to the efforts of many people, the program grew and became established as the one-stop training center I had envisioned. My role also expanded from a single trainer to a supervisor, then to a manager of a small training department, and then to an account manager responsible for the IT training function, large-scale IT project management, IT process improvement services, and technology account management with a dedicated set of clients. During that same time, I also completed my first college degree. It was an incredibly busy time of growth and learning.

Despite the incredible progress we had made, I still wasn't satisfied that we had closed the gap I saw between our service offerings and the needs of our clients and the organization. If anything, I was *more* convinced that we weren't meeting the organization's needs. That realization led me to expand my thinking about what might be possible. I talked with people about their observations and kept my eyes and ears open for ideas and solutions.

After some hard work, research, and deep thinking, I came up with the next iteration of my "big idea." I shared it with my manager and the head of the IT group. The head of IT told me—kindly and with good intention—that I needed to "slow down." He went on to tell me that I was moving too fast, leaving others behind, and making others in the department look bad. He warned me to be careful not to get too far ahead of everyone.

Let's pause here.

Has this happened to you? If not, it may. When you make the commitment to break through to your next level of success, people will notice. In my twenty-five years of experience, I've noticed that it usually goes one of three ways:

1) People cheer you on and want to support you with a "Go you!" attitude.
2) People quietly stand back to see what happens with an "I wonder if this will work?" attitude.
3) People try to hold you back with a "who does she think she is?" attitude.

We'll dig more into this conundrum later. For now, I want to acknowledge that this happens and encourage you to listen to other's advice when it's wise and discard it when it isn't. Don't let the opinions of others stop you from pursuing your "big idea" if you believe in it. You have to get used to attracting attention if you want to create enough momentum and action to achieve your breakthrough. As much as we want people to join us in the journey, not everyone will choose to. That's their choice. And yours is to keep going and not give up. Now, back to the story.

I was shocked by the feedback. As I left the meeting, I began processing what I heard. In fairness, I could see how my exuberance, intense focus, and commitment could be off-putting. For that reason, I tried to pull myself back but refused to give up on the idea. I recalled how, years earlier, I had almost let Charles, the safety trainer, sideline me. I learned from that and vowed not to let it happen again.

The next iteration of my "big idea" expanded on the original idea of consolidation and evolved into a new function with a dedicated training department that would report to the Senior VP and Chief HR Officer, bringing all training services into one group.

Personally, I really wanted to transition from IT technical training to HR leadership development training. At the time, the organization didn't have in-house managerial or behavioral training, often referred to as "soft skills" training. I wanted to learn and teach leadership skills, which was a passion of mine. I was a skilled technical trainer, so I had the creation and delivery of adult learning concepts down, but I needed the opportunity to transition my subject matter from IT to HR and leadership. I also saw a clear need for this service within the organization. Further, HR was one of my client departments, so I had some insight into how my idea could benefit the organization and our employee team.

At this point, I knew where I wanted the next phase of my career to go (leadership and HR soft skills training), and I knew I had a skill gap in HR and leadership development. As I contemplated how I could shore up that gap, I realized two things.

First, I probably needed to go back to school. Ugh. I had just completed my bachelor's degree while working full-time. The idea of going back to night school wasn't an exciting thought. I also thought it might be the fastest way to create the opportunity I wanted. It was something I needed to think about.

Second, there was an unmet need within my organization. Training functions were scattered, underfunded, disorganized, and inefficient. At that time, the only leadership training available was periodically and irregularly provided by outside consultants. The organization was working to grow through acquisition, and good management was needed at all levels to achieve the organization's strategic plan. Centralizing all training functions and sharing resources more efficiently could increase the effectiveness and utilization of existing training programs, while also meeting the need and creating more value for the organization.

As I thought about the organizational gap, I realized there was likely quite a bit of support for the idea. I had heard others express the same frustration I had experienced from the absence of readily available leadership training. As a new manager, I had dealt with some pretty tough employee relations issues but hadn't received enough training to help me navigate the situations I faced.

So, the opportunity I identified for myself of expanding training services to include HR and leadership topics was also an opportunity for my organization. It would consolidate all training functions to share resources and create greater value with minimal cost.

As I thought more deeply about the gap and its potential, I realized that I had stumbled on something pretty special. I had discovered a possible project that would create visibility for me with my managers, tangible value for my organization, and the potential for a breakthrough promotion with greater responsibility! Now, I needed to decide what to do with the idea and whether I had the courage to pursue it.

I'll continue the story in the next chapter and share how I turned my idea into a plan. For now, let's pause here and work on identifying your "big idea" for your visibility project opportunity. Let's get to work!

Our Goals:

In this chapter, we will work through a series of personal assessment and brainstorming exercises to help you gain clarity about the opportunities that exist around you that could be turned into visibility projects that highlight your skills and draw the attention and support of your managers. Here's how we will do that:

1) Identify your unique characteristics that differentiate you from others in your workplace.
2) Use a Perfectly Positioned Targeting Chart to help you identify possible skill and experience gaps in relation to your breakthrough goal.
3) Use the Opportunity Compass to help you identify gaps that represent potential opportunities within your organization.
4) Match up your skill and experience gaps with your organization's needs to identify your best visibility project opportunity.

As we work through the exercises in this chapter, we're going to assist Shawn from Chapter 2 in identifying his visibility project opportunity. Shawn's talents are strong in the Energize and Mobilize steps. Let's briefly revisit Shawn's situation. Note the areas that are emphasized.

Shawn is a bright, enthusiastic, extremely likable person who draws people with an innate charisma few possess. He is the first person to celebrate a team member's birthday.

He arranges team bowling events, and he knows the names of everyone's family members and pets. He regularly volunteers for the company picnic, and the planning team breathes a sigh of relief when he's working on the project. He will make it fun and execute it incredibly well.

Shawn's issue is that he is a *great executor of other people's plans*. He wants to lead a team, and the team loves him—but when given the chance to lead projects that *require planning* and *forecasting*, he stumbles and *misses the mark*. He is *overlooked* for bigger management roles because of his *lack of long-range thinking and planning*. He is viewed as a great team member and is well-regarded, but he isn't trusted with additional management responsibility.

Shawn is currently an HR Director, working in the corporate services division of his company. He aspires to become a VP of HR.

Now, let's begin our work by taking inventory of your skills, knowledge, abilities, and the unique characteristics that set you apart and differentiate you from others.

There's Nobody Like You

There are so many variables that make you who you are. It's hard for me to wrap my head around the incredible diversity that has to exist for each person on earth to be different and unique, and yet that is exactly how God designed it. It blows my mind. Here's my point: *You are special.*

You are different from everyone else. You are uniquely gifted. You are talented in ways others aren't. You've experienced things others haven't. Things that come easily to you are hard for others. Other people can't see, comprehend, communicate, and envision like you do. There are so many things that make you... you! It's impossible to catalog all of them. Instead of trying, we're going to lean on your insight and the knowledge you have about yourself to quickly uncover how we can turn your unique qualities into a differentiator you can authentically leverage in the workplace.

Activity 1: What Makes You Unique

Let's do a rapid-fire fill-in-the-blank journaling exercise to discover some of the things that make you unique. You can answer each of these statements with as many responses as you can think of. The questions focus on traits that are seen at work, but your answers should pull from every aspect of your life (note Shawn's response in question 7 about performing arts). Feel free to add to these questions. You may think of other questions that draw out responses once your brain engages fully in the topic.

Before you do this exercise, let's walk through an example based on Shawn's responses.

1) At work, people often tell me that I'm great at _motivating a team, boosting morale, and making work fun while still meeting deadlines_.

2) I lose track of time and become totally engrossed at work when I'm _coaching leaders on HR topics_.

3) People at work seek me out when they are having issues with _low team engagement or morale issues_.

4) If I were asked to share my "zone of genius" with a group of close friends, I would say it is _managing a department—budgets, compliance, performance, team morale, and HR systems. If I'm honest, I'm good at these things, but I don't enjoy many of them. I'd rather be working with people than doing desk work._

5) I've never admitted it aloud, but I really love working on *performance management reports—I get a kick from helping people grow, and annual reviews make that work a priority*.

6) I think what sets me apart from others is *my ability to bring a group of people together to accomplish specific tasks while also supporting the team's morale and building fun into the work*.

7) My background is unique because *I took performing arts and theater classes in college (I've not thought about that in a while!)*. It shows up in the workplace by *making me more comfortable speaking in front of others, and I tend to lean on my training when I'm put on the spot and have to think on my feet*.

8) The things that are easy for me but seem to be hard for others are *managing the logistics of running a department while engaging my team*.

9) My unique characteristics are:
   - *my ability to build team morale, but also get the work done*
   - *my ability to run my department smoothly*
   - *my ability to speak in front of crowds and be comfortable (and even entertaining) thanks to my theater training*

Now it's your turn. Grab a pen and start answering these questions as honestly as you can. Remember to pull from all aspects of your work and life.

1) At work, people often tell me that I'm great at _____.

2) I lose track of time and become totally engrossed at work when I'm _____.

3) People at work seek me out when they are having issues with _____.

4) If I were asked to share my "zone of genius" with a group of close friends, I would say it is _____.

5) I've never admitted it aloud, but I really love working on
_____.

6) I think what sets me apart from others is _____.

7) My background is unique because _____. It shows up in the workplace by _____.

8) The things that are easy for me but seem to be hard for others are _____.

9) My unique characteristics are: _____.

HACK IT TIP:

Answer these questions yourself. Then, ask someone who knows you well to answer them on your behalf. You may be surprised by their answers, which could lead to new insights.

Now, we need to expand on your work above by capturing some things that may not have come out in your rapid-fire responses.

Grab some note paper and jot down your current primary job duties and any other professional interests you have—whether they are used in your current job or not. We'll use your notes in the next activity to create a visual representation of your current job duties, professional interests, and unique characteristics using a tool called The Perfectly Positioned Targeting Chart.

The Perfectly Positioned Targeting Chart—Current Role

The targeting chart provides focused insights about where to put your time, energy, and resources in alignment with your goals. Even if you feel you are clear about your goals and how you will attain them, I encourage you to walk through the exercises in this section. Clarity about what you need to do and how you will tackle it can create a competitive advantage in achieving your breakthrough that helps you attain it more quickly, efficiently, and joyfully.

There are four variables in the targeting chart, and each asks a question (shown below). The intersection of all four is where you are most perfectly positioned for top performance.

Perfectly Positioned Targeting Chart

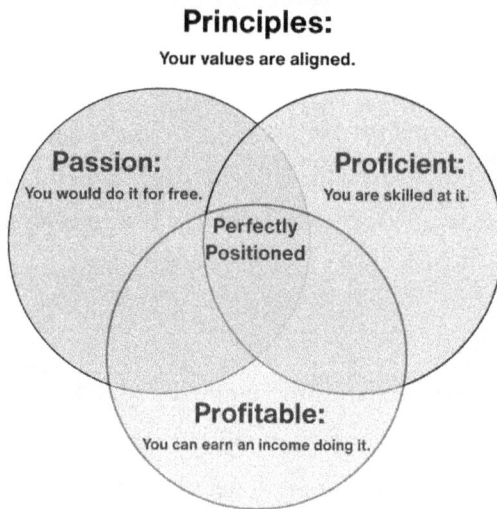

Principles:
Your values are aligned.

Passion:
You would do it for free.

Proficient:
You are skilled at it.

Perfectly
Positioned

Profitable:
You can earn an income doing it.

Questions to Ask:

1)   **Passion**: What would you do for free?

2)   **Proficiency**: What are your skills?

3)   **Profitability**: What can you earn an income doing?

4   **Principles**: How do your values align with the work environment?

Activity #2: Determine Your Current Positioning

To help you see the value this exercise can provide, let's look through Shawn's completed example and the insights revealed before you plot your own. Don't let the look of Shawn's activity fool you. This is actually an easy and quick (5-minute) activity to complete—but it can produce great insights for the small amount of time you invest in it.

Shawn took the notes he captured about his current primary job duties, professional interests, and unique characteristics and created a numbered list. He then plotted each number where he felt it best fit, using judgment to determine the exact placement.

Shawn's Perfectly Positioned: Plotting Exercise

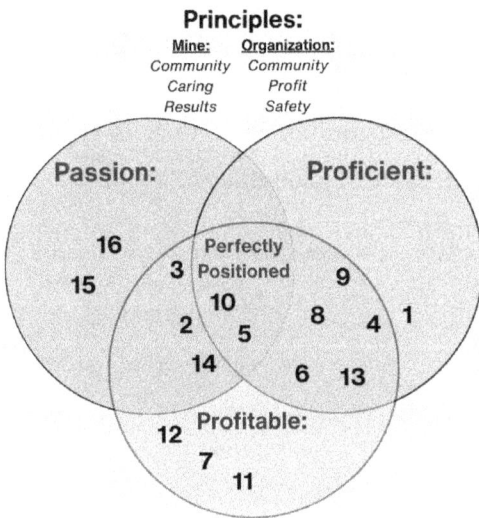

Principles:

Mine:	Organization:
Community	Community
Caring	Profit
Results	Safety

Passion:

Proficient:

16

15

3 Perfectly Positioned

9

10

2   8   4   1

5

14   6   13

Profitable:

12

7

11

Shawn's Current Role: HR Director

1. Draft communications
2. Facilitate meetings
3. Client relationship building
4. Manage department budget
5. Manage team engagement
6. Manage compliance processes
7. Develop strategy
8. Manage team performance
9. Manage HR systems
10. Coach clients in HR matters
11. Forecast trends
12. Support succession planning
13. Execute project plans
14. Provide subject matter guidance to executives
15. Public speaking
16. Volunteering in my community

Look at Shawn's chart above. What do you notice? What could this picture tell us about Shawn's current role? Let's analyze this together.

- Most entries are in the proficient and profitable areas. That tells me he is skilled in the majority of the job duties he is paid to perform. The theme present in these duties is managing a department and team.

- Only two of his current job duties hit all three circles. This begs the question of how much he is truly enjoying his work and feeling fulfilled by it.

- There are three job duties he is paid to perform that he doesn't feel passionate about or proficient in. These represent a skill gap for which he needs to creatively leverage a strength, potentially grow his skills, or find a hack to address. All of these skills also seem to fall into the area of strategy development.

- Three of his duties align with his passions. Interestingly, all are related to client-facing relationships.

- There are two items he is passionate about that don't currently relate to his job. He will need to meet these needs outside his role or seek ways to bring them into his work.

- His values and those of his organization seem to be in alignment and do not conflict. That's a good thing.

Your turn. Take a few minutes to complete this exercise. What do your results reveal to you? Does it provide any insights?

Perfectly Positioned Targeting Chart

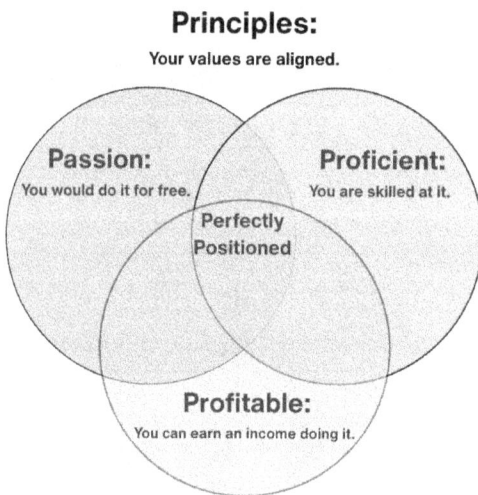

Principles:
Your values are aligned.

Passion:
You would do it for free.

Proficient:
You are skilled at it.

Perfectly Positioned

Profitable:
You can earn an income doing it.

1. _____
2. _____
3. _____
4. _____
5. _____
6. _____
7. _____
8. _____
9. _____
10. _____
11. _____
12. _____
13. _____
14. _____
15. _____
16. _____

1) Download a copy of the targeting chart, use the above chart, or draw a Venn diagram on a sheet of paper.

2) Grab your notes from the previous activity. This includes your insights about what makes you unique and your list of current job duties.

3) Create a numbered list of each item in your notes. Don't worry about the order in which you list your items, and don't censor your list.

4) Once you are done, take your targeting chart and plot each of your items on the chart where you feel they best belong. Position your numbers where they seem the most fitting. If something falls into both passion and proficiency, but you feel you are more passionate about it than proficient, then position your plot point closer to the passion circle than the proficient circle. Follow your intuition. (See Shawn's example above.)

5) Consider your principles compared to those of your organization. Are they aligned or complementary? Note your observations.

6) Take a step back and examine your targeting chart. What do you see? What stands out to you? (See the analysis of Shawn's chart for an example.)

Consider sharing your completed targeting chart with a friend. Ask them what they see when they look at the charts. I'm always amazed by what those closest to me see that I miss. Some things that we can't see for ourselves will be obvious to others.

The Perfectly Positioned Targeting Chart— Your Career Aspirations

Now, let's take this exercise one step further by asking yourself how your chart would look if you were to pencil in attributes from the career aspirations you wrote down as your "what" in Chapter 3. Understanding where your gaps may be when compared to your aspirations can be a powerful tool when making decisions about where you want to place your time and attention. Let's walk through Shawn's situation.

Shawn's aspiration is to become a VP of HR. Since he is currently a director who is performing well and has demonstrated strengths in both Energize and Mobilize, he can likely break through to the VP ranks in one move if he is ready when the opportunity arises, and he has demonstrated that his obstacle of strategy and planning have been overcome.

Your career aspiration may be possible in a single promotion, like Shawn. Or if you are like Emily, a senior operations manager who wants to become a CEO, it may be the next role needed on the path to CEO. Or it may not be a promotion at all. Your aspiration may be that you want more freedom in your work, the chance to work from home, or to have a greater impact without the strain you are currently facing.

Whatever your career aspirations are, we will use the next activity to capture a picture of your ideal future state so you can turn it into a tangible list of attributes to compare with your current skills. It will serve as a thought tool to help you build a plan to move from where you are today to where you want to be. Again, there is no perfect answer. Just do your best.

Activity #3: Determine Your Perfect Positioning

If, like Shawn, you are seeking a specific role, I encourage you to get a copy of the job description for that role, if possible. Doing so takes the guesswork out of the exercise. If the job description isn't available, you can draft a short aspirational job description based on your knowledge of the role. If there are specific qualifications, degrees, or certifications that are typically required for your ideal role that you don't yet have, capture those requirements as well.

HACK IT TIP:

- Quickly perform an online search for job titles you think align with your ideal job and use the information you find as the start of your numbered list.

- Use AI to create a job description based on your ideal title and attributes. There is no shortage of AI tools available. I tend to use Perplexity.ai, ChatGPT, Google Gemini, and the AI features built into programs. These tools are evolving rapidly, so use whichever tool works best for you.

Use the list you just created to plot out the job duties on your Perfectly Positioned Targeting Chart, just as we did in Activity #2 for your current role. Your plotted chart will still reside fully within the profitable circle but may be more skewed toward passion than proficiency. If so, that is a great indicator of the skills you need to build to move into jobs that fit your ideal role.

Side note: While we aren't doing an actual job search here, I have actually found job opportunities I wasn't looking for by doing this exercise. You never know what will happen!

Shawn has a copy of the job description for the VP of HR. He has created his numbered list and plotted it on the targeting chart. His results are below.

Shawn's Perfectly Positioned:
Breakthrough Aspiration Plotting Exercise

Principles:

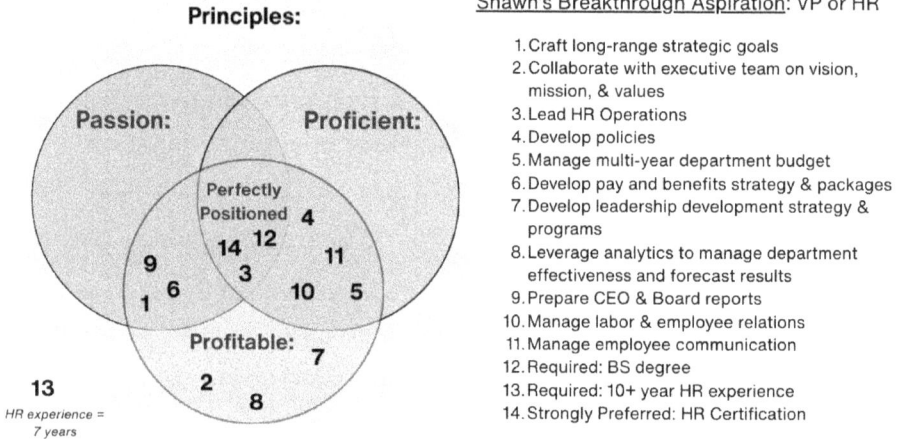

Shawn's Breakthrough Aspiration: VP or HR

1. Craft long-range strategic goals
2. Collaborate with executive team on vision, mission, & values
3. Lead HR Operations
4. Develop policies
5. Manage multi-year department budget
6. Develop pay and benefits strategy & packages
7. Develop leadership development strategy & programs
8. Leverage analytics to manage department effectiveness and forecast results
9. Prepare CEO & Board reports
10. Manage labor & employee relations
11. Manage employee communication
12. Required: BS degree
13. Required: 10+ year HR experience
14. Strongly Preferred: HR Certification

Look at the above example. What do you notice? What does this picture tell us about Shawn's readiness for his ideal role? Let's walk through it together.

- He appears to be relatively well positioned in about half of the ideal job duties. The duties that fall into the proficient (4, 5, 10, 11) and perfectly positioned areas (3, 12, 14) are escalations of duties he is already performing. Shawn feels confident that his skills in these areas will scale up.

- The three duties in the profitable area (2, 7, 8) are skill gaps. He has no experience with these duties. They are part of the job, so he needs to consider how he will gain these skills.

- Three duties fall into his area of passion (1, 9, 6) and are also skill gaps because he lacks proficiency. He needs to consider how he will gain these skills.

- Requirements: Evaluate these cautiously. While it is good to know that these items are generally sought by employers, they are variables that can change based on the company, industry, and role. Experience may also be a replacement for these factors. As it stands now, Shawn meets the degree and certification requirements (12, 14) and falls short of the years of experience requirement (13). This creates an opportunity for a conversation with his sponsor. (See chapter 7.)

After looking at Shawn's results for his current role and for his goal of VP of HR, it appears that his biggest opportunities and knowledge gaps can be summarized as:

- Long-range planning and strategy
- Forecasting and the use of analytics
- Development of strategic HR programs (pay and benefits, leadership development)
- Strategy consulting with executive leaders

Shawn has selected strategy development as his top priority. It is a common theme that has appeared in the feedback he's received in his current role. It's a critical skill for success in achieving his ideal role, and is something he is interested in and excited to develop. Shawn will set these results aside and return to them after the next activity.

Your turn. Take a few minutes to complete this exercise. What do your results reveal to you? Does it provide any insights?

Perfectly Positioned Targeting Chart

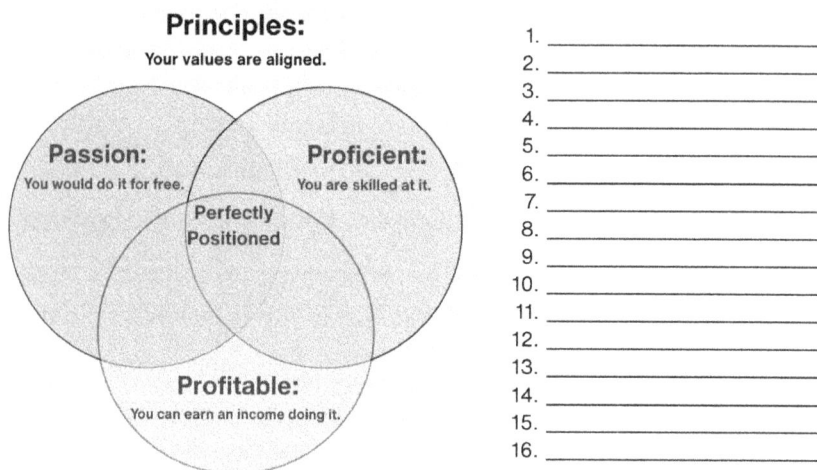

Principles:

Your values are aligned.

Passion:
You would do it for free.

Proficient:
You are skilled at it.

Perfectly
Positioned

Profitable:
You can earn an income doing it.

1. _____
2. _____
3. _____
4. _____
5. _____
6. _____
7. _____
8. _____
9. _____
10. _____
11. _____
12. _____
13. _____
14. _____
15. _____
16. _____

1) Download a copy of the targeting chart, use the above chart, or draw a Venn diagram on a sheet of paper.

2) Write your career aspiration on the top of the sheet.

3) Grab your notes about the attributes, education, and experience requirements you believe would be needed for someone to achieve your aspiration. Turn your notes into a numbered list of attributes.

4) Plot them on the chart according to where your skills are today. Your plotted chart will still reside fully within the profitable circle but may be more skewed toward passion than proficiency. If so, that is a great indicator of the skills you need to build to move into jobs that fit your goal.

5) Take a step back and examine your targeting chart. What do you see? What stands out to you? (See the discussion above about Shawn's chart for an example.)

Once again, consider sharing your completed targeting chart with a friend to gain the benefit of their wisdom and insight.

Now that you have an idea of your unique characteristics and how you are currently positioned in your current role and in relation to your career aspiration, let's set this work aside for the moment and move on to examining the opportunities created by unmet needs in your organization. For that work, we'll use the Opportunity Compass exercise. Once we've done that, we'll combine all the work you've done in this chapter to pinpoint your best visibility opportunity.

The Opportunity Compass Exercise

The Opportunity Compass exercise is an easy three-step question process that helps you identify organizational pain points and potential solutions. It helps you discover what *isn't working well* in your workplace and asks you to problem-solve.

Activity #4: The Opportunity Compass

The exercise has no right or wrong answers. This is about your opinions, observations, and ideas. Put anything and everything on the table. Even if it seems outlandish, there may be a spark of an idea that generates a great opportunity.

As you read through each of the items below and the questions they pose, capture your observations and potential solutions. An example of Shawn's situation is provided below.

1) Pain Points

Think about the conversations you've had with others about things that commonly get in the way of delivering an optimal product or service to your customers. Have you ever thought, "There has to be a better way of doing this!" If so, you've stumbled into a pain point that could be an opportunity. Here are a few questions to get your brain going. Feel free to change or add to these questions as appropriate for your situation.

1) What frustrations are you and your coworkers experiencing? What grumbles are being talked about when members of management aren't around?

2) Are there inefficient or missing processes you think you can improve?

3) Are there programs or policies that everyone "loves to hate?" or are they senseless rules that could be eliminated?

4) What frustrations are your clients and customers experiencing when they do business with you? Is there a pattern of feedback that points to a larger issue?

2) Potential Solutions:

Switch your perspective from finding the problems to identifying solutions. Consider the questions below as you brainstorm ways you could correct, resolve, or fix the pain points you've identified. No idea is too big or too small. Let your imagination run wild. Some of my best ideas have come from outlandish conversations that resulted in the question: "Why not"? We need to stretch our imaginations and employ our creativity to find a variety of alternate solutions.

1) What is the easiest way to fix the pain point you identified?

2) What is the wildest idea you can come up with to address the pain point?

3) If you had to fix it by staffing more people, how would you fix it?

4) If you had to fix it with a process improvement, how would you fix it?

5) If you had to fix it with a policy change, how would you fix it?

6) If money was unlimited, how would you fix it?

7) If you could spend no money at all, how would you fix it?

8) Could the issue be outsourced? If it happens outside the organization, could it be brought back into the organization? What would that require?

9) Of all the ideas you've generated, which one do you believe presents the best outcome *and* the best opportunity? Why?

You will notice in Shawn's responses, there are several things he could and should be doing that fall into his current area of responsibility. At the risk of stating the obvious, there are times when our work becomes hectic, and things fall through the cracks in our own areas of responsibility. Carving out time for this activity periodically (monthly/ quarterly) to challenge our thinking can create unintended benefits and bring new ideas and solutions to the surface.

The Opportunity Compass: Shawn's Responses

Pain Points	Potential Solutions
Frustrations: Outside of HR: As directors, we are frustrated by the budget process; the new signature authority that has cut back on what we can approve; and the reorg of the IT help desk.	• Engage with the finance department to better understand the budget process, how the inputs are used, and why they are needed. Could the timeline be changed to give us more time to get the work done? How much of it is actually needed? • Ask for training on the new signature authority training at the next HR staff meeting. The general training was confusing, and we didn't ask the questions we had about HR impacts. • Ask our IT account manager for better information about the IT reorg. We are experiencing crazy lag time in response, which is creating issues for meeting client needs. Could we ask for a dedicated staff person to be assigned to HR, or for a "high priority" status to be given to HR for immediate client needs?

<u>Inside HR</u>: Everyone is complaining about the new work-from-home policy restrictions; the move of recruiting from Jan's department to Thomas has had a negative impact on client relations; and the lack of career growth and job rotation within the HR group.	• Ugh. I'm not sure what we can do about the work-from-home policy. Any change made impacts someone. Consider small group discussions to help our team understand the new policy and field their questions—even if I don't know how to answer them! At least I'd better understand their specific concerns. • Invite Jan and Thomas to a joint meeting to discuss the rough transition and what can be done to resolve it. • Pull together the other directors to discuss a possible team member "loan" program where HR members can learn in another department. When we have something to share, present ideas to the VP of HR.
Processes: As a field-based HR leader, I "catch" most of the processes and don't have much to do with their development. I may have to revisit this one after more thought.	• I think Tom, the HR director for this area, would be open to doing a "job shadow" trade. I could follow him and vice versa, so we would both get a better idea of each other's pain points. An idea or opportunity could come from that.
Programs/Policies: Hmm... the performance management process. Everyone hates the amount of time it takes and the inconsistency in the quality of the feedback given. I enjoy the process (as I captured in my first activity), but I understand the frustrations people have with it.	• We've all given up on the performance management process. It's been revisited several times but never seems to improve. This is also in Tom's area. I wonder if he would be open to having a deeper conversation about this. I know he is sick of hearing all the complaints and is at his wit's end. There might be a crazy option here.

Client Feedback:	• Perhaps instead of getting annoyed (and to be honest, I am annoyed by the complaints), we should create an advisory panel of clients to share their perspectives and feedback on the "busy work" so we can capture their feedback. While we think we have efficient processes, given the constraints we have to navigate, they may think of something we haven't.
Too much busy work tied to HR process that isn't seen as value-add; perceived delay in processing applications for open jobs; difficulty finding HR materials on the intranet site	
	• We need to process applications faster. That's on us.
	• It's been a long time since we revisited the HR intranet. This could be a special project for members of the HR team and may address some of their desires to do work outside their normal scope. This is something to consider and talk to the other HR directors about.

3) Your Organization's Purpose and Values:

If you work for an organization, you are there to serve the organization's mission and purpose. So, if the ideas you generate to address or fix the pain points don't align with the core mission and values of the organization, you are unlikely to get the support necessary for the company resources needed to implement your proposed solution. For instance, if your proposal requires implementing a hard-sell campaign to increase revenue tied to an underperforming product, but your organization's values don't support that approach, your solution may not take flight.

Keep this in mind when considering your potential solutions. Nothing in Shawn's proposed list of solutions triggers any flags regarding his organization's mission and purpose.

Your turn!

Take a few minutes and brainstorm your organization's pain points and possible solutions while checking for alignment with your organization's mission and purpose.

So, you've listed your pain points, considered potential solutions, and checked your ideas against the organization's purpose and values. It's now time to match up your ideas with the work you did earlier to identify your unique characteristics and your growth needs from the perfectly positioned targeting chart. It's time to pick your opportunity.

Put It All Together

It's time to pull your thoughts together to compare notes and look for a good match between your needs and your organization's needs. Spend a few minutes analyzing the possibilities.

Gather the following:

1) Your "What Makes You Unique" Responses (Activity #1)
2) The Perfectly Positioned Targeting Chart for your current role (Activity #2)
3) The Perfectly Positioned Targeting Chart for your career aspiration goal (Activity #3)
4) Your Opportunity Compass notes (Activity #4)

As you review your notes, what jumps out? Look for opportunities that may be a good match between your unique characteristics, your development needs, *and* your organization's needs. The best visibility opportunities create a win/win scenario by meeting our needs and our organization's needs simultaneously.

While there is no guarantee that your organization will green-light your idea, it's a great place to start and can have unintended positive consequences. There have been organizational gaps I've chased that didn't pan out, but that did lead to new and different opportunities I didn't have access to previously. Many of those opportunities turned into customized roles that resulted in promotions because I identified an unmet need in my organization and put forward a proposal to address it.

Conversely, there have been times when I identified a match of my need and the organization's need that seemed like a perfect fit for me, but when I really thought about it in comparison to my *big* "what," I realized it wasn't something I wanted to pursue. Looking back, I'm thankful that I didn't chase those opportunities. They likely would have benefited me, but they also would have taken me in a very different direction than achieving my "what" would have required. And they may have taken up time that caused me to miss a different opportunity that I would have enjoyed more, and been an even better match for me.

Lastly, if nothing immediately jumps out, that's ok, too. Keep going. If you keep looking, you will find an opportunity (or you will create one just by looking for it). You can also use the insight you gained by comparing your Perfect Positioning Targeting Charts (Activities #2 and #3) to pick an area that you would like to further develop—even if it doesn't appear to be a match for your organization's needs right this minute. I've found that continuing to work on my professional growth in the absence of a specific opportunity has a way of preparing me for an opportunity that is around the corner. And one always eventually appears. Grow, and the opportunity will present itself!

Let's return to Shawn's example. After reviewing Shawn's charts, what would you pick for him to pursue? Did you see a match between his unique characteristics, his development needs, and those of his organization? Here's a breakdown:

- Shawn's Unique Characteristics:
  - He enjoys the performance management process and the opportunity it creates for him to connect with his team members about their work, growth goals, and career aspirations.
  - Shawn is strong in Energize and Mobilize.
  - Shawn's background in performing arts and his passion for public speaking could be leveraged in many ways to play to his strengths and create a differentiation between Shawn and his colleagues.
- Shawn's Development Needs:
  - Long-range planning and strategy
  - Forecasting and the use of analytics
  - Development of strategic HR programs (pay and benefits, leadership development)
  - Strategy consulting with executive leaders
- Shawn's Organization's Needs:
  - After reviewing his charts, Shawn believes there is an opportunity for him to explore tackling the performance management process. It's a known pain point.
  - Shawn is also fairly confident he can get his manager's approval to work on the project during normal working hours.
- Shawn's Selected Opportunity to Pursue:
  - The performance management process: After reviewing his work, Shawn believes there may be an opportunity for him to explore tackling the performance management process. It's a known pain point. Tom (the process owner) would likely be open to Shawn's interest in

revisiting it, and it would require Shawn to develop new skills in areas he needs to develop while also leveraging his unique characteristics to give him an edge. Partnered with his strong Energize and Mobilize talents, this would be a good opportunity for him to grow *and* showcase skills that aren't well known.

Pick Your Opportunity!

Great visibility projects create win/win situations that draw positive attention and provide the time, money, and resources you need to accomplish the project. The best candidates for your visibility project:

1) Highlight your unique strengths, talents, and skills.

2) Allow you to gain new skills and improve your performance.

3) Are supported by your organization and are interesting to your leaders.

4) Create measurable value for the organization and/or solves a known issue or problem.

When you are ready and have considered your work from this chapter, pick one opportunity you want to pursue. Then, start working on it by moving to the next chapter, where you will lay out your plan.

Let's Review:

1) *You are special.* You are different from everyone else. You are uniquely gifted. Understanding, embracing, and leveraging your unique qualities allows you to differentiate yourself from others in your workplace.

2) The Perfectly Positioned Targeting Chart has four variables: Passion, proficiency, profitability, and principles. When all

four are present, you are perfectly aligned to do your best work. The tool is also useful for mapping out your ideal future role or the next breakthrough you want to pursue.

3) The Opportunity Compass Tool focuses on uncovering opportunities for value creation in your organization. Uncovering needs in your organization that match up with the development needs you have can create a powerful win/win scenario that provides a strong foundation for your visibility project.

Think About It:

1) Go back up to the breakthrough journey installment at the beginning of the chapter. Locate the skill gaps and opportunities I identified in my own plan. How might you approach my situation differently? If I were your friend at the time, how would you have advised me?

2) Do you agree or disagree with the idea that your unique qualities can become a differentiator that helps you stand out? Why or why not?

3) Which of the activities in this chapter did you find most helpful? Will you use any of these activities in the future? Why or why not?

Take Action:

1) Complete the activities associated with the Perfectly Positioned Targeting Chart. Consider using the HACK IT suggestions to expedite your work and expand your thinking.

2) Once your activities are complete and your opportunities have been analyzed and prioritized, pick one opportunity to use as the basis for your visibility project.

3) If you aren't someone who enjoys introspective work, try completing this chapter's activities conversationally with a friend who enjoys this kind of thinking or is your go-to person when you are wrestling with something. The odds are good that your conversation with them will spark some ideas and lead to insights that help you settle on the opportunity you want to pursue.

Chapter 5

Layout Your Plan

My Real-Life Promotion Journey: *Installment 3*

After much thought and discussion with James, I decided to fully pursue the idea I had about consolidating the training departments into one training organization under HR.

I knew I needed to develop a well-considered plan that would communicate my idea, make a compelling case for the need I saw within the organization, and present myself credibly as someone who could do the job despite my lack of experience in HR. Fortunately for me, IT always has project work to do, so I had been drafted to help lead projects early on and developed a talent for drafting project plans and leading large-scale projects.

With a game plan in mind, we decided to hold off on pursuing a master's degree to see what would happen when I seriously pursued my idea. I was hoping I would be able to pitch the idea and my plan directly to Jack, the Senior VP and Chief HR Officer, and perhaps create a career opportunity for myself by doing so.

Before I could make the call to ask for a meeting, I knew I needed to explain my idea in a written document that was different from a typical, already-approved project plan. This was something I had never attempted before, and I was clueless about where to start. When I get stuck, I tend to run toward the wisdom of books… so off to the bookstore I went! I found a book about writing one-page pitch documents.

After returning home, with my new one-page-pitch book in hand, James and I talked through my next steps. After listening intently to my plans and asking detailed questions to spur my thinking, he settled down with me in our small kitchen nook to keep me company while I worked on my plan and my pitch. For the entirety of a three-day holiday weekend, James sat with me while I worked. He gave me his impressions of my work, encouraged me to keep going, poked holes in my logic, and asked really hard questions. My amazing husband has been a central, behind-the-scenes figure in every area of my professional career. He has been my constant encouragement and the boot on my back when I forget that I'm capable of doing hard things. This instance was no exception.

By the time the weekend ended, I was exhausted but ready with a one-page pitch document and a folder full of brainstorming notes, ideas, and crude drawings of process diagrams and org charts. I needed to get all of my ideas out so I could develop a big picture of what I wanted to do. That, in turn, allowed me to summarize my thoughts into my one-page document. It also prepared me to talk through my ideas at a deeper level when I got the opportunity to pitch my project.

Let's take the idea we selected in the previous chapter and begin putting structure around it by creating a one-page project description. We'll pick this story back up after we have our draft document in hand.

Our Goals:

In this chapter, we are going to organize our thoughts about our visibility project idea into a short summary that can be shared with others. It will serve as the backbone for the activities we'll add to the plan later.

We will also review some simple tools that create a clear, easy-to-use, can-build-it-in-under-an-hour plan description that we create with a simple document or notes app. If the idea of building a project plan in a word processor or Notes app is the equivalent of nails on a chalkboard, I understand. Remember, I started my career in IT. You don't need a fancy tracking app, a subscription to a cloud service, or a specialized project management app to create a basic plan. Using a simple approach forces you to spend your energy thinking and minimizes distractions. At this point in our journey, we need clarity and focus. Our aim is to create something that is clear, can be shared with others, and is *quick* to create.

In this chapter, we'll accomplish that by:

1) Collecting and organizing your ideas before you start drafting your plan.
2) Crafting a one-page description (or scope) document that provides all you need to communicate your topic, intentions, resources, and accountabilities.
3) Discussing how you can leverage AI to help you improve your document quickly and efficiently.

I will share quite a few ideas about the use of AI and how it can increase your productivity and efficiency when completing the activities in this chapter. I wholeheartedly believe there is tremendous benefit when AI is used appropriately. I would be remiss, however, if I didn't also provide a word of caution: Never upload anything online, whether into an AI engine or elsewhere, that has information specific to your organization. Once you put something online, you can't pull it back. Caution is imperative. Your organization likely has specific policies that govern how company data should be treated, including where, how, and which AI tools (if any) may be used with company data. Be sure you know the restrictions and maintain compliance.

Now that we've adopted an appropriate level of caution, let's move on to the topic of planning and its importance in building out your visibility project plan.

The Importance of Planning

Planning is an interesting activity in business. It is a necessary tool to help groups of people organize their collective thoughts and actions into a workable, multipart solution that will be carried out and made a reality by people who are very likely not even in the room doing the planning.

We pull from our plans to run every aspect of our business. What is your strategy? Oh, we have a strategic plan for that. What is your budget? We have a forecasting and budgeting plan for that. What results should your team achieve through the day-to-day running of the business? We have a goal plan... We have bonus plans, performance plans, project plans, communication plans, and on and on it goes.

Plans are a big deal. They are necessary. But they are also very easy to get tangled up in. I'm a big fan of plans. And planners. And planning software. And planning apps and all the gadgets that help me carry my plans in their various forms. I've studied formal project management methodologies and read many books on the subject. I love it. If you ask my husband where I keep my planners, he will walk you to a bookshelf full of the planning systems I've collected. Some people collect figurines or shoes. I collect planners.

If you have a bent toward all things planning, it is *so* easy to take it too far. I once had a personal development plan that took me eight hours to build and an hour to update every time I did something on it. I didn't get very far with that particular plan. We have to be so careful that we don't spend all our time planning and updating and not enough time *doing* the work. That's when we fall into the trap of being a one-hit wonder.

If we over-engineer our plans, we also run the risk of our brains believing that we've actually done the work (you know, since we spent all that time imagining the work through the lens of planning), so instead of priming our bodies for action, it instead sends signals to kick back and relax, as we discussed in chapter 3, *Ignite Your "What" and "Why."* (DLD Conference 2014; Kappes, Stephens, and Oettingen 2011; Oettingen et al. 2005; Oettingen and Wadden 1991; Kappes and Oettingen 2011; Clips 2022)

If we go back to the example I gave in Chapter 2 about the online training system project I inherited that had stalled for over a year, you will recall that their 100-page project plan was, at the same time, brilliantly detailed and completely useless. They unintentionally overwhelmed themselves with minutia and couldn't get moving to actually implement their plan. And yet, we still need plans to guide our actions, think through the logical steps, coordinate our activities, and track our progress. So we will build a plan, but we won't over-engineer it.

To build a plan that serves as our North Star, we're going to create a plan that resembles a coloring book page rather than a work of art. It needs to be simple and just engaging enough that it serves its purpose without getting in our way. If our plan overwhelms us or is too involved, we simply won't have the time, energy, or capacity to keep working on it. The planning approach I'm sharing with you is the same approach

I used to help our online training system project team get unstuck. It is simple, and only needs to perform a few jobs for us. The biggest of which is to get us *moving*. Our first step is organizing your project information.

Collect and Organize Your Thoughts

Let's get clear on what we are going to build. For our purposes, we are defining a plan as a set of intentional and interrelated actions you perform with the expectation of achieving a specific goal. So, to build our plan, we need

1) a visibility project goal and purpose statement
2) a list of actions we will perform to accomplish the goal.

In reality, we need a bit more than that, but not much.

We need to know the boundaries to work within, the resources available for the project, and who can approve the project. I know this may seem oversimplified, but that's the point. *We need to keep this simple.* We aren't talking about implementing a million-dollar solution. We just need something to organize our efforts, keep us on track, and be able to easily share that information with others.

Let's do this through a set of three activities. For the purposes of these activities, I'm going to assume that you identified your visibility project opportunity in the last chapter and have it ready to go. If not, keep reading. There is no shame in taking time to carefully consider what you want to pursue and what it might mean if you do.

Activity 1: Brainstorm The Possibilities

There are several ways to do this. Let's cover two different approaches that lead to the same place: Journaling and mind mapping. One is verbal; one is visual.

Journaling

For this exercise, I'm using the term journaling to describe answering questions in written form. This will help you get all your thoughts out. If you don't like to journal, you can use a form of verbal journaling. I have a friend who uses Otter.ai to record her voice, transcribe it, and produce a summary of the content with action items identified. Genius! If you journal best by talking, grab your phone, and let's go. Here are some starter questions to get you going:

- How will I approach this opportunity? What abilities, skills, knowledge, and/or experiences are needed to successfully close this gap?
- Based on the above, what exactly needs to be done?
- Is there anything tangible that my project will produce? Does my plan have any deliverables?
- Are there key dates or milestones I need to achieve? What are they?
- How long will it take to address the need I've identified and resolve it?
- What resources are needed? (Money, people, tools, time, etc.)
- Will any approvals be needed to support my plan? If so, from whom?
- Will anyone around me be impacted when I achieve the results? Will they be impacted positively or negatively?
- What risks are associated with my plan? What are the best, worst, and most likely outcomes?

Let's look at a partially completed example based on Shawn's idea to tackle the issues with his organization's performance management program. The rest of Shawn's examples will be based on the first phase of his project, which will focus on defining the problem so he can begin identifying possible solutions.

Shawn's example: *Performance Management Program Improvement—Phase I*

- How will I approach this opportunity? What abilities, skills, knowledge, and/or experiences are needed to successfully implement the idea?
  - *Gain Tom's agreement to work with me on the project or to let me lead the project with his sponsorship and oversight.*
  - *Collect information about the existing performance management system and methodology.*
  - *Research performance management principles, methodologies, and systems.*
  - *Collect information from both HR and non-HR employees to understand the primary issues people are having with the current system.*
- Based on the above, what exactly needs to be done?
  - *Ask for approval from the VP of HR after Tom agrees to work with me*
  - *Prepare a project description document to use in the above-mentioned meetings*
  - *Draft questions to be used in focus groups or a survey*
- Is there anything tangible that my project will produce? Does my plan have any deliverables?
  - *An assessment of the issues identified with the current system and a proposed plan to address them*
- Are there key dates or milestones I need to achieve? What are they?
  - *None that I know of. Tom will know more. There may be a window of opportunity based on the timing of the annual performance management cycle.*

- How long will it take to address the need I've identified and resolve it?
  - *I imagine I will need at least two months to gather information based on my current work and home responsibilities and workload.*
- What resources are needed? (Money, people, tools, time, etc.)
  - *I need access to Tom and his team to pull reports*
  - *I need time from Tom and his team to learn from them*
  - *I need meeting space, engagement from focus group (or survey) participants, and calendar assistance to organize a meeting time and place (even if it is all done via video conference)*
- Will any approvals be needed to support my plan? If so, from whom?
  - *Yes. Tom and the VP of HR*
- Will anyone around me be impacted when I achieve the results? Will they be impacted positively or negatively?
  - *Hard to say at this time. It will depend on the results of the evaluation and the proposed solutions. I imagine the impacts would likely be viewed more positively than negatively.*
- What risks are associated with my plan? What are the best, worst, and most likely outcomes?
  - *Best: Tom agrees to work with me, the VP approves the project and provides resources to support it, HR and non-HR employees are engaged and make time to participate, we identify significant improvements with little cost and high adoption*
  - *Worst: Tom doesn't engage with me or actively blocks me, and the idea dies immediately. I go back to the drawing board.*
  - *Most likely: Tom agrees to work with me and the VP approves, but resources are constrained; HR and non-HR employees are interested but struggle to find the time to*

engage; the project takes longer to complete because I am unable to hold their attention or complete the information gathering.

While I'm a big fan of journaling as a tool for uncovering deeper thoughts and insights, I realize you may not feel inclined toward it. If so, there's another method you can try called mind maps.

Mind Maps

Mind mapping is another of my favorite tools for collecting and organizing thoughts. In fact, this book is the result of 20+ mind maps. If you aren't familiar with mind maps, let me briefly explain them.

Mind maps start with a central idea that you build upon with greater detail as your thoughts flow. Again, use the journaling questions above as a guide for your mind map. Let's use my pitch preparation as an example.

- The central idea would be a "Centralized Training Pitch." Write that in the center of the page and circle it. You can also use a mind map app, like Xmind or MindNode. The same principles apply.
- Then, draw a line from the circle to a supporting idea to address the question of "What exactly needs to be done?"
- Responses might include: "Set the meeting," "Develop the Idea," and "Prepare Pitch Documents." Keep listing responses until there are no more ideas. Then, move on to the next question and repeat the process.
- Keep adding thoughts until you run out of steam. When done, there is a page filled with circles and lines that connect ideas and look like a spider web.

If you do an online image search, you will see all kinds of mind map styles and examples. Shawn's simple mind map is provided below and in Appendix A.

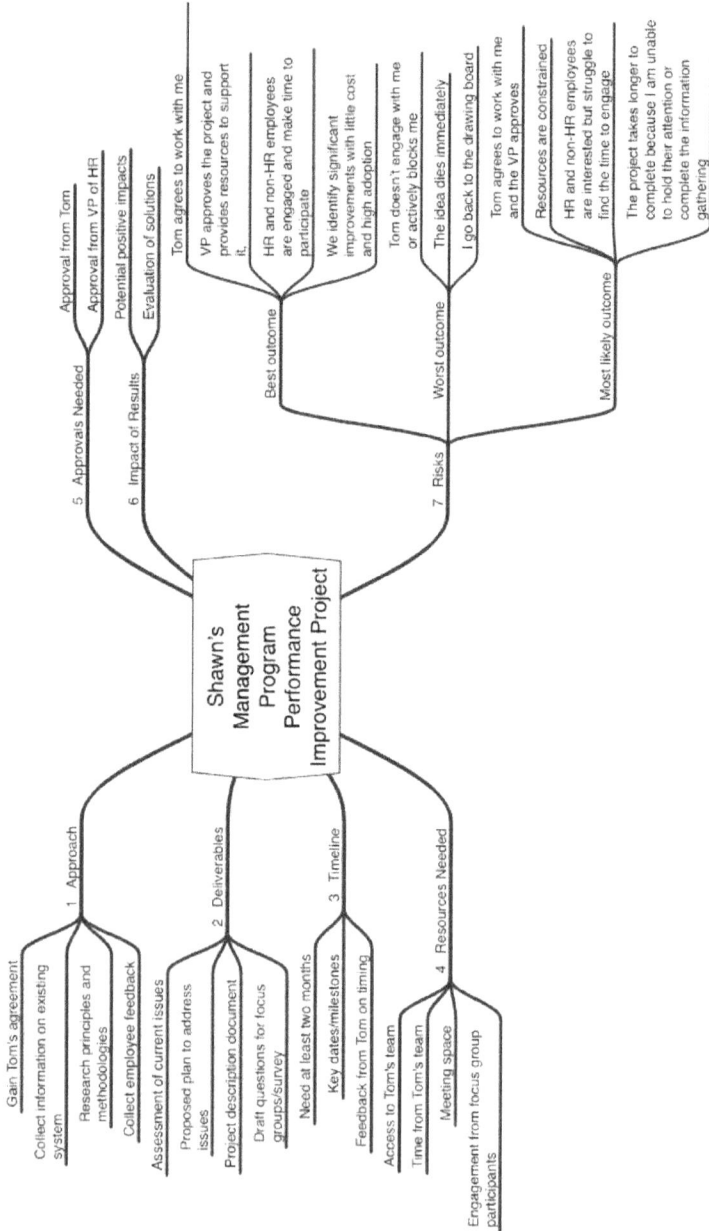

The central node reads "Shawn's Management Program Performance Improvement Project" with branches:

1 Approach
- Gain Tom's agreement
- Collect information on existing system
- Research principles and methodologies
- Collect employee feedback
- Assessment of current issues

2 Deliverables
- Proposed plan to address issues
- Project description document
- Draft questions for focus groups/survey

3 Timeline
- Need at least two months
- Key dates/milestones
- Feedback from Tom on timing

4 Resources Needed
- Access to Tom's team
- Time from Tom's team
- Meeting space
- Engagement from focus group participants

5 Approvals Needed
- Approval from Tom
- Approval from VP of HR

6 Impact of Results
- Potential positive impacts
- Evaluation of solutions

Best outcome
- Tom agrees to work with me
- VP approves the project and provides resources to support it.
- HR and non-HR employees are engaged and make time to participate
- We identify significant improvements with little cost and high adoption

7 Risks

Worst outcome
- Tom doesn't engage with me or actively blocks me
- The idea dies immediately
- I go back to the drawing board

Most likely outcome
- Tom agrees to work with me and the VP approves
- Resources are constrained
- HR and non-HR employees are interested but struggle to find the time to engage
- The project takes longer to complete because I am unable to hold their attention or complete the information gathering

HACK IT TIP:

Here is a version of a MindNode map I created from the responses in the journaling activity above. I copied the questions and answers into Perplexity.ai and told it to create a mind map outline from the text I provided. (Perplexity.ai, October 12, 2024) It grouped the information into the groupings you see in the mind map. I then copied the outline and pasted it into a new Mind-Node Outline. A few tweaks and voilà! While far from perfect, it gives Shawn a great place to start from in a fraction of the time. The mind map above was created in under five minutes.

I use mind maps to think through *everything*. I love their blend of simplicity, lack of formatting, and the visual information you get when you step back to examine where your thoughts took you.

Once you have your journaling notes or mind map completed, let's use the information we just compiled to populate our one-page project description.

Create Your One-Page Project Description

Now that you have completed your brainstorming, you will turn your notes into a description document that serves as the backbone for your plan. There is no magic here. We just need to boil your brainstorming down into something that shares your intent and provides guardrails for your project.

This is a simplified form of a scope document in project management methodology. There are many great templates available online for project scope documents. The one I'm sharing in this section is the tried-and-true document I've used for the majority of the projects I've led.

Activity 2: Summarize Your Visibility Project Idea as a Goal

Your document starts with a clearly defined, one-sentence goal that is specific and clear about what you will accomplish. I'm not going to spend much time on this, as I know you already know how to write a clear goal—and we now have AI to help us speed that process up.

I like to use the SMART methodology when drafting goals. (Doran 1981) It's clear, easy to remember, and helpful. The model was originally created by George Doran in 1981, but has since been altered and adapted by users. I tend to prefer the more well-known version below. For those of us who need to jog our memories, SMART stands for:

- Specific (What exactly am I going to do?),
- Measurable (How will I measure progress and achievement?),
- Attainable (Can I reasonably accomplish this?),
- Relevant (Does this goal relate back to the bigger picture I'm trying to achieve in the long-term?), and
- Time-Bound (What is my deadline for achieving the goal?).

You will likely need to play around with your wording until you fit it all into a clear and concise sentence. You can cut down on the time it takes to write your goal by using an AI tool to help you with the wording.

HACK IT TIP:

You can even feed the responses you wrote in the journaling exercise and tell the AI tool to write a SMART goal using the information you provide. I did so using Perplexity.ai. Here's what it provided without edits from me.

> *Develop and present a comprehensive assessment of the current performance management system, along with a proposed improvement plan, to the VP of HR within three months, after gaining Tom's sponsorship and conducting research involving at least 30 percent of HR staff and 10 percent of non-HR employees through surveys or focus groups.* (Perplexity.ai, October 13, 2024)

It requires Shawn's intervention and editing, but again… not a bad start!

Go ahead and write your goal using whatever method and tools you prefer.

Activity 3: Assemble Your One-Page Project Description

Your one-page description will quickly and efficiently outline the boundaries of your project. This is your working document and the one-page you will share in your initial discussions with possible sponsors, team members, and resource owners. I think of it as my quick reference guide for my project.

Let's start by considering the following common elements found in project scope documents. Don't worry about word count, grammar, or writing more than a single page. You can clean up the document and whittle it down to one-page after you've captured your thoughts. Keep in mind that you can add to or delete these elements based on your needs and the size of the project. I've found covering these few elements is all you need to bring clarity and focus to your efforts.

- *Project Name and Short Description*: Title the project with a clear and obvious name.
- *Purpose and Goal*: Describe the purpose of your project as the problem you are trying to solve. Include the goal statement you just wrote. (4-5 sentences)
- *Scope:* Summarize the project to communicate clearly what is "in" and what is "out" of scope. This is a guiding statement that helps keep you on track. (1-2 sentences)
- *Deliverables:* List the tangible results the project will deliver. (Bulleted list)
- *Timeline or Target Dates:* Provide the due date for the project and list key dates or milestones that correspond to the deliverables you included in the previous step. (Bulleted list)
- *Required Resources:* List the resources needed to support the project. Include things like budget, people, tools, access, and anything else you need to support the project and get it done. (Bulleted list)
- *Key Stakeholders and Sponsors:* List the people who will be most involved in the project and the leaders who will provide organizational sponsorship and oversight. (Bulleted list)

As you are creating the document, let me encourage you to keep it simple and easy. Don't overthink or over-engineer it. The point here is clarity, not perfection. Just get your thoughts down on paper. The back of a napkin, a blank page in your planner, or a notes' entry on your phone will work. The act of writing out the description of your project is powerful and demonstrates your commitment to yourself. It begins the process of self-accountability, is a great tool to share with people in your life who will support you, and is good practice for the next time you need a well-written one-page scope document.

__Side Note:__ If your project opportunity is tied to your organization, your company may have a specific template you should use. I recommend talking with someone in your organization to find out if a particular project management methodology or template is used and preferred by your company. Doing so may also create an opportunity for you to talk about the project you are pursuing and gain additional support, guidance, and resources.

After you've drafted your document, read it from top to bottom. Is it clear and helpful as a description of what you will do? If you feel it needs a bit more work or is too long to be helpful at a glance, edit it to be clearer, concise, and useful. Our aim is to keep this to one-page.

__HACK IT TIP:__

Writing a short, concise, punchy document is much harder than writing a long one. This is another place where AI can help. Consider uploading a generic version of your document to an AI engine with instructions to correct any spelling or grammatical mistakes, make it more concise, and limit the output to one printable page.

Another option is to upload your information from Activity #1 and instruct AI to organize the data according to the one-page project elements at the beginning of Activity #3. I did this with Shawn's responses and told Perplexity.ai to generate the text for the example below. (Perplexity.ai, October 13, 2024)

Here is Shawn's phase I project scope document:

1-Page Project Description

Project Name	Performance Management Program Improvement - Phase I
Project Purpose	Performance reviews impact every team member in our organization. While intended to be a valuable tool for employee development and organizational growth, the current annual performance review process has become a source of significant frustration for managers and team members alike. This frustration stems from several key issues, including time inefficiency, cumbersome systems, misalignment between performance measures and actual performance, and a lack of continuous feedback throughout the year. This project will attempt to better understand these issues and identify possible resolutions.
	Project Goal: Develop and present a comprehensive assessment of the current performance management system and provide a proposed improvement plan within 3 months by conducting research including:
	• Information about the existing performance management system and methodology
	• Performance management principles, methodologies, and systems
	• Feedback from at least 30% of HR staff and 10% of non-HR employees to understand the primary issues people are having with the current system
Project Scope	This project encompasses the evaluation of the existing performance management system, gathering feedback from HR and non-HR employees, and developing a proposed plan to address identified issues. It excludes the implementation of proposed solutions.
Deliverables	• Assessment report of issues identified with the current performance management system
	• Proposed plan to address the identified issues
Timeline / Target Dates	• Project duration: 2-3 months
	• Specific milestones to be determined in consultation with Tom, considering the annual performance management cycle
Required Resources	• Access to Tom and his team for report pulling and knowledge sharing
	• Meeting space (physical or virtual) for focus groups or interviews
	• Survey tool (if applicable)
	• Calendar assistance for scheduling meetings and focus groups
	• Time allocation from HR and non-HR employees for participation in feedback sessions
Sponsors & Key Stakeholders	• Shawn (Project Manager/Lead)
	• Tom (Project Sponsor)
	• VP of HR (Project Sponsor)
	• Key Stakeholders:
	o HR team members
	o Non-HR employees (participants in feedback sessions)

Also see Appendix A

Now that you have your one-page project document ready, it's time to start reaching out to others to share your idea and build out the rest of your simplified plan. That's what we'll do in the next chapter, *Add Specific Actions*. Keep going!

Let's Review:

1) Plans are necessary but don't have to be complicated.

2) Use journaling or mind mapping to brainstorm how you want to turn your identified visibility project opportunity into a plan.

3) Build a one-page scope document to share your project's key information with supporters and sponsors. Consider including the project name, purpose, SMART goal, project deliverables, timeline, resource needs, and key stakeholders and sponsors.

Think About It:

1) Do you need a plan document to support your project? If not, what could you use instead to track your progress, communicate with your supporters, and build accountability?

2) What is your favorite brainstorming approach? What has worked well for you in the past? What is a new method you could try?

3) What is your organization's AI use policy? Are you clear on what you can and cannot do to remain compliant?

<u>Take Action:</u>

1) Complete the brainstorming activity. Try picking a method you don't generally use. This is a great opportunity to learn and grow a new skill. If you aren't someone who enjoys writing, try using dictation on your phone in your Notes app or in a transcription app like Otter.ai.

2) Dictate or write a draft of your one-page scope document. Consider doing this in real-time with a friend. Talking through your ideas while recording yourself can help you quickly settle on ideas and generate content you may not have been able to do with a blank sheet of paper or computer screen. Then, use AI to test your thinking and improve your draft (if appropriate).

3) Share the document with a trusted friend for feedback to evaluate whether the description document conveys what you had in mind when you drafted it.

Chapter 6

Add Specific Actions

My Real-Life Promotion Journey: *Installment 4*

Coming back into the office after the long holiday weekend with my pitch document taunting me from my bag, I knew it was time to make the call. I knew that my idea wouldn't get off the ground without Jack's support.

It was time to take action. I had to pick up the phone and ask for a pitch meeting, but I was so nervous that I didn't think I'd be able to talk without a squeaking, shaky voice. So, instead of picking up the phone, I paced the hallway outside my office, practiced what I would say under my breath, and tried deep breathing exercises to calm down my racing heart. None of it worked, but there are moments in life when you know you *must* do something, even if it means doing it scared and nervous. So, without allowing myself to overthink it any longer, I returned to my desk and picked up the phone to call Jack's office.

His administrative support partner answered the phone.

"Hi, Katie. This is Jenn Landis. I'm wondering if I can get a few minutes with Jack to share an idea I have."

"Hi, Jenn. Jack is in a meeting right now, but I can visit with him and get back to you. Can you tell me more about what you want to visit with him about?"

I was hoping she wouldn't ask me that! I responded, "Um, I have an idea for an improvement in the training function I'd like to share with him."

I could tell by the awkward silence that followed that she wasn't satisfied with the amount of detail in my answer.

"Ok… well, all I can do is ask him if he's willing to meet with you. I'll visit with him when he has a break in his schedule and get back to you."

"Thanks, Katie. I really appreciate that." I hung my head as I hung up the phone. I felt like I was going out on a limb with my request, and I was terrified that I had just made a colossal mistake.

As the day stretched on, I found myself deeply distracted by what I would say if Jack returned my call. I moved through my tasks in a daze, as though I was sleepwalking. I had to re-read passages multiple times, caught myself not listening during meetings, and generally felt like I was in a stupor. It was as if all my energy had been expended by making the single phone call to Jack's office.

Finally, at the very end of the day, I heard back from Jack.

"Hi, Jennifer. This is Jack."

I shakily asked him if I could set up a time to meet with him to share my idea. There have been few times in my life when I was more exhilarated and terrified at the same time. It was one of those moments when the world slows down, and everything feels surreal. Or perhaps it was just the lack of oxygen from holding my breath.

"I'm happy to meet with you," he replied with interest in his tone. "Can you come to my office next week?"

I took my first deep breath since making the call to Katie and quickly agreed. We compared calendars and scheduled the meeting.

I raced home that night to share the news with James. He listened intently as I practiced my pitch over and over again, and then we took a break, and he took me shopping. No judgment, please! When some girls get nervous, we borrow confidence from a new outfit and a shiny new red pleather briefcase! We didn't have a lot of money at the time, so it was a big deal for him to literally invest in me to get me ready for this meeting.

When we returned home, I pulled out my folder, which was full of scribbled notes, drawings, and random thoughts and ideas from my brainstorming sessions with James. It was time to add more detail to my project in an organized fashion. I wanted to be able to walk in with my pitch document and some details about the thoughts that had gone into it. I didn't know if I'd get a chance to share it, but I knew that I would need it eventually and decided it was a good way to streamline my thoughts and get prepared for my meeting with Jack the following week.

When I was done, I proudly held a spiral-bound fifteen-page project plan, complete with my one-page pitch document and fourteen pages of support documentation. It included an organizational structure show-ing a new department that reported directly to the VP of HR, a diagram showing how information would flow between the various departments in his organization, a detailed project plan, budget, and a job descrip-tion for the director of the department—which I hoped would be me. I was proud of the work I had done and ready for my pitch meeting.

That meeting would end up being one of the most impactful and life-changing meetings of my life.

In the next chapter, I'll share my monumental meeting with Jack. Just as I needed to build out my plan before my meeting, so must we!

Before we dive into our plan, let's recap where we are and how far we've come.

So far, we've talked about determining our "what" and our "why," we've identified and evaluated the potential opportunities that will move us toward achieving our career aspirations, we've selected our most impactful opportunity, and we've begun drafting our plan to achieve it.

In this chapter, we will think through the specific actions needed to initiate action. In short, we're going to turn your visibility project idea from an *aspirational* dream on a one-page document into an *achievable* plan.

Our Goals:

It's time to turn our attention to building a *simplified* action plan. This plan will add structure to support your one-page document that will be used in the Energize and Mobilize steps of the Breakthrough Formula. We're going to do this by focusing on three activities.

1) Practice looking around corners to see potential issues and think more deeply about what needs to be done to achieve your goals and support your movement toward your career aspiration.

2) Think about what it will take to achieve your plan and turn those thoughts into categories of action.

3) Build out an action plan using a simplified form of a project management tool called a work breakdown structure (WBS). We'll add due dates and resource assignments to your action items so you can track your progress and request help with resources you don't currently have available.

By the end of this chapter, you will have a working, shareable plan to support your project that can be carried into conversations and used when planning your activities.

Why You Need an Action Plan

I can hear some of you in my head saying, "But, Jenn, isn't building out an action plan a waste of time?" And, "I know what needs to be done. This planning stuff is just extra fluff."

I know it can seem that way, but there is a method to the madness. How many New Year's resolutions have you stuck to? If you've nailed every one, you have my permission and my blessing to skip this step. You also have my admiration. If you are a normal human like the rest of us, we need to take the time to figure out the actions we need to take so we can actually *do* them. If you were killing it with your breakthrough efforts, you probably wouldn't have picked up this book. To get a different result, you have to entertain doing things differently.

Here's the kicker. I'm not asking you to do something you don't already know how to do. If you bought this book, you've written many action plans. The difference is that we often only do them for work. The sad truth is we don't put the same thoughtfulness and work into planning when the only beneficiary is ourselves. That's why doing so can be a difference maker. I want you to achieve your breakthrough. So, working through the basics methodically can help us identify where our past efforts have fallen short or aren't working for us.

Let's revisit why we are building a plan by revisiting Shawn's situation.

Shawn's Challenge

Do you recall our discussion in Chapter 2 about one-hit wonders and the trap of limited success? Those leaders have been frustrated and stuck in stalled careers because of one or more persistent, recurring obstacles that stopped them just short of achieving the breakthroughs they wanted. In most cases, they fell short because they lacked one of the three critical Breakthrough Formula steps—like Shawn.

Shawn's issue is a lack of consistent performance in the Strategize area, particularly his ability to plan ahead and guide his team by anticipating future needs. He demonstrates Energize and Mobilize characteristics but lacks the focus, foresight, and planning essential to Strategize.

Let's revisit Shawn's story briefly. Note the points that are emphasized:

> Shawn is a bright, enthusiastic, extremely likable person who draws people with an innate charisma few possess. He is the first person to celebrate a team member's birthday, he arranges team events, and he knows the names of everyone's family members and pets. He regularly volunteers for the company picnic, and the planning team breathes a sigh of relief when he's working on the project. He will make it fun and execute it incredibly well.
>
> Shawn's issue is that he is a _great executor of other people's plans_. He wants to lead a team, and the team loves him—but when given the chance to lead _projects that require planning and forecasting_, he _stumbles_ and misses the mark. He is _overlooked_ for greater management roles because of his _lack of long-range thinking and planning_. He is viewed as a great team member and is well regarded but _isn't trusted_ with higher-level management responsibility.

Shawn is a talented guy and someone everyone wants on their team. He executes while also energizing those around him—which isn't an easy thing to do. Shawn's gap is thinking critically about what needs to be done, when it needs to be done, and by whom it should be done, and putting accountability measures and tools in place to help him monitor progress so he knows when corrective action is needed. It's not that Shawn doesn't know how to plan. He does. What he lacks is the ability to anticipate future needs and the ability to plan for them accordingly.

Let's review some tools Shawn can use to build these skills.

Looking Around Corners

For two years, I worked in a tertiary healthcare system. (You will hear about that period of time in the story installments in the Energize section.) I learned many valuable lessons during that period of my career, and I want to share one of my favorite and most enduring lessons with you. It has to do with hospital hallways.

The healthcare system I worked for had a large campus with a premier hospital as the centerpiece. While most corporate service departments were placed in a separate building on campus, my department was housed in the heart of the hospital. I was accustomed to a typical office environment, so this change of surroundings was jarring. I continually stumbled over two things: the crazy number of acronyms used in a hospital setting (I gave my team many reasons to laugh at my mistakes) and navigating blind corners in the hallways.

Because we were in the actual hospital, we had to be very cautious when walking around hallway corners, as there were often people on stretchers or wheelchairs being moved from one area of the hospital to another. If you weren't careful when turning a corner, you could create a safety concern by running into people and patients. I'm a head-down, fast-walking, lost-in-her-own-thoughts kind of person, so this was an issue for me. There was already a mechanism in place to help me; I just had to learn how to use it. Any guesses what it was? The answer is convex safety mirrors.

In every hallway in the hospital, a convex safety mirror was mounted near the ceiling. Looking into the mirror would tell you immediately if the coast was clear or if someone was coming down the hallway. The issue was I wasn't used to using them. Other than inside some convenience stores, I had never seen convex mirrors installed inside a building. I discovered that there was an art to using them.

1) It helped if you knew the layout of the building and where most of the traffic was coming from.
2) You had to get used to looking up so you could see the mirrors.
3) You had to get comfortable translating the distorted vision of unfamiliar objects to interpret what you were seeing.
4) You had to make a decision about the specific action you should take.

After a while, I became dependent on the mirrors to efficiently navigate the hallways, and even missed them when I returned to a corporate environment.

My experience with the mirrors taught me several lessons that I still use to this day. Yes, I learned the obvious skill of watching where I was going so I didn't crash into people. I also learned a lesson about metaphorically looking around corners for strategic planning purposes.

When I think about strategic planning, I think about *looking around corners*. I need to pay attention to what is happening around me and when there is an increase in activity that signals a potential change. Based on the glimpses I get from scanning my environment, what do I think could be coming at me (or at my department/organization/industry) from around the corner? And how should I be preparing for its arrival? Is it something I should avoid (get out of the way), is it something I can participate in (and thereby gain an advantage), or is it something that I should prepare and brace for because it is unavoidable? You get the idea. Getting really good at looking around corners can create a strategic advantage.

Looking Around Corners Translation

Hallway Lesson:	Strategic Planning Equivalent:
Know the layout of the building and the direction in which most traffic comes from.	Learn your profession, industry, and company to get in sync with normal/typical operations.
Get used to looking up.	Learn to use tools to help you continuously scan the environment.
Translate the distorted vision to know what to pay attention to.	Use your knowledge and tools to anticipate changes and potential disruptions that may be headed your way.
Make a decision about the action you should take in response.	Make decisions about proactive actions to embrace or dodge what you anticipate is coming.

For the purposes of your visibility project plan, I want you to do more than just build an action plan that takes you from A to Z in your project—because I know you never go straight from A to Z. Crashes around corners you didn't see coming will happen. Guaranteed. By intentionally looking around corners before you begin, you develop skills that can reduce your response time and may even create a strategic advantage for you.

Activity #1: Look Around the Corner

Take a moment to consider your visibility project plan. We're going to expand our brainstorming from previous chapters and add additional insights from looking around the corner. I prefer to engage in this activity with a trusted thinking partner. It helps me to talk and think it out.

Grab the brainstorming exercise you completed in the last chapter. Is there anything you should add to your brainstorming list that you see coming around the corner or that could help you look around the corner? Here are some starter questions to get your brain going:

- Think about what you know regarding the environment surrounding your visibility project idea. How would you describe it? Is it supportive, is it chaotic, is it preoccupied? Get specific.
- What are potential opportunities, challenges, threats, or obstacles to your project?
- Revisit your notes from the last chapter about the risks to your plan and the best/worst/most likely scenarios. What is the most likely thing that could go wrong? What could you do to prevent it or to lessen its impact?
- What actions should you consider building into your plan based on your responses above?

Try to be realistic when you walk through this activity. Being realistic (versus optimistic or pessimistic) will help you build a better plan. That said, please don't talk yourself out of pursuing your visibility project. Our purpose here is to prepare for the "what ifs" so you can get ahead of them or work around them. This exercise will help you get more comfortable looking around corners and is a fantastic way to strengthen your strategic thinking skills.

Break it Down! The WBS Task List

One of my favorite and most helpful project management tools is the work breakdown structure, or WBS. (Webster 1994) It's a method for breaking down a project into smaller buckets, or packages, of work that together represent the entire project. We're going to walk through a simplified version of this tool.

A full WBS is a hierarchically numbered outline that starts with Level 1 (to represent the highest priority work) and descends in numeric order (1 > 1.1 > 1.1.1. > etc.....) with ever-deepening detail until every activity needed to execute the plan is captured and has a reference number. The WBS is structured so that each deliverable in the project is captured in its own section of the outline, which is called a work package (see the example below).

WBS Outline Example:

1. WBS Level 1
    1.1. Level 2
        1.1.1. Level 3
    1.2. Level 2
        1.2.1. Level 3
            1.2.1.1.   Level 4
2. WBS Level 1
    2.1. Level 2
        2.1.1. Level 3

Additional details, like who is responsible and when the task is due, are also usually included. When you are done creating your WBS, every task associated with the project is represented and categorized by the deliverable it supports. The WBS forms the underlying structure that organizes and tracks all the tasks needed to accomplish the project.

The reason I love using a WBS as the foundation for a plan, even a small plan, is that your WBS can be used in a variety of ways. For simplicity, we'll call this your task outline.

Your task outline can be copied and used as a template for a number of project-tracking purposes. It saves you time and ensures consistency. Here are some examples:

- *Timeline chart (or Gantt Chart):* Need a visual, time-based task chart that shows where your project will encounter bumper cars? No problem! Use your handy-dandy task outline to create one.

- *Progress report:* Need a progress report to track what has been done and what is up next? Easy-peasy! Copy your task outline and paste it into a spreadsheet program. Most programs come with list and drop-down functionality that makes it easy to create these kinds of reports. I like using red, green, and yellow icons to create a "stoplight" report that quickly shows which tasks are on track (green), falling behind (yellow), or at risk (red).

- *Budget:* Need to create a budget? Task outline to the rescue. Copy and paste it into a spreadsheet program and delete the lines that don't apply. Your task outline numbering system ensures your tasks are identified and consistent so you can keep track.

- *Resource List:* Need to separate your tasks based on the resources needed for their execution? Piece of cake! Drop your task outline into a word processing document or a spreadsheet application and organize your lists based on resource needs.

Please note that in the above examples, the task outline that was copied and used as a template isn't automatically linked. If the original task outline changes, it won't update in the copy/paste applications. Even with that limitation, using the task outline as a starter template still saves tons of time. If you choose to use an online project management application, and there are loads of them available, your task outline likely *will* be linked. Just make sure you keep it simple and easy. You don't want to fall prey to spending more time managing your plan than actually executing it.

Activity #2: Creating a Simplified Task Outline

Step 1: Grab your project description document and your brainstorm journaling question responses from the last chapter that you (hopefully) added to above after looking around corners. You will reuse your work for this exercise.

- Grab a highlighter and start identifying obvious categories of work for your plan. If you created a mind map in the last chapter, your nodes will provide a starting place for your WBS categories.
- Continue to build out your outline by listing the supporting tasks to be done.

Step 2: Take one more trip through your outline.

- Where could you ask for resource help from friends and supporters? Note those tasks in some way. You will come back to them in the Energize section when you "Unleash your Community."

Step 3: The last step is deciding if you want to include target deadlines in your task outline.

- Add deadlines or target dates to any of the tasks you view as critical.

HACK IT TIP:

Once you have built out your task outline, check it against an AI-generated WBS for your goal with a prompt like, "I have a goal of ... Create a work breakdown structure populated with tasks that will help me accomplish this goal." This will return a detailed list of items you can compare to your task outline and/or consider adding to your task outline.

Below is an example of a portion of a WBS task outline using Shawn's Performance Management Phase I project. I fed Shawn's one-page project document into Perplexity.ai and asked it to create a WBS outline using the information supplied. Shawn's complete Phase 1 project WBS task outline is in Appendix A.

Work Breakdown Structure (WBS):
Performance Management Program Improvement - Phase I project:

1. Project Initiation
    1.1. Define project charter
    1.2. Identify key stakeholders
    1.3. Establish project team
    1.4. Develop project schedule
    1.5. Secure necessary resources

2. Current System Assessment
    2.1. Gather existing documentation
    2.2. Review current performance management system
    2.3. Analyze current methodology
    2.4. Identify system limitations and pain points
    2.5. Document findings

3. Research Performance Management Best Practices
    3.1. Review industry standards
    3.2. Analyze modern performance management principles
    3.3. Explore alternative methodologies
    3.4. Investigate available performance management systems
    3.5. Compile research findings

4. Employee Feedback Collection
    4.1. Design feedback collection strategy
        4.1.1. Develop survey questions
        4.1.2. Plan focus group sessions
        4.1.3. Create interview guidelines
    4.2. Conduct HR staff feedback sessions

(Perplexity.ai, October 13, 2024)

As we close out this chapter, let me again state that this is *your* plan and *your* project. If you don't want to use the approach I've outlined in this chapter, then don't. Just use something. As I said earlier, plans are a big deal for a reason. My passion is in seeing you succeed. Plans help move you from dreaming to action. And I want you to live your dream.

Speaking of dreams, my dream of pitching my idea to Jack is about to happen. Turn the page to get the next installment of my breakthrough journey.

Let's Review:

1) Planning is important even when the project is small. Committing to a plan helps us maintain accountability and can help us identify where our past efforts have fallen short or aren't working for us.

2) Looking around corners is a practice of looking ahead to gain strategic insights from continually scanning your environment to identify opportunities and threats that may be coming, so you can determine how to address them. Getting really good at looking around corners can create a strategic advantage.

3) We discussed using a simplified version of a Work Breakdown Structure (WBS) that we are calling our task outline. It serves to organize your project task list.

Think About It:

1) What was your most surprising insight from your Looking Around the Corner exercise? How might you use this exercise in other areas of your work? What additional corner-peeking questions could you add to the list?

2) How many categories did you use for your task outline? Have you over or under simplified your outline?

3) How can you best use AI to expedite and improve your work in this chapter?

Take Action:

1) Complete Activity #1: Looking Around the Corner. Add to your brainstorming work from the last chapter by incorporating new insights after looking around the corner. After you've created your list, expand your ideas using an AI tool to see if there are things you missed or could add to your work.

2) Complete Activity #2: Build out your task outline with due dates and resources needed. Once you have built out your task outline, check it against an AI-generated WBS for your goal.

3) Take another step by building out at least one other document that will help you track and monitor your progress, like a stoplight report, resource plan, or project budget. You will need this in the Mobilize section. You get extra credit for doing it now.

Chapter 7

Network for Assistance

My Real-Life Breakthrough Journey: *Installment 5 (Part 1)*

The day of my big meeting had arrived. I got to the headquarters early and paced around outside, trying to get my nerves under control. My hands were sweating, my face flushed, and I felt a mix of excitement and fear. I prayed for guidance, for the right words to say, and the ability to recall everything I had practiced. Finally, I clutched my new red briefcase (which carried just two copies of my fifteen-page proposal), took a deep breath, and headed to Jack's office.

He greeted me kindly but with reservation, as we settled around his conference table. Jack was a kind and warm man. He was also a fantastic poker player. He could wear an expressionless mask like no one I've ever known. It totally freaked me out. I was used to a smiling, warm, and approachable man. The man sitting across from me was wary and strictly professional. This was up to me. He wasn't going to help me make this pitch.

I took a shaky breath, stared at the window over his shoulder, and began my pitch. I rambled with a quivering voice and trembling hands for what felt like two hours but was really only about ten minutes. At the end of the pitch, I took a deep breath and squeaked out something like, "and I want to run this new department and report directly to you." Then I sat back, and the peanut gallery in my head started heckling me and telling me to get ready to grab a box for my belongings because I was probably going to get fired.

After an awkwardly long pause, Jack gently asked me if I was done. Looking back, I'm not surprised he asked that, given my rambling explanation and stuttered words.

"Yes, thank you for giving me the opportunity to share my idea." I held my breath and waited for the disappointment that comes when you know you've blown it.

Instead, he cracked a grin that turned into a huge smile, accompanied by a statement I'll never forget and an action that changed my confidence forever.

He said, "Today is a good day! Anytime an employee brings forward a great idea supported by good work, it's a good day. Give me a high five."

And then, to my complete astonishment, he raised his hand to offer me a high five. I returned the gesture and started breathing again.

At that point, Jack took control of the meeting and started asking detailed questions and offering suggestions and revisions he wanted me to make to my proposal. Jack supported my proposal and committed to sharing my idea with our new CEO. I couldn't believe it, and I left the meeting on cloud nine and with the memory of a very unexpected high-five.

I went home and immediately made the revisions Jack asked for. Within two days, I delivered a new spiral-bound copy of my proposal to Jack. He asked me to give him a few weeks so he could visit with the CEO and get back to me with next steps. For the next few weeks, I was on pins and needles. I jumped every time the phone rang. After an eternity, I heard back from Jack.

"The CEO and I love your proposal. We really appreciate your deep thought and the extra work you put into creating it. Unfortunately…"

Let's pause here. Don't you hate that word? Nothing good *ever* follows the word "unfortunately."

Jack continued, "…now isn't the right time to pursue this. I fully intend to revisit your proposal when the time is better. Now just isn't it."

I immediately deflated and was so glad our conversation was happening via phone instead of in person. I had the presence of mind to thank Jack for his time and interest. He reiterated his support and tried to convince me that the "no" was really a "not yet." In truth, I didn't believe him.

Please tell me your heart is breaking just a little for me. It was such a discouraging phone call. After all the hard work, extra hours, and intense hope I had poured into my pitch, I got a "no."

What I came to realize is that my disappointment wasn't just because I was told "no." I was discouraged because I had started to envision a new future for myself, and the "no" represented a return to a reality I no longer wanted or was inspired by. I know you've been there. Who hasn't? Disappointment is a part of life, but so is picking yourself back up.

My dad taught me that you can't always control what happens to you, but you can control how you respond to it. I may not like that lesson, but I know it to be true. So, I gave myself a few days of being sad and disappointed and then got back to work. I've found when I'm upset, the best course of action is to *take* action. I change my focus to what I'm grateful for and decide what I need to do next to keep moving forward. So that's what I did.

I also believe in silver linings. I had proven to myself that I could do something I didn't believe was possible. I pitched to Jack! I was now on Jack's radar, and I had impressed him with my initiative, preparation, and coachability. He and I had many more conversations as a result of my pitch than I would have had otherwise.

James added to my silver lining by telling me, "Now you know what you want to pursue. You have clarity you didn't have before. That's a good thing."

And with those words of encouragement, we began talking about other ideas and possibilities. We made the decision to find a master's degree program that would prepare me for the time when Jack and the organization were ready to revisit my proposal.

That action had unintended consequences that changed my career path yet again. I'll share that portion of the story at the end of this chapter.

For now, let's talk about the critical role others, like Jack, play in shaping our perspective, our career opportunities, and our growth through coaching, mentoring, and sponsorship.

Now that you have determined your plan and the resources you need to achieve it, it's time to leverage advisors to help you think through your ideas, share experience-based insights, and provide access to resources you may not have on your own.

Having help from the right set of advisors can be invaluable and speed up your ability to execute your plan. They can also serve as slingshots for future opportunities. By working with you, your advisors get a front-row seat to your thought processes, work product, ability to follow through, and how you handle successes and setbacks. This access provides them with a unique opportunity and gives you an invaluable resource for feedback, recommendations, references, and sponsorships for new opportunities.

Our Goals:

In this chapter, we'll dive into how different advisory relationships work and why you need each of them. I'll share my experiences as someone who has been on both sides of all three of the advisory roles discussed in this chapter.

1) Explain the difference between sponsorship, mentorship, and coaching.
2) Walk through the process of earning a sponsor and brainstorm advisors who may be able and willing to help you.
3) Discuss how to ask your advisors for help.

Characteristics of Advisory Relationships

Let's spend just a minute talking about the characteristics of advisory relationships and how they differ from most relationships you have with family, friends, and work colleagues:

1) Advisors are topic-specific. Your relationship with them is based on a specific need. Once that need is addressed, the relationship naturally tapers off—unless and until another need arises that fits both you and your advisor.
2) You will not be close friends or lifelong pals with your career advisors. A healthy dose of respect will characterize the relationship. You will respect the advisors as they are experts in an area you are not and likely have much more experience and organizational power than you do. They are likely in roles you aspire to one day achieve.
3) Both you and the advisor serve a purpose for each other, and when that purpose is met, the relationship dissolves. You will

retain a friendliness and sense of gratitude that will keep you connected to your advisors, but the relationship as you knew it will change and dissipate.

4) Advisory relationships are very intentional. They don't just happen. They are characterized by an invitation and a response. Meeting with your advisor will be much the same. They will be scheduled discussions with a specific purpose.

5) And finally, there is a sense of professional obligation that exists. There is an understanding that in exchange for your advisor's time and expertise, you will listen and at least consider the advice they provide. After all, you asked for them to serve as an advisor!

There are several types of advisors. We are going to discuss the three most common: sponsors, mentors, and coaches. While there are similarities between the three, there are also distinct differences.

What's the Difference? Sponsor, Mentor, Coach

The best single-sentence definition I have found about the difference between sponsors, mentors, and coaches comes from the US Air Force: "A sponsor talks *about* you, a mentor talks *to* you, and a coach talks *with* you." (LeMay Center for Doctrine, n.d.) This elegantly simple definition captures the essence of each of these three roles. But let's take it a bit deeper.

A mentor is someone who teaches based on their own experiences, serves as a guide, and provides advice based on their own past learnings. Mentor relationships are often initiated by people who want to be mentored, rather than selected by the mentor. While offers of mentorship can be extended, the onus is on the person being mentored (the mentee) to schedule meetings and initiate discussions about the mentoring goals. Goals are often mutually agreed upon.

Additionally, mentors are usually hierarchy-based: a senior professional mentors a more junior professional. Said another way, more experienced people mentor less experienced people. (I've been mentored by people who are fifteen years younger than I am but are much more experienced in the topic of the mentorship.) Mentorships also generally don't involve compensation and can last for many years. It's a voluntary relationship on both parts for the benefit of passing along information and advice from someone who has been there, done that, and lived to tell the tale.

A coach is generally someone who specializes in a specific topic or skill set and who serves as a teacher to someone who wants to learn or become more skilled in the coach's particular specialty. Coaches often operate outside an organization and are generally paid engagements. They are initiated by the person being coached and are usually defined by a set time period, like six or twelve months. They often involve testing or assessment of some sort, so the coach can determine proficiency and build a coaching plan tailored to the needs of the person. The objectives of a coaching relationship are defined by the person being coached.

Sponsors, on the other hand, are advocates. They are usually influential leaders in positions of power that allow them to lend support, increase visibility, and create unique opportunities for the people they sponsor. Sponsors operate quite differently from mentors and coaches in several ways. They do most of their sponsorship work when the person they are sponsoring isn't in the room.

Let's walk through an example:

- The VP of HR that Shawn reports to is in a closed-door meeting discussing staffing needs for a series of special projects.
- Leaders in the meeting are talking about different people in the organization who might fit the needs of the project.

- Shawn's VP knows Shawn's interest in growing his strategy and planning skills because Shawn recently shared his idea for the performance improvement project and requested the VP's support.
- The project under discussion isn't currently on Shawn's radar, but the VP thinks it might be a good fit for Shawn and is willing to advocate for Shawn's consideration on the special project team.
- Shawn may never know that his VP advocated for him.
  - If the project under discussion goes in a different direction, or if someone else is given the opportunity, Shawn will never hear about it.
  - Or he may get a great opportunity simply because he made his interest known, and his VP chose to sponsor him without his knowledge.

Sponsors are particularly potent when you are trying to achieve a goal that you are unlikely to achieve without outside support and help. Sponsors can also significantly reduce the amount of time it takes you to achieve a goal by opening doors that aren't available to you without their access and influence (e.g., the closed-door meeting in our example).

Sponsorship is unique. It is more about the actions taken by people of influence and less about a specific relationship. They don't generally announce themselves or make promises. Rather, they quietly observe, decide to advocate on your behalf, and open doors for you, often without you being aware.

See the table below for a simplified explanation of the characteristics for mentorship, coaching, and sponsorship.

	Mentorship	Coaching	Sponsorship
Role	Guide	Teacher	Advocate
How they operate	Mentors talk to you.	Coaches talk with you.	Sponsors talk about you.
Foundational structure	Hierarchy based.	Contract based.	Potential based.
Nature of relationship	Mentee driven. Unpaid volunteer.	Participant driven. Often compensated.	Sponsor driven. Often anonymous.
Length of engagement	Decided mutually and often lasts many years.	Defined by a contract, usually 6 or 12 months.	Determined by the performance and potential of the person being sponsored.
Attribute shared	Shares past experiences.	Shares expertise from topic knowledge.	Shares advice and influence.
Resource support	Tell you where they got resource support.	Help you determine how to gain resource support.	Removes obstacles and provides resources.

Activity: Advisor Brainstorming

Let's do some brainstorming about the advisors you've been blessed with in the past, those who may be able to advise you going forward, and what you need from advisors to support your project plan. This brainstorming should help you think through who may be able to help you obtain the resources you need to put your plan into action.

Before you start your brainstorming session, let's organize our thinking by asking some preliminary questions.

1) What skills, experiences, resources, or attributes would be most helpful for your visibility project?

For instance, when I was thinking about going back to school for my master's degree, I wanted to talk to hiring managers for my ideal role, people in HR who could give me insight into the kind of degree I should pursue, and people who had completed their master's degrees while working and their do and don't recommendations. That list of advisors is very different from the list I might create for a different kind of project. Ground yourself in what you most need for *this* project.

2) Start brainstorming using the table below.

List everyone you can think of who has been an advisor to you in the past, whether as a mentor, coach, or sponsor. Then, list their areas of expertise, the advice you could seek from them for this project, and if there are any resources you may be able to request their assistance with. You won't reach out to all of these advisors, but this exercise should give you a good idea of a few that you may want to approach.

In my example above, I reached out to a former mentor who had a degree in a similar field to the one I wanted to pursue. I asked her to share her experiences and advice (expertise), asked her opinion on the program I was most interested in (advice needed), and asked her if she would be willing to be a reference for me (possible resource assistance).

Name:	Expertise:	Advice Needed:	Possible Resource Assistance:
1.			
2.			
3.			
4.			
5.			
6.			
7.			

Earn Your Sponsors

There are a few ways you can approach obtaining advice and resources. I believe the most effective, efficient, and sustainable way is through sponsorship. If you can attract and earn a sponsor, they will help you by providing feedback, advice, *and* resources!

The issue is that, unlike coaches and mentors, sponsors aren't something you can ask for—the sponsor has to choose to use their credibility, reputation, and influence on your behalf. They have to believe you have potential, will perform well if given an opportunity, and are worth the risk.

I've had many conversations with talented up-and-comers who didn't understand this concept; a few even demanded they be given a sponsor. It probably doesn't surprise you that no one who could have sponsored them wanted to do so. You can't be demanding, egocentric, and self-promoting and have a sponsor want to snap you up and become your advocate.

Conversely, I've known talented leaders who had several sponsors who were actively advocating for them but had no idea how many people were trying to help them behind the scenes.

But how are they earned? In my experience, sponsorships are a chain reaction. If you exhibit a strong work ethic, add value, and demonstrate the potential to do and become more, someone who is in a position to directly observe your work will take notice. It could be your immediate supervisor, the supervisor of a neighboring department, a mentor, or perhaps your supervisor's manager. I've even experienced sponsorships that came from a side gig that led to a higher-paying and higher-impact full-time job in a different organization.

It went something like this: "Oh, Dan, I was thinking about the new team you are building. I have someone you should meet. Her name is Jenn. She is working with me on the XYZ project, but she may be a great fit for your company and the new team you are building. She has really impressed me with her organizational and technical skills, and I know you are looking for people with those skills. I highly recommend her!"

The sponsorship chain reaction works like this:

- You do good work and demonstrate potential.
- Someone who can help you notices.
- They hear about an opportunity and think of you.
- They advocate for you when talking to the decision-maker about the opportunity.
- You get the opportunity.
- You do well, and the cycle starts over again and leads to another opportunity.

This cycle repeats and snowballs until you have a series of supporters who turn into sponsors!

Your job is to do good work and be someone others want to sponsor. Then, when you start getting opportunities because of sponsorship, be worthy of your sponsors' support by continuing to do good work and grow and develop your potential. If you do, the sponsorship chain reaction will continue.

The Sponsorship Chain Reaction:

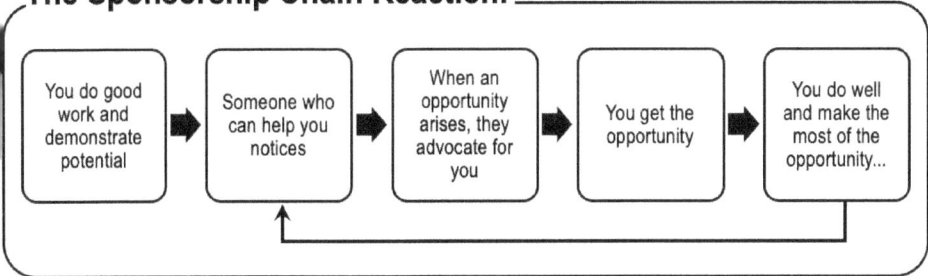

You do good work and demonstrate potential ➤ Someone who can help you notices ➤ When an opportunity arises, they advocate for you ➤ You get the opportunity ➤ You do well and make the most of the opportunity...

Mack was the first vice president I ever reported to. He hired me specifically to get a stuck project moving again. He took a chance on me. (You will hear more about Mack and this project in Part 3.) Long story short, I was able to deliver the results he needed within a few months. By doing so, I earned Mack's sponsorship. I didn't realize it at the time. Looking back now, it's more obvious to me.

Mack was an incredible sponsor and mentor to me. He played both roles. Under his tutelage and support, I was able to try doing things that were way above my pay grade or skill level. He was willing to take a chance on me, and those chances paid off when I did good work.

Let's shift our attention now to a different type of advisory role: mentors.

The Gift of Mentors

Sponsors may be the best-positioned advisors to provide access to opportunities and resources, but mentors are the best-positioned to teach, guide, and develop you in deep and lasting ways. Most of my stories are about my mentors. Most of the lessons I pass on to others were gifted to me by mentors. I don't have relationships with my past sponsors—but I do with my mentors.

If you don't currently have a mentor, get one. Getting a mentor is so much easier than most people realize. If you work with people you admire and want to learn from, try asking them if they would make time to have a short conversation.

This approach works inside and outside of organizations. Some of my most meaningful relationships right now are with people who are mentoring me (or I'm mentoring them), and we met casually at a networking event or entrepreneurial class. I've not known them long, but we are quickly forming deep relationships based on shared experiences and trading expertise. Mentors are everywhere. If you look, you can always find someone who is willing to engage with you. The added benefit of having a mentoring relationship outside your organization is the anonymity and ability to speak freely.

Additionally, mentors are more likely to advocate for you when the opportunity arises. So they can become both mentors and sponsors.

For those of you who are experienced with mentorship, let's look at how you may want to use mentorship differently. Sometimes, you need a mentor purely to help you gain a sponsor or access to a very specific kind of opportunity. Let me share an example.

I was talking with a bright and experienced mid-level manager yesterday. She is one step away from a VP role. We were talking through her lack of mentorship options inside her organization. She acknowledged that she can learn something from anyone, but the areas in which she needs growth aren't represented in the pool of likely mentors she has access to at her company. As we walked through various scenarios, we discovered one or two people who may be able to help her and who would be fantastic sponsors *if* they knew her better.

As you become more senior in your role and/or management level, there may be times when you need to engage a mentor not because of what you will learn from them but rather because of what they will learn about you. Remember, sponsors choose you. And they can't do that if they have no visibility into your work. And you never know; you may be surprised by what you learn through the mentorship—even when you don't think you will.

So far, we've talked a lot about how you can benefit from an advisor relationship. It is equally important that you give back by serving as an advisor to someone else.

Become an Advisor

You don't have to be an expert to offer value to someone. You just have to be willing to serve and be genuinely interested in the other person's growth. It took me a while to understand this.

I had a boss who set me straight: "Jenn, it's time for you to stop looking for mentors and become one!" He was right—kind of. I still had mentors, but I also became a very active mentor and sponsor to others.

I just hadn't thought of myself as experienced enough at the time to offer value to someone else. I think we can get so focused on growth and achievement that one day, we look up and realize we're the one others are now interested in learning from.

Besides the joy that comes from paying it forward and the satisfaction that comes from being someone's biggest fan, you also get the added benefit of working with and supporting different kinds of talent than you may have been able to work with before. Leaders notice other leaders who grow leaders. It's a tongue twister, but it's true! Once you enter the serious game of leadership, you gain additional scrutiny from other leaders, which isn't all bad.

Lastly, as you mentor others, remember that this book can be a reference for you. I've done much of the work, and I encourage you to use the book as a framework to guide your mentorship discussions. Just replace my examples with your own, use The Breakthrough Formula Generator to build a baseline and discussion tool to focus your efforts, and leverage the exercises you feel are most appropriate for your goals. Voilà! You now have a custom mentorship program!

Asking Advisors for Help

We've talked quite a bit about where to find advisors, the benefits of having them, how they work, and the need to pay it forward. We've not yet talked about the moment in which you approach them to make your ask. Let's do that now.

Once you have identified someone you want to approach with your project, reach out to them and ask for a meeting. If you don't have a relationship with the person, do you know someone who could introduce you? Is there an alternate person you could approach that may also be able to assist you?

Pick someone and take a leap of faith. This is the belly-dropping moment of stepping into the unknown. The good news is that most influential leaders know how hard it is for you to ask for a meeting.

Within an organization, you may need to work through the leader's administrative professional, who is adept at fielding these kinds of inquiries. In some cases, it may be a good idea to ask another leader you know to reach out on your behalf to make the request. Be prepared if they point you to someone you weren't expecting instead of giving you the meeting directly. Go with the flow and meet with anyone who is willing to visit with you about your project.

Ok. You've got a meeting scheduled, you're prepared with your pitch documents, you've practiced, and you know what you are going to ask for. Let's cover one last preparation tip: Practice how you will respond if you are disappointed by the outcome.

Here are some questions to consider:

- What will I do if I'm turned down?
- What will I do if my work is substantially edited?
- What will I do if my idea is accepted but given to someone else to implement?

I know very few people who can handle all of the above situations with grace in the moment without any preparation at all. It's natural to be emotionally tied to your work. You've put a lot of yourself into your project already. I encourage you to figure out how you will respond to each of these questions. And then practice it.

Your final items of preparation are easy: Plan out your clothing, take deep breaths, do jumping jacks to get out your nervous energy, make good food choices before you enter the meeting, check your materials, phone a friend, say a prayer, and deliver a final pep talk to yourself. You can do this!

Then, go into the meeting and kill it. Do your best and leave it all on the field. Give yourself the gift of no regrets. You worked hard for this meeting, so make the best of it and try to enjoy the experience. You're about to do something other people have wanted to do but haven't done. No regrets.

Fast-forward… The hardest part is done. You've delivered your pitch!

Now brace yourself and your emotions for the leader's response. If the outcome of the meeting is disappointing, try not to let it overshadow your gratitude for their time and interest. If they didn't have an interest in supporting you, you wouldn't have been granted the meeting.

Disappointment is tough to face, but a gracefully accepted "no" can build a reputation faster than an excited expression after a "yes" is received. We show our true colors when we hear the word "no," and leaders know that and pay attention to it. That's what happened to me after Jack delivered his disappointing news following my pitch.

I didn't know it at the time, but the company was going through a large acquisition that wasn't yet public knowledge. That was the reason my pitch was turned down or put "on hold." So when Jack told me "not yet," he meant it! He also selected me for a team leader role for the post-acquisition integration team on the strength of my work with him following the pitch. I didn't know any of that until much later. If I had handled the disappointing news poorly, those unknown opportunities could have been pulled back, and I never would have known about the opportunity I lost.

I want to close this chapter with the end of that story and tell you about an unexpected twist that happened just days after my final phone call with Jack.

My Real-Life Breakthrough Journey: *Installment 5 (Part 2)*

Let's backtrack to my situation after receiving Jack's rejection of my proposal, gently delivered as it was. I knew the direction I wanted to take with my career, and I knew I needed to start preparing now. So, after talking with James, we revisited the idea of pursuing my master's degree and started looking into programs that would support my move from IT to HR.

I wanted to be smart about the degree I would pursue, so James and I did a ton of research to find the right program in the right school, at the right price, and with the right delivery method so I could continue to work my more-than-full-time job.

As part of the research, I told James I wanted to do a job search so I could backward engineer the education requirements. I wasn't looking to leave my company; I just didn't want to spend two years of my life earning a degree that wouldn't support my future job ambitions.

Through that research, James found a job description that was almost identical to the job description I had included in my pitch documents to Jack. He shared it with me one night after work.

"Take a look at this job opening, Jenn." He sat me down at his computer.

I started to read but stopped several times to gasp and gawk. "James, this is *just* like what I sent to Jack!"

"I know," he said, "keep reading."

This happened several times. I would gush, and he would tell me to keep reading. When I finally got to the bottom of the job posting, I murmured, "This position is with a healthcare system in our town."

I stared at James in wonder. What in the world was going on? James found this job posting on a national website. We weren't looking for jobs in our area. We weren't really even looking for a job. We were using job postings as a way of testing the education requirements against the master's degree we were evaluating.

James was smug. "I know! That's why I wanted you to keep reading!" He smiled, then asked, "So, are you going to apply for it?"

I gaped at him, "I'm not qualified yet."

James responded, "What would it hurt to apply? Technically, you aren't unqualified. It says the master's degree is preferred. What if you just tried to get an interview? Wouldn't that be a good experience?"

Yes. Yes, it would. So I put in my application for my master's degree program and then applied for the job. I also put together a portfolio of my work, created a web page showing it, created business cards for myself as an applicant, and prayed for an interview.

I'll fast-forward the story here and tell you that I got the interview. And I got the job. It turned out they needed someone with a background in IT to help them get their online training system launched, and my lack of experience in HR wasn't an issue for them. They felt my qualifications more than met their criteria. And they loved that I was already accepted into a master's degree program that fit the role!

Next Up: Launch Your Visibility Project with Energize FUEL Actions

We've made it through the Strategize section and the PLAN actions. You have identified your opportunity, drafted your plan with specific actions that support it, and started reaching out to pitch your idea to advisors who can help you.

Before we launch into the next part of the book, let's pause to pull out your personalized breakthrough formula. Have you been using it as we've worked through each chapter? Take a moment to revisit your formula report and capture any activities, tools, or topics you want to remember from the Strategize section. Then, decide which sections of the Energize step you want to pay particular attention to.

Ready? Let's keep going.

As we move into the second step of the Breakthrough Formula, Energize, I want you to think of the FUEL components like a virtual ride in a hot air balloon. The Energize step is all about gathering the FUEL we need to lift us up and carry us through the Mobilize step, where we will intentionally execute our visibility project plan.

To generate FUEL, we are going to:

- Fan the Flame
- Unleash Your Community
- Encourage Input
- Lighten Your Load

When you combine encouragement, community, input, and letting go of things that weigh you down, you create the FUEL needed to lift off. So, join me on a hot air balloon ride and climb in so we can lift off. I'll see you in the next chapter, where I'll take you with me into the first meeting I have with my new boss, Mack.

Let's Review:

1) We defined and discussed the differences between types of advisors: Mentors (talk to you), coaches (talk with you), and sponsors (talk about you).

2) Sponsors have the most impact on resource allocation. They have the influence and position power to remove obstacles, provide guidance, and directly support resource needs. Mentors are the best positioned to teach, guide, and develop you in deep and lasting ways. Mentors can also provide advocacy and sponsorship, depending on the circumstance.

3) Sponsors must be earned, and the process of obtaining a sponsor can be described as a chain reaction:
   ◦ You do good work and demonstrate potential.
   ◦ Someone who can help you notices.
   ◦ They hear about an opportunity and think of you.
   ◦ They advocate for you when talking to the decision-maker of the opportunity.
   ◦ You get the opportunity.
   ◦ You do well, and the cycle starts over again and leads to another opportunity.

Think About It:

1) Who was the best advisor (sponsor, mentor, or coach) you've ever had? What characteristics made them better than others? What could you learn from them to apply to your own practice of advising others?

2) Can you look back at a past experience of pitching an idea for approval? What might you do differently? What did you do that was particularly effective that isn't shared in this chapter?

3) How do you self-manage your expectations and emotions when you hear disappointing news? How would you advise someone else to temper their disappointment?

Take Action:

1) Complete the advisor brainstorming activity to create a list of possible advisors you can approach to share your ideas and learn from.

2) Once you have your short list of possible advisors, start working toward getting discussions scheduled with them. Reach out to someone you know and trust and ask for their help through coaching or introductions to people in their network who may be willing to assist you.

3) Consider how you can begin advising others as a mentor, coach, or sponsor. Understanding the role of an advisor will help you better understand how to approach new advisors who could potentially help you.

Section 3

Energize!

Chapter 8

Fan Your Flame

My Real-Life Breakthrough Journey: *Installment 6*

"Welcome to the team, Jennifer." Mack, my new boss, greeted me as I entered his office for my onboarding meeting.

We were scheduled to discuss his expectations, the reasons he hired me, and the most pressing matters facing my new department. I was the Director of Education and Development. It was still surreal. I couldn't believe I had been hired and had broken into the director ranks and into my ideal career field and position. I was incredibly grateful for the opportunity.

Then Mack started speaking, and the other shoe dropped. "There are a few things you need to know about your team."

I sat forward with my pen, poised to take notes.

Mack continued, "They didn't pick you. And they didn't want me to hire you."

My heart sank, and my throat grew tight. I took a hard swallow and put my pen down, working hard to school my features and quiet the negative chatter and alarm that had exploded inside my head.

He continued, "You're going to have to get them on board. Also, your department was on the chopping block not long ago. There is still concern that the team isn't providing enough value to warrant the expense. We've made some changes, but your department isn't out of danger yet."

Surprise! None of this came up in the interview. My head was reeling as my thoughts chased each other. What had I gotten myself into?!?

Undaunted, he continued, "Getting the online training system implemented will go a long way to silencing our critics. That's one of the reasons I hired you. I love that you have a background in IT and that you've implemented several of these systems. I believe in you and will support you."

I was numb for the rest of the meeting. We talked through some new employee paperwork and I asked as many questions as I could before the meeting ended and I had to leave.

As I walked slowly back to my new office, I thought about the challenges ahead of me and tried to process everything I had been told. "So much for my 'dream job,'" I mumbled to myself. "Time to take inventory… "

1) I'm leading a team that doesn't want me.
2) I'm responsible for turning around a department that is under-performing and on the shortlist for possible budget cuts.
3) I need to have a quick win with the training system implementation to buy time while I figure out how to get the department back on track.

Ugh. "I wonder if Jack would let me come back?" I thought.

Have you ever felt that way? You can't wait to have that cool glass of lemonade on a hot day, only to take the first sip and realize the sugar was left out. I needed to assess the situation, build a plan, and win over my team so we could implement it together.

Before I could realistically do any of that, I needed to process what I had been told and figure out how to deal with the negative chatter in my head that was telling me I had made a colossal mistake in taking this job, that I was way over my head, and that failure was just a matter of time.

It didn't take me long to feel like there was a threat around every corner. My team didn't want me, and the organization wasn't sure they wanted my team. I didn't have friends or allies, I didn't yet know the unwritten code that every workplace operates with, and I was still learning absolutely everything about my role, the job itself, and how to lead a much larger team. I was also going to night school to earn that master's degree I signed up for. It was overwhelming.

I had to make a choice: Was I going to cave under the pressure and quit, or was I going to dig deep and fight through it? I won't lie. Running sounded pretty darn good. But in the end, I was just too stubborn to quit, so I decided to change my outlook and my negative attitude.

My dad always told me that my attitude was a choice—and sometimes, that choice had to be made 100 times in the course of a single day. I knew I needed to change my attitude from negative, angry, and victimized to positive, determined, and accountable. I could tackle these issues. Perhaps not alone, but I wasn't alone in this. I had a team. I just needed to win them over by demonstrating respect, building rapport, and enlisting their help in turning our situation around. I could do this.

The next two years became a period of my career I call my "boot camp" experience. It was one of the most challenging periods of my life. It was also a period in which I grew exponentially.

Through that process, I learned that you can't fan the flames of positivity and encouragement if you are constantly snuffing those flames out with a wet blanket of negativity. I had to find ways to minimize and eliminate negative chatter to make room for positive thoughts—and then protect them fiercely by fanning my flame to keep it roaring.

Our Goals:

In this chapter, we're going to lean into some positivity techniques and consider new ways you can sustainably fan your flame. We need to kick your hot air balloon burner into high gear so you get the lift you need for takeoff and to keep you soaring.

There are countless reasons for mental obstacles and many fantastic books that deal with this subject. We'll only be able to scratch the surface, but sometimes that's all you need: awareness of the issues and a few simple techniques you can use to snap out of it and return to a positive and uplifting headspace. For this reason, I'm zeroing in on three concepts I think can be immediately helpful:

1) Understanding how your brain filters information in the world around you—an ounce of prevention is worth a pound of cure!

2) Fine-tuning your brain's filter so the right information reaches you. We want to spend less time searching for positivity and more time noticing it around us.

3) Consider different ways you can saturate your brain with positivity and encouragement for just-in-time encouragement boosts.

Your Brain at Work

Before we dig into techniques and tools for clearing up and protecting your headspace, I think it's helpful to have a shared understanding of how our brains process information.

The field of neuroscience has revealed fascinating insights about how our brains work, and we can use that knowledge to accelerate our performance and better manage our mental health. Much as we manage our physical bodies by what we eat, how we exercise, and our maintenance routines, we need to be just as intentional and regimented with our brains. By better understanding how our brains are wired, we can work with our brain's natural functioning to achieve better performance. Let's take a quick spin through the area of the brain responsible for filtering what gets in and what stays out.

If you've not yet met your brain's focus filter, allow me to introduce you. Meet the Reticular Activating System or RAS. Think of this as the "Google" of your brain. Just as Google has access to an infinite number of data points, so does your brain. Your brain is bombarded by millions of data points collected by your senses, and it needs some instruction to know what it should present to you and what it needs to filter out. (Thome et al. 2019; Mary McKone 2024; Health Tips 2022) In this way, your RAS is just like a Google search. You tell Google/RAS what to look for, and it provides the information you requested.

The better you become at making requests, the better your search results match your intentions. If you tell your RAS to look for the positive, you will begin to see it everywhere. And vice versa. You are in control of what you let into your brain with your control of your RAS.

So, how, exactly, do we do a search using our RAS? Well, we give our brains instruction about what to let in or keep out based on what we intently focus on. For example, I'm writing this chapter, and my focus is solely on my computer screen and my subject—what I'm not paying attention to is the music in the background, my dog sitting at my feet, and the birds chirping outside. As soon as I try to focus on those things, I can see, hear, and sense them. A minute ago, all I could hear was the distant sound of my clicking keyboard and the sound of my own voice in my head. My RAS was helping me focus by filtering out non-essential information.

So, how does this work when we apply it to the topic of our headspace? Let's compare two examples.

1) If you focus on negative thoughts and beliefs, your RAS will helpfully supply you with data points that support that focus. For instance, if you tell yourself you are tired, guess what… your RAS will search for data to back that up, and you will feel the signs of fatigue in your body.

2) If you focus on something positive, like an affirmation or something you are grateful for, your RAS will search for data to back that up, and you will feel more energy, hope, and positive emotions.

We can solve many headspace challenges simply by being more disciplined about what we let into our minds and by making better choices about what we focus on.

Focus on the Right Things

Let's return for a moment to the opening story of this chapter. In fact, after you read this paragraph, scroll back up to that story and examine it.

As I walked away from my boss's office, I processed the conversation and focused on the issues that seemed reasonable and relatable. But do you see any positive thoughts mentioned? Can you catch me engaging in any solutions-based thinking? Nope! Because I stopped short. I only focused on negative thoughts and emotions. I was too busy visiting Pity City and feeling sorry for myself.

If I had passed through the negative thoughts, acknowledged them, and then let them go and moved on to what I *could* do and *could* control, I would have regained my energy and reached solutions faster and with less heartache. By focusing on and being stuck inside a negative headspace, I could easily see the naysayers and critics all around me, but I couldn't even fathom that supporters may also exist. The hard truth is that we can fix a lot of the issues we cause ourselves with a little proactive work to focus on positive, helpful, supportive concepts.

So how? How can we turn the tide of negative thoughts? I won't insult you by offering a magic pill that will fix it overnight. It takes work and time to focus on things that are positive. And sometimes, you just have to fake it, which is ironically also a way of telling your RAS what to search for.

When you are feeling stressed, forcing yourself to fake a smile sends signals to your brain that release hormones that lower stress and improve your mood. (Wiswede et al. 2009; Kraft and Pressman 2012) There are quite a few research studies that support this. (Coles, Larsen, and Lench 2019) So you really can "fake it till you make it" when it comes to your outlook.

Retraining your RAS by consistently asking it to search for positive information, including smiling when you don't feel like it, will sharpen its ability to provide better search results and shift your focus to a more positive place. As you do so, you will find returning to a positive headspace happens more easily and quickly. This step is proactive in nature and builds momentum over time.

You can use visualization exercises, repeat daily positive affirmations, journal to set your intentions, pray, write down your goals, and so much more. As we work through the rest of this chapter, I challenge you to think of things that you do now that work for you, things you can add to your routine that have worked for you in the past, and new ideas you want to try out.

To help jump-start your thinking, let's walk through three techniques that saturate your brain with positivity and have worked for me: Picking a word and affirmation, pops of joy, and gratitude.

Saturate Your Brain with Positivity

1) Pick a Word to Set Your Intention:

Selecting a word and writing an affirmation for it that encompasses what you want to achieve can be a powerful way to set your RAS filter. The statement should be positive, aspirational, powerful, and exciting. I do this every January. I also use this technique when I'm working on a particular project, and I need additional focus.

Once you have your word and affirmation, memorize them so you can recite them daily. I like mixing this with a little Mell Robbins *High 5 Habit* by staring into the mirror in the morning and stating my word and affirmation with gusto as if I was passionately convincing a friend how amazing they are, and I end it with a High five to myself. (Robbins 2023)

I've done some variation of this for years, but I became truly committed to this approach in 2020 when I met a woman named Pamela Crim, owner and founder of Big Life, a faith-based women's mentorship program. ("Big Life Headquarters," n.d.) Prior to meeting Pamela, I had picked a word to focus on without an affirmation, and I didn't use it daily. With Pamela's instruction and guidance, I added an affirmation that locks in my intention by defining how that word will guide my decisions and daily actions.

Emily's Word and Affirmation:

To bring this concept to life, let's create a word and affirmation for Emily. If you recall Emily's story in Chapter 2, she has struggled with limited success. She demonstrates strength in the Strategize and Mobilize areas but would benefit from improvement in the Energize area.

Let's briefly revisit her story. Note the points that are emphasized:

> Emily is a hard-charging, get-it-done professional who is technically brilliant and rarely (if ever) wrong. She knows her subject matter deeply. If Emily gives an answer, it is right. She is trusted to do the most complicated work and deliver it on time and with the highest quality. She is extremely valued for the consistency of her results and her unquestionable accuracy.

> Emily's issue is that she can be *rude, impatient,* and *unintentionally unkind* to others who do what she considers to be inferior work. People have quit after being assigned a project under her leadership. She has stated quite clearly that she expects to be promoted and has CEO aspirations. Because of her *inability to effectively engage others*, she is overlooked for executive positions, and her bid for CEO isn't treated seriously. She *doesn't get* the *feedback* she needs about her people skills because even her managers are unwilling to deal with the *backlash* they fear the feedback would produce.

> Emily is currently a senior operations manager with a background in finance. Her ultimate goal is to become a CEO.

For the purposes of our discussion, let's assume that Emily has gone through the Strategize PLAN steps and has decided that her next breakthrough opportunity is to lead a project team on a topic that is outside her area of technical expertise. Doing so will benefit her growth in the following ways:

1) It will force her to lean on the technical expertise of others instead of being the most knowledgeable person on the team. This means that she can't fall back on her own knowledge to ensure success. Instead, the project's success will be dependent on the performance of the entire team.

2) It will give her a chance to put all her time, energy, and effort into the people aspects of leading a team. Since this is an area she struggles with, it will require focus and a lot of effort to do things that don't feel natural or comfortable.

3) If she can pull it off, it will demonstrate her ability to respond to the feedback she's received and will begin to change the way others view her and her potential as a leader of others.

After meeting with her mentor and sponsor, she has been assigned to lead a marketing campaign project for a new operations service offering. The team has ten operations and communications team members assigned.

Ok. Let's pick a word and write an affirmation for Emily to use during this period of growth. Here are some options:

- Inspire
- Encourage
- Patience
- Collaborate
- Achieve

Let's further assess these options:

- **Inspire**: This feels like it may be too aspirational. Will people accept inspiration from someone they are weary of? Perhaps over time, they would, but in the beginning, this may be too far a reach.
- **Encourage**: This could work, but it still feels like a bit of a stretch.
- **Patience:** This word is interesting as it is something she could apply to both herself and those around her. Let's keep this one in mind.
- **Collaborate:** This is also an interesting word. It requires her to lean on others and invite active participation.
- **Achieve:** This doesn't seem to fit as well because achievement has never been her issue. This word may put too much emphasis on "winning" and not enough on the process of winning by working with and through others.

After considering the options, Emily has selected "Patience." Now for the affirmation. We want the affirmation statement to be aspirational but achievable. The statement will set Emily's mindset for the day and help her RAS actively seek out information to support her word and aspirations.

Here is Emily's completed word and affirmation:

Patience: Today, I will lead with patience and understanding, allowing each team member the space to grow and contribute, fostering a culture of respect and collaboration. I will also exercise patience with myself by recognizing that it takes time and practice to learn new skills.

If Emily uses her word and affirmation daily, it will help retain her focus on what she is trying to accomplish. It will also serve as an accountability tool. You cannot recite your word and affirmation without immediately thinking about how you did the day before.

Additional examples for Shawn and Magda are provided in Appendix A.

Activity #1: Pick Your Word and Write Your Affirmation

1) Spend a few minutes doing a brain-dump journaling exercise about what you want to accomplish by choosing a word and writing an affirmation. Let your thoughts flow. Don't restrict or edit them. Just pour out everything that comes to you.

2) Once you've emptied your thoughts, go back and look for ideas that jump out at you. I like to use a highlighter to identify anything that seems important.

   ◦ What words catch your eye?

   ◦ Are there repetitions that tell you something?

   ◦ Are there phrases that you really like?

   ◦ Is there a theme that stands out?

3) Pick a word. It will likely come from your journaling, or it could be a word that describes what you journaled.

4) Go back to your journaling and write an affirmation.

   ◦ Make it positive.

   ◦ Make it actionable.

   ◦ At the end of the day, can you evaluate whether you acted according to your aspiration with a clear "yes" or "no"?

5) Write it down in a place you will see it each morning and speak it aloud. (Extra credit if you do it in front of a mirror!) Over time, try to memorize it.

> ## *HACK IT TIP:*
>
> If you don't enjoy these kinds of writing exercises, this is a good opportunity to borrow other people's talents, verbally journal with a recorded note or coffee with a friend, or tap into AI to assist you. You could even drop your journaling ramble into an AI engine and ask it to find themes or even write an aspiration for you.

Now that you have your word and affirmation, let's move on to technique #2, pops of joy.

2) Just-In-Time Pops of Joy

Have you ever received a small surprise that delighted you unexpectedly? Something you didn't plan on or expect but that made your day brighter? I call these "pops of joy." They pop up out of nowhere and bring a little ray of sunshine, usually when I need it most.

A few years ago, I decided that these little blessings were needed more frequently by me and everyone around me. For years, I worked in high-stress environments where much of my job involved dealing with tough issues and high emotions. To combat this, I couldn't count on moments of joy stemming from good news and happy people. I had to make my own moments of joy. That's when I started creating "pops of joy."

Here are three corny things that manufacture smiles in chaos and combat negativity with sheer fun and silliness. If none of these bring you joy, use them as examples to create your kind of "pops of joy."

1) *Pop of Joy Grab Bags*: This sounds really corny, but it totally works.

   ◦ Hit the dollar store and fill your basket with silly things that make you smile. It could be chocolate, party favors, smiley face pencils, or a cheerful notebook. The point here is to gather inexpensive items that are fun and out of your norm.

   ◦ Then, place each item into a brown paper lunch bag with POP OF JOY written on it. You can even add a positive and encouraging note or a quote you love. Better yet, do this with a friend and prepare bags for each other so it is a total surprise.

   ◦ Put the bags in your work area, around your house, in your car, wherever they will be most needed. And then just live life.

   ◦ The next time you are having a tough day or a hard time, break open one of the bags. It never fails that the message or the item is just exactly what I needed at that moment. The odds are good it will startle a laugh from you and lift your spirits. And every time you look at the silly little something, you will remember the pop of joy that came with it. Sometimes, all you need is a jolt to break your negative thoughts and get you back on track.

2) *Daily Inspirational Cards:*

   I have several decks of cards written by a comedienne that have very funny illustrations and "words of wisdom" on them that always make me smile or even laugh out loud.

   During a tough time at work, I got into the habit of randomly drawing from the deck when a friend of mine, or I, were having a bad day. I would shoot it over to her via text. It never failed to lighten our spirits and adjust our attitudes.

You can find these kinds of tools everywhere: at bookstores, in daily tear-away desk calendars, and online. Where are my Dilbert cartoon fans? See! If you love Dilbert, I bet that made you smile.

3)   *Daily Devotionals or Inspirational Messages:*

Do you have a favorite daily message that gives you inspiration or a positive thought for the day? I subscribe to several different inspirational text messages from people I follow, tune into positive podcasts, and check in with other short and snappy leadership and self-care inspirational messages delivered by various apps I use. Begin looking for short, consistently delivered positive messages that you can subscribe to so the message comes to you, and you don't have to remember to go looking for it!

Regardless of the method you choose, help yourself out by intentionally designing pops of joy into your day and life. These small moments of joy can yield big results over time, just like our next topic: Gratitude!

3) Gratitude Practice:

No chapter on Fanning Your Flame would be complete without a discussion about gratitude. Having a healthy and vibrant gratitude practice has grown in popularity for very good reasons. When you focus on things you are grateful for, you find more reasons to be grateful. You also benefit from improved mental health with less anxiety, and more positive emotions and mood. (Diniz et al. 2023)

There are so many ways you can practice gratitude. There are one-sentence daily gratitude journals, daily page practices that focus on gratitude, gratitude workbooks, and so much more. You likely already have a favored method. Let me share one of mine: Gratitude photos!

A friend introduced me to the concept of taking a daily gratitude photo. She took one picture each day that represented what she was grateful for that day. After a year, she created a collage of her 365 photos.

I've taken this in a slightly different direction. I take a photo anytime I am feeling grateful. Sometimes, that is multiple times a day, and sometimes I miss a day. At the end of the month, I review the images I've taken, and I create a photo album of that month's gratitude photos. It reminds me of my blessings and the many people, places, and experiences I was grateful for that month. It amazes me how much joy reviewing those images brings me. I will go back to previous months, rewatch my gratitude albums, and relive all of those precious moments. It's also a great way to review my blessings at the end of the year.

If you aren't currently engaged in some form of daily gratitude practice, I encourage you to start right now. If you've let your practice falter, then turn it back on. The biggest challenge in practicing gratitude isn't a lack of methods; it's a lack of consistency. So pick something that is easy.

When I have my hardest days, the fastest way for me to get out of my funk is to focus on everything I'm grateful for and then take action to do something positive for someone else. I reach out to encourage someone. I pay something forward. I volunteer for something. I do *something* that takes ME out of the equation. When I'm most down, it is usually because I'm too focused on myself, and I've lost sight of who I'm serving and why I serve. Gratitude realigns me and immediately moves me into a positive headspace.

It's amazing how quickly gratitude puts everything into perspective. I said I wouldn't offer a magic pill, but practicing gratitude may just be one!

Now that you have spent some time Fanning Your Flame, it's time to take your positive energy and share it with others. In the next chapter, we're going to dive into how you can unleash your community as a source of FUEL. We're going to turn our solo positivity efforts into a party that engages others.

Let's Review:

1) The Reticular Activating System, or RAS, acts like the Google search engine for your brain. It filters millions of data points collected by your senses to reduce what enters your conscious mind based on what you focus on.

2) We can solve many headspace challenges simply by being more disciplined about what we let into our minds and by making better choices about what we focus on.

3) Tips for saturating your brain with positivity and encouragement include picking a word and writing an affirmation that sets your intention, daily pops of joy, and engaging in a consistent gratitude practice.

Think About It:

1) Is the state of your current headspace helping or hurting your performance? Why is that?

2) In what ways would you like to retrain your RAS?

3) How can you create moments of joy in chaos? What new routines or techniques will you use to intentionally focus your RAS on a more positive message?

<u>Take Action:</u>

1) Pick a word and write an affirmation statement that breathes life into your word and sets your intention. The statement should be short, positive, aspirational, powerful, and exciting.

2) Find and subscribe to a pop of joy inspirational message that is delivered on a consistent basis, and that doesn't require effort on your part. Share your pop of joy with someone else to make their day and create a shared moment of positivity.

3) Engage or evolve your gratitude practice. Pick a method that you enjoy and start focusing on everything for which you are grateful. Find a time to routinely review your gratitude log, journal, or photo album to reinforce your focus and train your RAS.

Chapter 9

Unleash Your Community

My Real-Life Breakthrough Journey: *Installment 7*

As I contemplated how to break the ice with my new team, I opened my email inbox and found an email waiting for me with the results of the company's most recent employee engagement survey. The survey happened before I joined the team, but the results had only just been released to the organization. I decided to dig into the results for my team to give me an idea about where to start.

My heart sank as I read the report. The results were worse than I expected. I knew from my discussion with Mack that the department wasn't doing well, but I wasn't prepared for results that were this poor. Their engagement scores were heartbreakingly low.

I spent quite a while digesting the engagement survey results and reflecting back on what I learned from Mack. My mind kept returning to how downtrodden my new team must feel about their jobs, the team, and the organization. With an improved attitude and a softened heart for my team, I scheduled our first team meeting and got to work preparing for it.

I knew that the entire team was long-tenured and tight-knit. Some of them had worked together for twenty years. All of them had at least fifteen years with the department. They were also all older than I was. I was definitely the odd one out: I was new to HR, new to healthcare, new to the company, and the youngest member of the team. To date, the team approached each interaction with me with wariness and caution. I knew it was going to be up to me to break the ice, build trust, and join their team.

Given the issues facing the department, I decided to take a very direct approach to the meeting. I would then have one-on-one conversations with each member of the team after we had met as a team. I was hoping that the initial meeting would answer their most pressing questions and give us something to talk about in our individual one-on-one meetings.

The day of the meeting arrived, and I showed up early. I was nervous and knew I needed to strike the right tone of confident, excited, purposeful, and caring. I needed the team to open up to me.

As I arranged the room and set up the food I had brought, I recalled a recent conversation with one of my mentors. She told me that people can't listen or accept what you say when they are mentally closed. She illustrated this by handing me a pen and telling me to give it to her. She extended a closed fist. The pen hit her hand and rolled off. She went on to explain that prying a closed fist open to take a pen only makes the fist instinctively close even harder. You have to be gentle and patient and convince the hand to let down its guard and open just a bit. With time and care, the closed fist can become an open hand.

I was about to face a group of "closed fists." I said a silent prayer for guidance as I waited for the team to arrive.

They slowly trickled into the room. They greeted each other warmly and me cooly. They sat together, leaving spaces between me and them. I knew their physical distance was indicative of their emotional caution.

"Ok, then," I thought, "This is where we are right now. Let's see if we can change it." Deep breath in, deep breath out.

I began, "Hello, everyone. Thanks for coming. Help yourselves to the treats in the back. I'm looking forward to our time together."

I received half-hearted greetings and closed body language, followed by an awkward silence. Time to rip off the band-aid.

"Well, let's be honest with each other from the start. Mack told me that you didn't want me as your boss."

Shocked expressions greeted me. I forged on.

"I was disappointed to hear that, and I'd like to understand why and what I did that made you feel that way. I'm very excited about the chance to work with you, and I hope we can learn from each other and build something great."

Deciding it was best to get it all out there, I kept going, "Mack also told me about the challenges the department has had with the workload and budget constraints. I understand that it has been a tough time. I think if we work together, we can figure out a solution we can all believe in."

I sat back and waited for someone to accept my invitation to have an honest and real discussion. This tactic was a bit of a gamble. It doesn't always work. In this case, it did.

Jane, the administrative assistant and the most vocal and direct person on the team spoke up, "We didn't feel like you really wanted the job. You kept talking about how great your team was at your organization. We wanted Mack to hire someone who really wanted this job and this team."

Ahhhh. In my attempt not to appear too eager or to appear as a pushover when I met with the team during the interview process, I had miscalculated and came across too confident and even cocky. When you add that to the backdrop of this department already feeling unwanted, I could easily understand where they were coming from. So, I chose to respond with transparency and vulnerability.

"I'm really sorry I gave you that impression. It's true that I am proud of my other team and what we accomplished together, and I wasn't looking to leave my company. But I was also crazy excited about this job and working with you. It's my dream job. I really want to be here." I infused as much emotion and feeling as I could into the statement. I wanted them to hear my sincerity.

I saw their shoulders fall a bit, and their faces relaxed, with some even giving me a smile.

Jane responded, "Well, it would have been a lot easier on all of us if you had just said that in the interview!"

I smiled. "You're right. Thank you for the feedback. I didn't handle that interview well."

Our honest exchange broke the tension in the room, and the team started adopting more relaxed and engaged postures. The metaphorical fist opened just a bit.

I continued, "Tell me about the department, your struggles, and your frustrations."

They opened up by sharing things that were getting in their way, the work they didn't feel they should be doing, and their concerns about a variety of issues. After some digging, I was able to piece together that the team didn't have a clear purpose.

In an attempt to salvage the department, the prior director had muddied the water by taking on any administrative task that didn't have a home. I understand and applaud the effort of trying to keep the department afloat, but taking on administrative duties that no one else wanted backfired and generated the opposite effect. If the team had time to do everyone else's work, then the unintended message was that they didn't have enough work of their own. The purpose of the department had been lost under the weight of a bunch of stuff that other departments didn't want to do. It was difficult for the team to take pride in the work no one else wanted. We needed to change that.

"To keep moving forward, I think we need to have a discussion about what we ultimately want to achieve as a department. What do we want our impact to be on the organization? We've been talking about pain points and frustrations, but I think we can aspire to more. What do you think?"

Everyone spoke up, and the discussion was vibrant and hopeful. Ideas were plentiful and free-flowing, with each person adding to the growing idea list from their own perspective. What a change from just an hour before!

I grabbed a marker, and we moved our discussion to the whiteboard.

"So if we were to create a vision of what we want to accomplish, what would that look like?" I encouraged the team not to focus on our current limitations but on what they wanted and what they felt would best support the organization.

That conversation led us into a vision casting session. Here's the vision statement we created:

The Education and Development Department is a team of highly skilled professionals that create and curate award-winning leadership development content, provide expertise and consultation to health system educators, and lead enterprise-wide HR projects that improve the employee and patient experience. We are the top-performing corporate department in customer satisfaction, employee engagement, and budget management. Other people want to work in this department and with this team!

This message is a far cry from what they were doing, how they saw themselves, and how others saw them. It felt like a huge leap, but they could see themselves in the statement and wanted this future to be true. At that moment, we became a team united by a common and compelling purpose.

In the following weeks and months, we met frequently to build out a plan that included specific assignments for each team member. Everyone was given a lead role in some part of the plan. We set clear expectations and held each other accountable. The success of our plan was dependent on every team member showing up and contributing their expertise and effort. It was an incredibly energizing experience. The energy and excitement was palpable. Best of all, no closed fists remained. Their palms were open, and they were contributing to the new direction, and those open palms would eventually turn into high fives!

Our Goals:

In this chapter, we're going to unleash the power of a committed community to help you achieve your visibility project. We'll discuss the importance of being part of an active community, asking your community for help, and providing support and value to them in exchange. There are few things as powerful or fulfilling as working with a group of people who are inspired and committed to taking action on each other's behalf so everyone wins.

To engage and unleash the power of our community, we must do three things well. If any of the three are missing, we will fail to harness the power of our community, and our project will falter.

1) Find the right community to engage with for your visibility project.

2) Clearly articulate and share your vision in a way that invites, encourages, and facilitates your community's engagement and support.

3) Ask your community for their support, give them a role to play and work to do, and then offer the same support back to them.

Let's begin this chapter with the power a community can provide to members in need by looking at a historical application of community support.

Building a Barn

Have you heard of a barn raising? It's a tradition that dates back to the earliest European settlers in North America, in which a community would gather supplies, food, and labor and come together to help a neighbor construct a barn to protect their livestock and resources. The task was huge and incredibly difficult, if not impossible, for one family to complete alone. Community members from far and wide would gather with food and music and turn the work into a community celebration. And there was much to celebrate! They were coming together to help provide for and protect each other. Each member knew that others in the community would do, or had done, the same for them. (White, n.d.; Cass 1937)

I learned about barn raisings as a child, sitting beside my mom as she watched old black and white films she loved. Many of them were musicals that included romanticized scenes of dances and potlucks that happened after a barn had been raised.

I love the imagery of a group of people who are struggling to survive, leaning into each other for support. I live in a semi-rural area, and I still hear of barn raisings, though they are less literal and often include modular buildings.

The idea of a community coming together to help each other is as old as time. And it's something we all crave. Connection, community, fellowship, support. We crave giving it, and we crave receiving it. It is a blessing to give to others, and it often blesses the giver more than the receiver.

Even though I deeply believe the sentiments I just expressed, I still struggle with asking for help. I have a defiance and obstinance that tells me I should be self-sufficient and not need anyone's help. I tell myself I'm bothering people. They're busy and are too involved in meeting their own needs to help me meet mine.

All that may be true, but we all still need to be needed by others. We need to be sought out and invited into relationships. And we all need the character building that comes from acknowledging we can't do it alone! This is also an area of faith that I'm constantly working on. Acknowledging that I can't do it alone and need heavenly support, guidance, and intervention. So the act of asking for help is not only practical for me, it's also character-building.

As you think about your community and ask them to move from passive support ("You can do it! I believe in you!) to active support ("Let me help you do that. I will make that call for you."), I want to encourage you to think about a community effort that speaks to you. Maybe it's a barn raising; maybe it's volunteering at a soup kitchen, or an adopt-the-highway campaign, or volunteer duty at an animal shelter. You get the point. Pick something that makes you lean into the power of community support. Then take that feeling and think about giving it to others and giving them the chance to do the same for you.

You may be thinking, "But what if I don't have a community of people to lean on? What if my community isn't one that I would trust with the fragility of my visibility project?" Great questions. Let's talk about what a community is, two different types of communities, and how you can find a community that is right for you and your project.

Identifying Your Community

A community is a group of people who are connected by a shared characteristic. It can be interest-based (e.g., hobby groups or industry groups), geography/location-based (e.g., your team at work, neighborhood association, parent/teacher associations, local volunteer groups), experience-based (e.g., college alumni groups, employee resource groups), values-based (e.g., political groups, church groups, advocacy groups), or a combination of these. We often belong to many different communities, even when we are not active in those communities.

For your visibility project, I want you to examine which of these groups you belong to now and how many of them align with your career aspirations. When I'm working with leaders, I often find that some of their communities are not a good fit with their aspirations. Rather, they are based on easy access and pre-established relationships that are convenient but may not offer what is needed to support their visibility plans. I call these "communities of convenience." Let me give you a personal example.

When I transitioned out of my corporate executive role and into entrepreneurship, I found myself struggling to maintain the depth of my connections with my previous communities. I was looking to them for support and companionship, but we were no longer a good fit for each other. In fact, it was a *poor* fit for me and the community. I reached out to them because it was convenient. They knew me. The relationships were established. But when I changed my goals and pivoted my career, my visibility plan required a different kind of community.

The search for new communities that fit my new path was disorienting and discouraging. I felt alone and a bit lost because I wasn't sure what kind of community I needed or where to find them. It took some patience and research until I found a new set of communities that shared similar goals and were pursuing similar end goals for themselves. I call these "communities of shared commitment."

The communities of shared commitment I found were vibrant, welcoming, engaging, and a *perfect* fit for me. My acceptance into the group was smooth because it was so obvious that my goals and theirs were aligned. The new communities gave me the opportunity to contribute value and receive support in meaningful ways that caused my visibility plan to take off like a rocket. I now spend my days conversing, supporting, and being challenged by a totally new group of people, many of whom have become dear friends.

In truth, it has never been easier to find a tribe of people with your shared interests, thanks to online social platforms like LinkedIn and Facebook. My seventy-five-year-old introverted mom recently signed up for Facebook and is having a ball and joining new Facebook groups for gardeners and bird watchers. It's easier than you think to find new communities and genuine support from people who share your interests—with the opportunity to support them in turn.

Here are some tips for finding new communities:

- Do a Google or AI search for groups based on your visibility project topic or support need. Most groups are looking for members to add to their communities, so you are likely to find a group.

- Ask people you know and trust if they are aware of any communities that specialize in what you are looking for. Community referrals can be a great way to find the right community quickly.

- Pay attention to courses that include community member-ship as a benefit or feature of the course. If your plan includes additional training or education, this can be a great way to accomplish two goals at one time: education and community.
- If, during your search, you find individuals interested in the same goals as you but don't find a ready-made community, consider starting one by inviting those you meet to a group call. Before you know it, you will have your community of support.

I've done all of the above, and all of these approaches have worked for me. Pick one or two and try them for yourself.

Lastly, let's not forget your home team. Often, the community you need to engage in first is the one you live or "do" life with. For me, that is my husband, my parents, and my sisters. When you are pursuing a visibility project, it helps a great deal if your home team is supportive and cheers you on. I know that isn't always possible, but it's worth the effort to get their backing and support if you can. Breakthrough journeys can be lonely, so having the constant, unwavering support of those who know you best and love you most can be a game changer.

Once you've identified your communities, you need to be able to articulate what you are working toward and how they can support you, so let's turn our attention to articulating your vision!

Sharing Your Vision

Aligning your visibility project with the right community will go a long way toward ensuring your community's support when you need it—but it doesn't guarantee support. In addition to your communities of shared commitment, you also have groups of people who will be impacted by your project that may not be interested (or could actively oppose) your project. For that reason, you must be able to clearly explain what you are doing, why you are doing it, how it will impact them, and why they should support your efforts.

For example, I needed James' full backing to pursue my master's Degree. To get him on board, I had to share my vision and explained how it would impact both of us in the short and the long-term, explained how I was going to get the course work done while I kept my full-time demanding job and described the benefit it could have on our ability to earn more income and provide increased job security by making me more marketable.

For maximum effect, your message is most effective when it:

1) Paints a clear picture of the problem your project will solve or the benefit it will offer.
2) States clearly how and when you will achieve it.
3) Communicates how your project may impact others.
4) Invites others to take part in the solution.

Whether the goal you are pursuing is an individual endeavor or a team project, you need support from others. So, it's important to articulate and share a compelling picture of the future once your goal is achieved. It's tough to support something you don't understand and can't see—even when you want to.

I once had a boss and mentor who had visions of the future that were so clear to him that they were like 3D models. The downside was that only he could see his vision. He wasn't good at explaining his vision in a way that painted the same picture for the rest of the team. He believed he was sharing his vision clearly, but we felt like we were looking out of a car window going 70 mph. We got glimpses of the scenery but couldn't give you many details about the landscape we were passing or where we were going. He would get so frustrated with us because he just couldn't understand that we couldn't see his vision as clearly as he did.

I think most leaders struggle with this at some point in their careers, and some never quite figure it out. You can't share with others what you can't clearly put into words. Think about my boss and his 3D vision. He could see it, but he couldn't explain it. You have to be able to explain your vision.

Think of it in terms of the classic elevator pitch. You have 2-3 minutes with someone at a social gathering, the coffee pot at work, or during a stroll to your next meeting. They ask you, "So, what have you been up to?"

You seize the opportunity and say, "I've actually been working on a project. I'd love to tell you about it."

They say, "Really, that's cool. What is it?" … drumroll please …

And what do you say? If you had an answer already forming in your mind, you're halfway there!

To be honest, this is where I often stumble. I'm always working on a project or goal of some kind, and I love to talk about it. But I like to paint with words and will use plenty of them to make my point. If I'm not careful, I'll bore the person I'm talking with to tears. I struggle to be succinct and exact in my wording when I'm excited about something. Articulating your vision well requires you to be "succinct" so people listen and can recall what you said, and "exact" because you need to be consistent.

When the message is clear, and the "ask" for support is reasonable, I've found that most people will genuinely want to support your goals. Supporting other people's goals makes us feel good about ourselves.

Think about Girl Scout cookies. How many boxes have you bought because a kiddo told you they were working to win a contest, earn a prize, or go to camp? I know the cookies are delicious, and it's not a hardship to have them on hand, but would you have made the purchase without the sales pitch? Sometimes, sure. But probably not as many times as you've actually made purchases.

We didn't just buy cookies. We sent a kid to camp. The message was clear, the "ask" was reasonable, and it felt good to help a child go to camp. I have candles, wrapping paper, popcorn, and knick-knacks I didn't want or need because I was willing to help someone reach their goals. Frame your message so others can help you, too.

Put it Together

Activity #1: Sharing Your Vision

To make sure you are armed and ready for your opportunity to share your vision at the coffee pot, during pre-meeting chatter, at lunchtime gatherings, or at backyard BBQs, we're going to draft a short script you can use to share your vision and gauge the interest of the person you are visiting with to join your support community. I've found the process of thinking through the questions below helps me distill what I want to communicate and get clear on which aspects of the message need more work.

1) Go back to Activity #3 in Chapter 5, Layout Your Plan, and grab what you wrote for your project purpose to describe the problem you are solving or the benefit your project will provide. (I'm going to use Emily's project for our example.)
   - *Emily is leading a joint operations/communications campaign for a new service offering for her company. Her purpose is to:*

Create a clear and compelling campaign for the new XYZ offering that benefits customers by providing a service they have requested and need. The campaign must:

- *Communicate the new service in a compelling way that drives sales*
- *Maintain technical accuracy so the organization doesn't unintentionally sell something operations is unable to support or that fails to deliver on customer's expectations.*
- *Receive final signoff and approval for release within six months*

2) Explain why you want to solve it. Consider the impact that solving it will have on you, your family, your workplace, and your community. (Don't get hung up on wordsmithing. We will clean it up later.)

- *Emily wants to solve this problem for the company because:*
  - She knows what it is like to deal with customer frustrations when operations can't meet the expectations created by a marketing campaign that was disconnected from operational reality.
  - She deeply cares about customers and her company. She sees the value and the opportunity this new product can produce for both if the launch is successful.
- *Emily wants to solve the problem for herself because:*
  - *This project is giving her a chance to grow her skills and rebrand herself as a leader who can be successful even when she isn't the technical expert on the topic.*
  - *Succeeding on this project could create future opportunities for promotion and get her back on track for her career plan to be CEO one day.*

- ○ *She is tired of hearing the feedback that others don't want to work with her. She doesn't want to alienate others, and it actually upsets her when she learns that it has happened. She wants to overcome this issue and figure out what she needs to do differently.*

3) Write a few sentences to describe how you will do this. Depending on the word you chose and the affirmation you wrote, it may come in handy here.

- *I will lead with patience and understanding, allowing each team member the space to grow and contribute, fostering a culture of respect and collaboration. I will also exercise patience with myself by recognizing that it takes time and practice to learn new skills.*
- *I will demonstrate the above by using my strong Strategize and Mobilize skills to help the team collectively map out an action plan to achieve the project's purpose and goal.*
  - ○ *Instead of writing the plan and developing the strategy myself, I will facilitate a group session in which the team will write the high-level plan together. This will allow me to share my process knowledge while also tapping into the subject expertise of the team.*
  - ○ *Instead of providing answers to every question, I will ask questions of others in a way that demonstrates my respect for their expertise and input.*
  - ○ *Instead of assuming that I'm performing well, I will seek guidance from others on my performance.*

4) Write one sentence that describes when you plan to complete the project.

- *We will complete the project in six months. At that time, I will assess my personal performance with the help of others to determine if I also met my personal goals of practicing patience with myself and others and leading a team with respect and collaboration.*

5) What is one action that you will need from every member of your community? How can you write that as a request? (We will address specific actions you may need to request from individual members of your community later in this chapter.)

- *If you are interested in supporting my work on this project, I'd appreciate assistance in one of three ways:*
  - *Willingness to give me honest and candid feedback on my leadership performance.*
  - *Being a "beta tester" for our campaign messages and visuals as we develop different drafts.*
  - *Lending the project team your technical expertise and perspective when we encounter obstacles or get stuck.*

6) Ok. Now, we need to boil it all down to a few sentences that you can use for written and verbal communication when the opportunity arises. You can either use AI or write it yourself.

HACK IT TIP:

If you choose to use AI, here is the AI prompt I used with Emily's responses. You may have a better script, so feel free to improve on this.

Take the text provided below and turn it into an elevator pitch with no more than four sentences. Use first person point of view. Use positive language. Meet this criteria: 1) Paints a clear picture of the problem the project solves or the benefit it offers. 2) State clearly how and when the project will be completed. 3) Communicate how the project may impact stakeholders. 4) Invite stakeholders to participate in the solution. "[copy and paste your sentences here, using quotation marks to set it apart]."

I ran Emily's responses through two different AI engines, Perplexity.ai and Google Gemini. The version shown below has been edited to incorporate the aspects I liked best from both options. (Perplexity.ai, October 21, 2024; Google Gemini, October 21, 2024)

I'm leading an exciting new campaign for our highly-requested XYZ offering that will transform how we serve our customers. I'm passionate about getting this right, so we'll be working collaboratively to ensure our campaign is both compelling and technically accurate so we don't overpromise and underdeliver. This project is a fantastic opportunity for me to grow my leadership skills and build a strong, collaborative team. With your support and expertise, we can deliver a successful launch in six months that exceeds customer expectations and drives incredible results for the company!

This is a great start, and it's something Emily could use in a variety of ways. It also meets the four criteria for an effective message. The next time she is in a conversation with someone and an opportunity arises for her to share her project, she will be ready, and so will you.

When you encounter this situation, you can provide more detail based on the interest of your conversation partner and the time you have available for the conversation. Since you've thought through how you would answer a variety of questions, you will be ready to flex conversationally and should be able to enjoy the discussion.

If you get the sense that the person is open to actively supporting you, don't be afraid to ask them how they might help. Knowing the ways members of your community are willing to roll up their sleeves to help you will be a critical starting point for encouraging that transition. There is no better way to know how they can help than by asking them!

Before you close the discussion, I invite you to add more thing… "So, how can I *support you?*" Let me tell you why this matters.

Mutual Value Exchange

I belong to several networking and support groups of entrepreneurs, authors, executives, and all-around amazing women who inspire me to do more, reach for more, impact more, push myself more, and who totally intimidate me. I've learned, from belonging to these groups, that hanging out with people who routinely operate at the level you aspire to challenges your thinking and levels up your performance.

One of the groups I joined was committed to the principle of mutual value exchange. It means that you give and get in equal measure. You couldn't be part of the group if you were only looking to benefit yourself. You had to also actively contribute to support others.

I love the idea of mutual value exchange, not because it means that I will get if I give, but because it settles my nerves by focusing my efforts on how I can genuinely contribute to others by using my gifts, expertise, resources, and ideas. I've gained great friends and have had front-row seats to their incredible successes—and I know that, in some ways, I've contributed to that success.

When you are asking your community to move from passive to active support, remember to offer a mutual value exchange. I love to end my conversations with, "What can I do to support you?" It has led to some interesting conversations and fun opportunities. There isn't always something I can do right then to support them, but they know I am available and interested in helping them "raise a barn." I have also been the one to spot something that I can do to support them that they were unwilling to ask for or that they didn't recognize. Again, it's fun to find something we can do together to push each other. And we usually have a blast as we're doing it.

Put Your Community to Work

You've now identified your community, developed a vision you can share in a few sentences, and asked members of your community to support you. After you engage with members of your community, you will have a good idea of who may want to lean in and help more.

Let me share a recent example of this. I was visiting with a friend, and she asked me the "So what's been going on?" question. I shared my vision and this book project with her, and she wanted to know more. When we were done with our discussion, she told me she wanted to be a beta reader of my book. At the time, I didn't take her offer seriously and forgot about it. The next day, she texted me and asked me when I was going to send her the book. Well, then, I sent it immediately. And

I plan to celebrate my next book milestone with her in thanks for her accountability partnership. It was a reminder to me that when a member of your community leans in and asks to help, let them!

What about when you need help that no one yet has offered to provide? Not everyone will know how they can help. They need you to guide them. You may be surprised how willing people in your community are to help you if you ask them for something specific.

Let's walk through a scenario that demonstrates how you can phrase your request for help.

Constructing Your Request

Asking for help is not something most people are good at doing. We are independent, self-starters and we fear that everyone is as busy as we are. We don't want to "bother" people with our projects. We have to break that mindset. So, as you read through this section, imagine if someone approached you for help. Would you help them? I bet you would. Use that knowledge as comfort to help you get over the hurdle of asking someone to help you.

Let's walk through a template that can help you construct your request using Emily's project. Emily has identified a training need for her project team. They don't understand an aspect of the new service offering that she believes is critical to their ability to accurately develop the messaging for the campaign. She doesn't feel like she should be the one to instruct them—particularly given her own goal of working through others and not serving as the expert. She needs to approach her colleague, Terra, to ask for help. Let's work through that conversation together.

Activity #2: Ask Your Community for Help

Script:	Example:
1. Open with why you are making the request.	*Emily: Hi Terra. Thanks for making time to visit with me. I'm calling to ask for your help and expertise with the XYZ campaign project. [Share your vision from Activity #1.] I'm hoping you can help me.*
2. Explain the nature of your specific need.	*Emily: I've noticed that the team doesn't fully understand the technical aspects of the new service offering.*
3. Create a link between what you need and their particular area of expertise, skill, talent, or knowledge.	*Emily: I've heard you speak about the new service, and I've appreciated how you made the complicated topic easy to understand. I think our project team would benefit from hearing you explain how it works behind the scenes.*
4. Ask them to consider helping you with a few specific actions they could take to actively help you. Present the actions in a multiple-choice format with different degrees of activity required. I like to start with the "biggest" ask and progress down to the "easiest" ask. Always include an option most people won't turn down.	*Emily: Would you be willing to:* *(option 1) Lead a two-hour training and answer the team's questions, or* *(option 2) If you can't give us that much time, could you join the meeting for thirty minutes to answer the team's questions?* *(option 3) If that doesn't work, can you recommend someone else in your department who might be able to help us?* *(option 4) And if none of that is possible, could you point us to some other references that may help the team?*
5. Stop talking. Give your community member a chance to absorb what you are asking for and time to process your request. Sometimes, we view quiet conversational moments as an awkward silence rather than a polite pause.	*[Insert a polite pause]*

6. Respond to any clarifying questions they have.	*Terra: I'd love to help you out. But the date doesn't work for me. Any chance you can change the date of the meeting?* *Emily: Yes!* *Terra: Then I can provide the two-hour training. I just delivered a similar training, so it's not a problem as long as the date works.*
7. Commit to an appropriate follow-up action on your part to cement the agreement and communicate that you will be in touch.	*Emily: Thank you! If I captured our conversation correctly, I'm going to do [a, b, c], and you will do [x, y, z]. I'm really looking forward to working with you again. I know the team will appreciate your time and expertise.*
8. Ask them how you can help or support them. Whenever possible, end the conversation engaging and thinking about them and not yourself.	*Emily: So, Terra, what are you working on that I can help you with? I want to support you, as well.*
9. Follow through! Do whatever you said you would do, even if they fumble the follow-through on their end.	

We've covered a lot of ground in this chapter. You've identified and perhaps expanded your community relationships by joining a community of shared commitment, you've gained clarity on your vision for your project and how you will share it with others, you've adopted a practice of mutual value exchange, and you've asked for specific help. In short, you've set up your project for success by unleashing the power of your community.

In the next chapter, we'll capitalize on the attention you've gained with your community and further engage them by asking for their input on your plan. We have more conversations to conduct, so let's keep going.

<u>Let's Review:</u>

1) Articulating your vision clearly will help you gain the support of your community to launch your project or goal and inspire action that builds momentum. When the message is clear, and your ask for support is reasonable, most people will genuinely want to support your goals.

2) For maximum effect, your message is most effective when it:
   1. Paints a clear picture of the problem your project will solve or the benefit it will offer.
   2. States clearly how and when you will achieve it.
   3. Communicates how your project may impact others.
   4. Invites others to take part in the solution.

3) Be sure to offer your support in return. Mutual value exchange creates opportunities for both you and your community!

<u>Think About It:</u>

1) Think about a time in your past when you have done the things discussed in this chapter. Was it easy? Was it effective? Why or why not? What can you learn from your own prior experience to either replicate your past success or improve upon it?

2) When was the last time you asked for help from a member of your community? What can you learn from that experience?

3) How can you improve your communication skills so your internal vision can get out of your head and into your conversations with others?

<u>Take Action:</u>

1) Identify your community. Are you engaged with a community of shared commitment? If you need to expand your community, start working to identify communities you want to join so you can meet people with similar interests and goals.

2) Draft your pitch (vision statement) to clearly articulate and share your vision using Activity #1 in this chapter. Consider leveraging AI to sharpen your message quickly and efficiently. Then, practice your pitch with friends or family members who will help you refine it. Create an accountability partner that will help you actually use your statement and will encourage you to start building your support team.

3) Ask for support. Start reaching out proactively to members of your community who could lend you their expertise, time, energy, enthusiasm, etc. And offer to support them in turn.

Chapter 10

Encourage Input

My Real-Life Breakthrough Journey: *Installment 8*

After my team and I walked out of our vision casting discussion, I knew I needed to gain support from other leaders and department heads in the organization if we were going to turn our vision into a reality. I also firmly believe in the sentiment that "you don't know what you don't know"! I was new to the organization, and I didn't know a lot of things. So, I set out to collect input and learn from others.

I reached out to a wide section of people, starting with Mack. If he wasn't on board with our desired vision, I knew we would have an uphill battle. Thankfully, he was fully supportive and eager to offer his input and advice. This is when Mack really became my mentor. He helped me build out my list of people to talk to, made introductions when I needed them, and lent me his complete support. We mapped out leaders in each of our client areas, and he helped me schedule conversations with their senior leaders. Those leaders, in turn, helped me set up conversations to gain the input of their department directors… and so my input-collecting journey began. Not surprisingly, most of the discussions went like this:

"Hi, I'm Jenn. I'm the new director of the Education & Development Department."

The other person would respond, "Oh, good. I've been wanting to talk to you." At this point, a litany of feedback, frustrations, and complaints were provided. Many of which had nothing to do with me and everything to do with a backlog of years of frustrations. (Sound familiar? Has this ever happened to you?)

I took it in stride, drawing confidence from our new vision and Mack's support. The exact complaints and frustrations were new, but the knowledge that the department was struggling was not. So, I adopted a posture of learning and problem-solving and vowed to myself that my team and I would win these internal clients over with our improved services and new direction.

I took notes and promised to follow up on anything I couldn't address at that moment. Then, I shared the vision for where the department was headed and how we would get there. I invited their input and listened intently.

As you can imagine, some of the conversations went better than others. On the whole, however, I accomplished my goal. Our client group and fellow services groups now knew what we were attempting to do and how we would go about it. Only a few of them were downright ugly about it. Unsurprisingly, most of those departments were getting back the work they had pawned off on our department. I saw that coming and was prepared for it. Still, others jumped on board and became big fans. Those may have been the most surprising conversations. There was a hunger in the organization for the things my team was attempting to do. And those new fans opened up opportunities for the department we couldn't have achieved on our own.

Now that we've shared our vision and we've started the process of unleashing our community, I'd like to take that one step further to truly cement their engagement and buy-in while also improving our plans. We need them to view our project as a pet project of their own. We need them to do more than agree to support us in concept—we need them to support us with action. We need personal investment in our plan so they take physical action to help move us forward.

Our Goals:

In this chapter, we're going to discuss how we can embrace input from our community to further energize our project and build momentum as we get closer to executing our plan. Specifically, we will cover:

1) The difference between input and feedback.
2) Engage our community so they are willing to invest in our plan by inviting their input.
3) How to use the input we receive to refine and tweak our plan.

The Gift of Input

One of the easiest and most powerful ways you can encourage your community to involve themselves in your plan is to invite and encourage their input. By asking for their advice, opinions, and perspectives, you can test a wider range of ideas and use them to refine your own. Getting input on your plans allows you to essentially borrow other people's expertise and leverage lessons they've learned. By sharing freely with your community and creating mechanisms to collect their input, you circumvent issues before they happen, build a team of people who will physically help you move forward by taking action on your behalf, and can tweak and improve your plans before you move into execution mode.

We all love to offer advice, and we all get a kick from seeing that advice put to use. It creates a sense of ownership and camaraderie that creates a stronger bond between you and your community. This is especially true when the input is offered freely, and the investment people make is by choice. When members of your community choose to support you, I hope you see it as the incredible gift it is. Our job is to invite it, appreciate it, learn from it, and be good stewards of it.

Input vs. Feedback

The terms input and feedback are often used interchangeably, but they have some subtle differences that are important for our discussion. Input is data, insights, suggestions, or information shared at the beginning and during a process. Think of it as something you *put into* a process to generate a result. You collect input before or during a process. Feedback is an opinion, evaluation, or assessment that is provided in response to something that has already happened. Think of it as a reaction to a process that changes or improves performance next time or at the *back*end of a process.

It's interesting and good to know the difference, but if we are honest, few people will stop and think about whether the statements they offer are technically input or feedback. That is for you to determine. Still, there is a difference, and knowing that difference can help you structure your request so you get more input and less feedback. Never fear, the topic of feedback has its own chapter, and we'll get to that in the Mobilize section. But for now, let's focus our efforts on collecting input.

Inviting Input

We all know people who can be resistant to receiving input when they are working on a project. Their project plans are "theirs." They have a deep commitment to their plans, and they aren't interested in other's views if they differ or aren't 100 percent supportive. I understand that perspective. Many breakthrough plans have a personal component, and we have a deep association with those plans. To hear less than positive remarks about our plans feels like an attack personally. Again, I understand it. But I also know it's a mistake, especially if we want our plans to succeed spectacularly so our gaps can close and we can break through our obstacles to achieve next-level success.

If you collect input you don't agree with, you can find ways to thank the provider and not incorporate all or any of the input. Additionally, there are three compelling reasons to invite input. We discussed the first reason in the opening of this chapter: You need to convert your community of supporters from interested and willing to bought-in and invested. Let's look at the other two reasons.

The second reason makes me chuckle because it's inevitable. Do you have anyone in your life who has an opinion about everything? Of course, you do! And do you think not being invited to offer suggestions will stop them from vocalizing them anyway? Nope—you've got that right. They care, and they just can't stop themselves from involving themselves in your business. So guess what… you're going to get their input whether you want it or not. I think of them as my "vocal few" supporters. These dedicated and involved folks aren't afraid to ruffle feathers and wade in without an invitation.

When this happens, if you haven't invited input from your broader community, you will be left with a lopsided perspective, and you risk alienating the members of your community that you didn't actively invite to provide input. Inviting a broader set of your support community will provide a more balanced set of inputs from a variety of perspectives.

The third reason is that inviting input can be incredibly validating. When you are given suggestions you've already baked into your plan, it reaffirms you are on the right path. Nothing gives you a boost like hearing your private thoughts reflected back to you from someone who has no idea you were thinking similarly. This is especially true when you are working on something new or that you don't have a great deal of experience with.

Inviting and collecting input can be an accelerator that strengthens the odds of your plan's success, while also building invaluable support. Asking for input also demonstrates your openness to learning from others, your appreciation of their support, and your genuine interest in their perspectives. All of these build trust and deepen your relationships. Trust me, it's worth it.

Input Seeking Questions

By asking the right questions, you can keep the discussion in the territory of input and gain valuable insights about what may be missing or perhaps need to be tweaked in your project before you launch into execution. Here are a few starter questions to consider.

- Based on your experience, expertise, and perspective, what is missing from the plan?
- What suggestions do you have for me about how to approach/ do/think about [insert an aspect of your plan]?
- What data should I be considering that isn't currently accounted for in my plan?
- What experience do you have that is applicable to my plan? What did you learn from your experience that would help me build a better plan?

- What is included in my plan that shouldn't be? What, if any-thing, should be removed?
- What haven't I asked you about that I should? What am I missing?
- What about my plan concerns you or gives you pause?
- How might you be willing to help me as I implement the plan?
- Is there someone you know that I should visit with? Would you mind introducing me?

Activity 1: Map Out Your Input Conversations

I encourage you to grab a sheet of paper and make a list of all the people in your community from whom you would like to seek input. Also, include anyone who comes to mind who isn't currently in your community and whom you could learn from and perhaps add to your community. List as many people as you can think of. Don't limit yourself. Some of the people you reach out to won't respond for one reason or another. By having a long list, you increase your odds of getting the valuable input you need.

Name	Area of Expertise	Questions to Ask	Discussion Requested?
1.			
2.			
3.			

How to Collect Input

There are so many ways you can ask for and receive input from mem-bers of your community. The situation and the size of your community will often dictate the input collection methods you use. It doesn't have to be face-to-face. You can often collect input more quickly via email, texting, social posts, surveys, etc. Do what makes sense for your project, your needs, and your community.

That disclaimer given, I'll admit that my favorite form of input collection is through person-to-person discussions and conversations. I enjoy the back and forth of a conversation and often learn things I didn't think to explore because the conversation takes on a life of its own. I've had a ton of these conversations during my time preparing for and writing this book. Every few days, I engage with a member of my community to share thoughts and seek their input, bounce around ideas, and play with concepts.

My community of input providers spans a wide range of people, including my mom and dad, James, close friends, my sisters, some Ph.D. colleagues, past and present mentors, coaches I've engaged in teaching me things I don't know, business owners I network with, and even some strangers who have been referred to me by others and who are quickly becoming valued friends. Each of these discussions brings me joy, gives me better ideas, pulls ideas out of me that I couldn't have accessed alone, validates what I'm doing, and encourages me to keep going when I'm stuck.

Every single conversation has helped me, even though I've not incorporated every suggestion I've received. And you know what? My support community doesn't expect me to incorporate everything we discuss. They are just happy to visit with me and to help me succeed as I chase my dream of helping you achieve your career aspirations, promotions, and breakthroughs. And every one of them will buy this book and cheer me on when it launches. Just as I will support them in their endeavors. We support each other. Inviting your community to invest in you will lead you to places you cannot imagine.

Incorporating Input

Now that you have invited others to contribute their ideas and suggestions, you need to evaluate the input and decide what to keep and what to set aside. There is no right or wrong way to do this. It's your judgment call. And a good community of supporters will recognize that, as I shared above. However, if you discount every single input you receive, I would question your integrity in asking for input. You need to be genuine and truly consider the input you receive.

<u>Activity 2: Incorporate Input to Your WBS Task Outline</u>

1) Pull out your one-page project description document and the WBS task outline you created during the Strategize step.

2) Review both through the lens of the input you've received from your community.
   - What could you cut out?
   - What should you exchange for something else that may be a better idea?
   - Is anything missing from your plan that your community spotted, but you missed?

3) Use the input you received to fine-tune the plan. Let's learn from the shared wisdom and experience of your community to make your job easier and your project more efficient.

4) Once you've thought about the input, take action and then cycle back to let your community know what you decided to do.

The last task of this exercise is important but often not done. Cycling back to let your community know that you listened and took action is a fast and powerful way to build credibility and trust. When you take action on advice you are given, people are more willing to offer support again in the future.

For instance, I was talking through one of my chapter outlines with my mom. She is a retired teacher and has an uncanny way of seeing the gaps in my wording or the potential holes in my stories. She identified a gap in my outline and asked me if I had any intention of covering that particular topic. She went on to explain why she felt it should be considered and then left the decision up to me. I included it in the chapter but am now revisiting it during the editing process. I'm not sure if it will remain or be cut. Either way, I have appreciated and learned from every one of her suggestions. Her comments show me how my writing is being understood and interpreted by someone who had a very different career than my own.

This same process has happened countless times during the writing of this book. When I'm done, my community will see their fingerprints all over the book because they will identify a concept, wording change, or exclusion they recommended. It's still my work, but my book and my growth are a product of their investments.

One last note about investments… make sure you return the favor and become someone else's biggest fan and active supporter. Community relationships should never be one-sided. It's about a two-way relationship. And that relationship brings incredible joy. I know I've mentioned this concept several times in different ways. I just don't want you to miss out on it. My sister coined a phrase that has become a promise between us: "We do life together. The good, the bad, and the ugly." When you have a community that is willing to do life with you, you are truly blessed.

With that in mind, I invite you into a community with me via social media. I know it's not the same, but it's a start, and I'd love to support you.

Now that we have cemented the buy-in of our community by encouraging their input, we are well on our way to generating the sustainable momentum and FUEL we will need as we move into the final Breakthrough Formula step, Mobilize. Before we launch into execution, we have one more very important stop.

In the next chapter, we're going to finish up the Energize section by talking about things we need to let go of. Generating lift also requires us to let go of things that weigh us down. So, let's review how we can Lighten Your Load.

Let's Review:

1) There is a difference between input and feedback. Input is data, insights, suggestions, or information shared at the beginning of a process that is used to generate an output. Feedback is an opinion, evaluation, or assessment provided in response to something that has already happened and is usually evaluative in nature.

2) By asking the right questions, you can keep the discussion in the territory of input and gain valuable insights about what may be missing or perhaps need to be tweaked in your project before you launch into execution.

3) There are three reasons to ask your community for input.

   ◦ To convert your community of supporters from interested and willing to bought-in and invested.

   ◦ Inviting input from your entire community provides a balanced set of inputs from a variety of perspectives.

   ◦ Receiving input can be incredibly validating by demonstrating that your thinking is in alignment with people who may know more or be more experienced than you are.

Think About It:

1) Think about the difference between input and feedback. How have you seen this play out? Have you ever asked for input and received feedback? Have you ever asked for feedback but meant to ask for input?

2) Review the list of input seeking questions. What could you add to this list?

3) What is your favorite method of collecting input? Why does it work well for you? Is there another collection method you should consider using more often?

Take Action:

1) Complete the activity to map out your input conversations.

2) Then schedule and complete those conversations. Take notes to capture the input. Then, show your appreciation for the conversation and for sharing their knowledge.

3) Incorporate the input into your plan as appropriate.

Chapter 11

Lighten Your Load

My Real-Life Breakthrough Journey: *Installment 9 (Part 1)*

Things in my new role were starting to look up. My team was engaging fully in our new plan forward. My manager Mack and our clients were largely supportive, and it seemed that we were making good traction. There was just one catch. We had a powerful adversary: one of the top executives named Frank.

Frank was engaged in a political battle with another senior executive. They had carved dividing lines between their teams, with Frank and his team on one side and his rival, whom my boss reported to, on the other. Frank was the most aggressive and antagonistic of the two rivals. He ruled with fear and intimidation, and most of the hospital staff were terrified of him.

He seemed to take delight in discrediting members of his rival's team by shooting arrows and verbal barbs at anyone in the management ranks. That meant my boss and I received unwanted scrutiny. Further, Frank was leading the charge in trying to eliminate my department during budget cuts, which meant I was fair game for his political machinations.

Mack and I had often discussed how to navigate situations with Frank, but our attempts to stay beneath his notice failed. While Mack tried to shield me, he was lower in the organization and was also at a loss for how to deal with Frank. So, I received Frank's unwanted scrutiny, criticism, and hostility every time I interacted with him.

When I presented to the executive team, Frank would ask critical questions laced with his undisguised disapproval. His questions felt harsher for me than for other presenters, and usually double in number. I felt like he was constantly trying to discredit me by asking questions he believed I couldn't answer. When I provided an appropriate response, he looked visibly irritated. Further, he was considered a bully among the other executives. I was advised to be very careful and not draw his notice. Frank rarely lost a battle he was determined to win.

I remember standing in my postage-stamp-sized office, which was a converted closet, staring at a locus of control chart I hung next to my office door. I would stare at that chart every time I left my office and practice deep breathing exercises to get my nerves under control. Then, I would plaster a smile on my face and leave the safety of my nook to wander the halls on my way to the next meeting. All the while, I prayed that I wouldn't run into Frank. And yes, I occasionally reversed directions, ducked into empty rooms, and avoided eye contact. I'm not proud of it, but I totally did it.

The constant strain and stress from the ongoing fear and conflict caused by my interactions with Frank started taking a toll on my health. I also knew I couldn't continue to cower in fear and still do what needed to be done to turn my team and our department around. Something needed to change.

I started devising mind games to turn the very real threat Frank posed into something that would make me laugh and break the tension in my mind. My biggest success with this came when I was scheduled to deliver an important presentation to the senior executive team.

I knew from past presentations that Frank wouldn't be supportive and may even be openly unpleasant during the presentation.

A friend of mine had suggested that I picture him in his underwear. I'm sure you've heard of that trick. It's intended to remind you that the person you are fearful of or intimidated by is just a regular person who puts his or her pants on one leg at a time. I was appalled by the idea and decided to visualize him in a ridiculous red sequined suit instead. Frank was straight-laced, serious, and would *never* wear something as eye-catching as red sequins. On the other hand, I love glitter and sparkly things, so it seemed like a good choice.

Before I went into my meeting, I made sure that I was over-prepared, that I could give my presentation without conscious thought, and that I had answers ready for the hardest questions I could imagine Frank throwing at me. I felt as prepared as I was capable of being. Here goes.

I entered the meeting and took my place at the front of the room. I pulled up my presentation, took a deep breath, and began my remarks. Frank behaved exactly as I expected. Within moments, he interrupted to correct me, questioned my statements, and asked overly critical questions.

My response, however, was different this time. Instead of taking his behavior toward me personally, I visualized each of his questions and comments as though it was an arrow that he was shooting at me. I visualized my response as a shield that deflected his arrow before it could harm me. I soon realized that Frank wasn't really shooting at me. He was shooting at Mack and his rival by trying to discredit me. After all, I was just a convenient bystander. He didn't care enough about me to want me gone. I was simply a tool he could use to annoy or hurt the executives he was at war with.

And in my mind, he did it all while wearing red sequins.

My visualization exercise worked so well that I was able to handle and deflect his rude behavior with poise, which was a first. My handling of Frank's questions changed the mood in the room. The executives could tell that I had relaxed and was more effectively managing Frank's behavior, which, in turn, helped them relax.

By the end of the presentation, Frank was frustrated, and his unprofessional behavior had drawn attention. In the end, my project got approved and the experience signaled the end of my irrational fear and feelings of intimidation of Frank. He was still a powerful and dangerous foe, but I was able to separate my fear from the actual threat, which allowed me to better navigate my interactions with him.

Looking back, I'm actually grateful for my dealings with Frank. He was the first really tough executive I had to work with, but he wasn't the last. Frank forced me to figure out how to operate with grace under pressure and taught me to overcome fear and intimidation. I can confidently say that I no longer fear the "Franks" I encounter. That lesson was a gift!

As my experience with Frank demonstrated, sometimes progress comes when you let go of things that aren't serving you. I had to let go of my fear and intimidation to have the space to think and move forward. My lesson was learning to let go of things that weren't in my control and to refocus my efforts on things I could control.

The final stage of our FUEL journey is just that. You may need to let go of some things, just as I did. To relate this idea back to that of a hot air balloon ride, you need to release the weights that hold the balloon down. To create lift, you must also limit drag.

Our Goals:

In this chapter, we're going to clear a pathway that supports your FUEL efforts to create sustainable energy and momentum, and we're going to do it without adding anything to your plate. Instead, we're going to release some things you've been holding onto. We will acknowledge them, accept that they served a purpose for us in the past, and accept that they are no longer something we should carry into our future. Let's tackle this decluttering project in categories:

1) Letting go of relationships with people we wish well but need to part ways with. This doesn't mean people are expendable. It means you need to purposely decide how to engage with them in the healthiest manner possible.

2) Letting go of fear by recognizing things that trigger us and reframing them. (I'm not a therapist, and we're not going to engage in therapy. We'll just apply what we know about the brain and some good old common sense to redirect our thoughts. If you need therapy, and there is incredible strength in that knowledge, please seek someone who can help you. I have, and it helped me tremendously.)

3) Letting go of excess worry over things we can't control by correcting our vision of what is and isn't within our ability to control.

It seems appropriate to begin our discussion about lightening our load with a metaphor about baggage. So, let's take a look at what we are carrying around with us.

The Freedom of Carry-On Bags

Let's return to the idea of preparing for a journey. Have you ever taken a long trip that limited the amount of luggage you could take?

James and I enjoy international travel, but the process of travel can be tough. Catching connections, finding tickets, and keeping track of luggage while navigating unfamiliar surroundings can become overwhelming. Our best travel experiences tend to be when I restrain myself from overpacking. Trying to find the right train in a foreign country when carrying a single backpack is far easier and more enjoyable than lugging multiple wheeled suitcases, a backpack, and a tote bag. Carrying less gives you greater mobility and flexibility.

Why don't we apply that same principle to other areas of our lives? There is only so much we can carry with us. Yet, we love to haul around old junk that is no longer serving us and is literally weighing us down. How can we acquire new traits, habits, skills, and knowledge if we are carrying around outdated versions that conflict with the new versions we are trying so hard to adopt? We can't, but we will spend a LOT of time, energy, and heartache trying to do so. It's a drag, and it needs to go.

Letting Go of Relationships: Anchors, Tides, and Wakes

As you engage with your community, you are absolutely going to run into people who steal your joy, rain on your parade, or attempt to convince you to play it safe by not chasing your visibility project and career aspirations. There are a number of reasons this happens, and to be honest, it hurts when it does. Worse yet, it sometimes comes from people you know best and least expect resistance from: your closest friends and immediate family.

There are many reasons why people will push back and try to shut down your dreams. And that is exactly what they are trying to do, whether they realize it consciously or not. We can't cover all the reasons why, but we can look for patterns and determine how we pivot our relationships to retain what we can while not taking on other people's opinions.

I was recently talking to a fabulous, daring friend who is on the path to creating the life and career of her dreams. She was in Spain on a three-month tour of Europe while working full-time to build her new company and realizing her dream of living and working while traveling abroad.

I opened our conversation with this, "Have you noticed connections and close relationships you had with people in your previous career have evaporated, or they've ghosted you?"

"YES!" She replied with enthusiasm and exasperation.

We started comparing notes and boiled it down to three groups.

1) Those who were well-meaning but just couldn't relate to our decisions to make a career pivot.

2) Those who were envious, yet scornful, of our decision and resented the abandonment of our corporate success after working so hard to attain it.

3) Those we thought we were close friends with but misread the strength of the relationship when we were no longer around them professionally.

We had both received comments like, "So you couldn't make it in corporate?" or "When are you going to stop playing around and get a real job?" Yikes. Talk about true colors being revealed. And then, our conversation changed to the benefits of expanding ourselves in new and unexpected ways through our career pivots. We talked about receiving support from unexpected people from our past. And we talked about the new people and friends we were making—like each other.

In the days following our conversation, I thought about the professional relationships and friendships I needed to let go of and those I wanted to retain. I found myself recalling a beach trip that involved anchors, tides, and wakes. That reflection turned into the basis of my thinking about the relationships that hold us back (anchors), push us forward (tides), or push us around (wakes). Let's look at each of these.

Anchors:

The purpose of an anchor is to hold you still and keep you from drifting away on a current when you intend to stay put. But when they are used incorrectly, they can become a problem. Let me share an illustration of this.

I was with a friend on a girls' adventure weekend in the Florida Keys. We were on a kayaking excursion. The day was perfect; the water was calm, and the temperature was just hot enough to enjoy the cool water. We stopped to snorkel near an underwater grotto and let down the small anchor in our kayak to keep the boat from floating away on the current. After snorkeling, we returned to the kayak, a little tired but happy and relaxed. We hopped back in, grabbed our oars, and prepared for our return paddle to the marina.

As we began paddling, we noticed that we were falling behind the other kayakers in our group. So we picked up our pace, but the additional effort wasn't making us go any faster. For twenty minutes, we threw out excuses and rationalizations for why we were going so much slower than everyone else. It must be a strong current, or we were more tired than we realized, or we weren't paddling in sync.

Then it struck us. We hadn't pulled up the anchor. It was dragging behind us, picking up more and more debris!

Anchors are relationships that keep you stuck. They are friends who want the status quo to remain unchanged. They aren't interested in growing in the same direction you are, and instead of supporting you, they hold you back—just like the anchor on our kayak. Whether this is done intentionally or unintentionally, it's still an anchor.

Reflecting on Anchors: It's up to you to determine if your professional relationships and friendships fall into this category and what to do about them if they do. Here are some questions to ask yourself:

- Is the relationship truly holding you back, or is it simply not keeping pace but also not interfering with your growth?
- Is the relationship worth holding onto?
- Will the nature of the relationship naturally change given time, distance, or the success of your visibility project?

Consider which relationships may require action and reflect on some steps you could take with each of your anchor relationships. We'll discuss this further in Activity #1.

Tides:

Tides are consistent and predictable and occur twice daily. You can count on their coming and going. They are caused by the gravitational pull of the sun and moon, not by circumstance. You can generally count on the tide to behave in a relatively predictable way.

When I am facing large life changes or am troubled, no scenery is as soothing to me as the vastness of the ocean when the tides come in and out. The dependability, rhythm, and sheer size of it all remind me to put my problems into perspective. It's calming. Even when I leave the beach and return to my home in the mountains, I know the ocean and beach are there. I know when I return, the tides will still be coming in and out.

There are people in life who serve as our tides. They are steady, calming, and dependable. They support you no matter what, and you can count on them. They are the loyal supporters who push you to pursue your dreams whether or not they understand them. They are friendships that can withstand a year between conversations but feel like no time has passed when you see them again. You don't have to work to remain "in sync" with them. You just pick back up where you left off. The power and generosity of their support give you momentum and accelerate your progress. Tides are powerful forces!

Reflecting on Tides: When you have tide friendships in your life, you hold onto, invest in, and treasure them. Here are some questions to reflect on the tides in your life:

- Who are the people I know will support me, no matter what?
- Who are the people I sync with the easiest and know they will come running if I need help?
- Which of my friends do I honestly believe will still be in my life in five years?
- What do I need to be feeding into these relationships to keep them healthy?

Consider what you should be doing to support your tide relationships. Is it time to make a call, reconnect, or perhaps express your gratitude for the relationship?

Wakes:

In keeping with our nautical theme, a wake is the disturbance of water caused by a moving vessel. The size and energy of a wake is in direct proportion to the size of the disturbance. When the disturbance ends, the wake loses energy and the water settles down. Wakes are man-made.

They can also be very destructive. To minimize the damage a wake can cause, "No Wake Zone" signs are often posted in canals and confined bodies of water.

My family and I visited Amsterdam and took a boat tour on one of the canals. Our guide became angry and upset at a speed boat that ignored the "no wake zone" signs and barreled through the busy canal. Our boat rocked precariously as the aggressive wake shook us when the boat sped past. After getting us settled once more, the guide explained the delicate nature of the canal's relationship to the city built around it and the destructive power of the wakes caused by those who disregarded the rules.

Conversely, creating wakes can be great fun and produce an amazing amount of energy. The people in the speed zone were having a grand time. Had they been in an area of open water, there would have been no issues with their speed. In fact, speed and wakes are needed for many water sports. Our family's lake visits are much more fun when we go full-throttle and pull an inner tube behind the boat. Wakes serve a purpose when used appropriately.

The metaphor holds true when navigating relationships. I think of wakes as the relationships that come in and out of your life and have a time limit. They are seasonal relationships. Sometimes, they are positive and create energy that pushes you forward. When appropriately managed, they serve a purpose for both parties for a period of time, and then they drift away. Sometimes, they are negative and rock your boat, requiring you to take abrupt action to mitigate their effects.

Wakes can also be misclassified as tides and vice versa. I have had wake relationships I would have sworn were tide relationships, but didn't survive the tests of time. Conversely, you can misjudge tide relationships as wake relationships because they went dormant for a while but returned to full strength when you needed them.

Reflecting on Wakes: Think critically about any relationships you think might be wake relationships. Then, consider the following questions:

- What is the foundation of the relationship? Is it based on something enduring (e.g., our values) or something more transient (e.g., a class we are taking or a group we belong to right now that will end)?
- Is the tone of the relationship positive, neutral, or negative?
- Does the relationship produce energy or drain it?
- What is the relationship costing in time, energy, and resources? Is it worth the cost? Is it mutually beneficial?

Evaluate each of your wake relationships to determine the value it provides, the energy it produces, and the cost to maintain it.

Now that we've reviewed anchors, tides, and wakes, let's examine our relationships. Are there any you need to let go of? Are there any you want to invest further in preserving?

Activity #1: Identify Actions for your Anchors, Tides, and Wakes

While you pursue your career goals, try to limit the weight you drag with you by positively reinforcing your tide and positive wake relationships and redefining your negative wakes and anchors. You can also limit your exposure to negative wakes and anchors by setting specific boundaries or kindly disentangling yourself.

1) Create a list of your prominent relationships.
2) Determine the nature of each relationship. Is it an anchor, tide, or wake?
3) What action will you take with each relationship?
   - Are there supportive relationships you need to nurture? If so, how will you do so?
   - Are there any unhealthy relationships you need to put boundaries around or extricate yourself from? How might you do so?

4) What is your immediate next step for each? What is something simple you can do right now to start taking action? (Text someone, schedule a coffee date with a tide you've not seen in a while, cancel a coffee date with an anchor or negative wake, etc.)

5) Do you have any gaps that you need to fill by looking for new relationships? How can you use your tide relationships to find new connections? Can you use the information about building community from the previous chapters to look for new connections?

A note about letting go: When it is time to let go of a professional or friend relationship, there are several ways to do so. You can end the relationship with a hard stop, transition the relationship by putting new boundaries in place, or allow the relationship to taper off naturally as you proceed down your own path. Pick the method that is the healthiest for you and them.

Now that we've considered our relationships, let's move on to consider the fears we may need to release so we can lighten our load further.

Letting Go of Fear: Threat Traps

We've all experienced a moment of fight, flight, or freeze response when faced with danger. Anyone afraid of spiders, snakes, or bees? I'm horribly afraid of any flying insect with a stinger. If I see or hear one, I jump up and run without thinking it through. I've even been known to do so when a horse fly buzzes past. The sound alone sends me packing. That's my fight, flight, or freeze response at work, and it's the job of your brain's amygdala.

The amygdala receives sensory input about potential threats faster than you can consciously process what is happening, thereby triggering your body to react to the threat before you even know what you are reacting to. (Wang et al. 2023; Alexandra Kredlow et al. 2022) Yet, what qualifies as a threat isn't universally predetermined and doesn't have to be an actual legitimate threat to our physical safety (e.g., rattlesnake at our feet). Our fight, flight, or freeze response is triggered by whatever we have learned from experience to identify as a threat (this is called an amygdala hijack): Speaking in front of people, meeting with someone we are intimidated by, tackling a work assignment we don't feel qualified to do, and so on. (Goleman 2011) Unfortunately, the possibilities are endless.

Let's go back to my fear of insects with stingers. My responses have always been to jump up and flee. I've tried to react differently. I've even been successful to some extent, but it has always been incredibly hard to control my reaction. Except once, at my wedding. In the middle of our outdoor marriage ceremony, a wasp decided my dress was fascinating. I was determined to stay in the moment and forced myself not to react—much to James' amazement! I still sensed the wasp, but I overcame it because my wedding was more important than my fear, which gave me a split-second pause and a chance to choose my reaction. You can do this, too.

When your mission is more important than your fear, you can reprogram your brain's response to alter your reaction.

I think of these fear triggers as "threat traps." They are perceived threats that trap me into a reaction I don't want and find difficult to control. Letting go of your threat traps by retraining your responses can be a liberating way to lighten your load.

Understanding Threat Traps

Now that we've started cleaning up what we feed our RAS (see the Fan Your Flame chapter), we need to build on that work by increasing our awareness of the particular threats we've programmed into our amygdala that cause a fight, flight, or freeze response.

We are going to focus on threats that clutter our headspace and prevent or slow our progress toward achieving our visibility project. To do this, we need to examine what makes us feel threatened, why, and how we want to respond differently.

Let's walk through a four-step process using my example of overcoming my fear of the wasp at my wedding and my fear and intimidation of Frank from the opening story of this chapter. (Comninos 2017; Holland 2019)

Overcoming Threat Traps

Step	Wasp Example	Frank Example
1) Acknowledge the trigger; notice what is happening and breathe through it.	*The wasp likes my dress. Just breathe.*	*Frank is about to speak. Focus on breathing.*
2) Take stock of how you feel, then narrow your focus on what is most important.	*I'm scared, but my wedding is more important. I don't want to embarrass myself or James by letting my fear control me.*	*I want to leave, but I'm not going to. Getting my project approved is more important - focus on that.*

3) Redefine the threat and engage your logical brain.	• My usual threat definition:
	  ○ *A wasp sting is painful and deadly (irrational fear since I'm not allergic to wasps)*
	• Redefining the threat by thinking logically:
	  ○ *A wasp sting would be an inconvenience and a nuisance, but there is no real danger.*
	  ○ *The bigger danger is responding badly and ruining the marriage ceremony with my fear and embarrassment*
		• My usual threat definition:
		  ○ *Frank will show everyone that I'm a fraud and don't know what I'm doing. (irrational fear since I was well-prepared and knew my subject)*
		• Redefining the threat by thinking logically:
		  ○ *I was prepared and could answer Frank's questions. Even if I couldn't answer one of his questions, I could get an answer for him.*
		  ○ *The bigger danger is responding poorly and letting my emotions control me, which could impact access to future opportunities.*

4) Take back control and choose your response.	*Ignore the wasp and stay in the moment!*	*Respond to the question, not his tone. Stay in the moment and remain focused on the goal of getting the project approved.*

I find this process works best when you prepare for it in advance, so you can more easily anticipate the threat and prepare for it. This isn't easy, but it is possible with practice. Just a small change in your definition of a threat can buy you that infinitesimal space you need to insert conscious thought and exert your will to choose how you respond.

In her book *"Take Control of Your Life,"* Mell Robbins discusses how you can sense fear in your body before your mind takes charge. She urges you to listen to your body and identify where in your body you feel the sensation, and then use that as a leading indicator that a threat is near. I find this technique to be helpful. (Robbins 2019)

Take a moment to fully consider what happened the last time you felt anxious, scared, or threatened. What did you feel in your body? Was the threat triggered internally (from your thoughts) or externally (from your surroundings)? Anything can activate your brain, and only you will be able to pinpoint what it was. It may take you a bit of sleuthing to figure it out, but as you start paying attention, you will likely be able to identify what caused your threat response. Here are a few examples:

- Driving past an office building where an unpleasant confrontation took place.
- Preparing for a meeting in which you will have to speak in front of a crowd.
- Sending a text message and not getting an immediate reply.
- Receiving an email with a statement that is unclear and that you interpret negatively.
- Seeing a co-worker or manager's facial expression that you can't interpret and assume is a result of something you said or did.

Once you start to identify threats that trigger a response, take note. When you know what they are, you can start to unpack them, reframe them, and take preventative action. Let's work on this using a journaling activity.

Activity #2: Identify Your Threat Responses and Triggers

Here are some questions to help you think through your threat traps to better define and identify them.

1) Describe the situation in which you felt a threat response. Where were you? What time was it? What happened?

2) What was the threat trap you encountered? Did it originate from an internal, external, or physical source?

3) Where did you feel the emotion in your body?

4) Rate the severity of your emotional reaction on a scale of one (low) to five (high). This uses your logical brain and helps put the threat trap into perspective.

5) Looking back, were there any clues that the threat factor was present? (e.g., I had just driven by my old workplace where ...)

6) How can you reframe or redefine the threat to make it less concerning or threatening? What do you want to replace the threat trap with? When you walk by the meeting room, do you want to feel confident, ambivalent, calm, etc.? This will start the work of retraining your brain.

7) What can you do next time to lengthen the space between the threat and your reaction so you can choose to respond differently?

Once you've worked to reframe your threat traps, you really can lessen their impact. My fear of wasps and my reaction to them has greatly improved over time. I still run when I'm surprised by them, but I have a much easier time controlling my reaction. Similarly, my interactions with Frank taught me a great deal about dealing with feelings of intimidation. I've dealt with many more people like Frank, and I can do so easily now. It is rare that I feel intimidated by anyone. The work to reprogram your threat traps is worth the effort!

We've got one more stop on our letting-go journey. The last topic is one I've used throughout my career. It's my go-to when I need to regain perspective.

Letting Go of Worries that Weigh You Down: Locus of Control

One of my all-time favorite tools in psychology is the concept of locus of control. It was created by American psychologist Julian B. Rotter in 1954. ("Julian B. Rotter," n.d.; Lopez-Garrido 2022) The concept deals with the degree to which an individual believes they have control over events in their lives in comparison to external forces they cannot control. Said another way: Locus, as in "location," and control, as in where control resides—within you or outside of you.

I'm a world-class worrier, and that's perhaps why this tool has been so helpful to me. In addition, my natural instinct is to assume that everything in my world is within my control. No matter what happens (good or bad), it must be tied to something I did. We all know that's not how it works, but in the dead of night inside my control-freak brain, it makes a strange kind of sense. So, I have to work to retrain my brain and tame my thoughts. That's where the locus of control tool comes in.

For years, I had a locus of control chart hanging near my office door so I could see it every time I left. I mentioned it in the opening story. I still have that chart. It looks like the image below. Let's dive into each of the rings to explore how to use the chart.

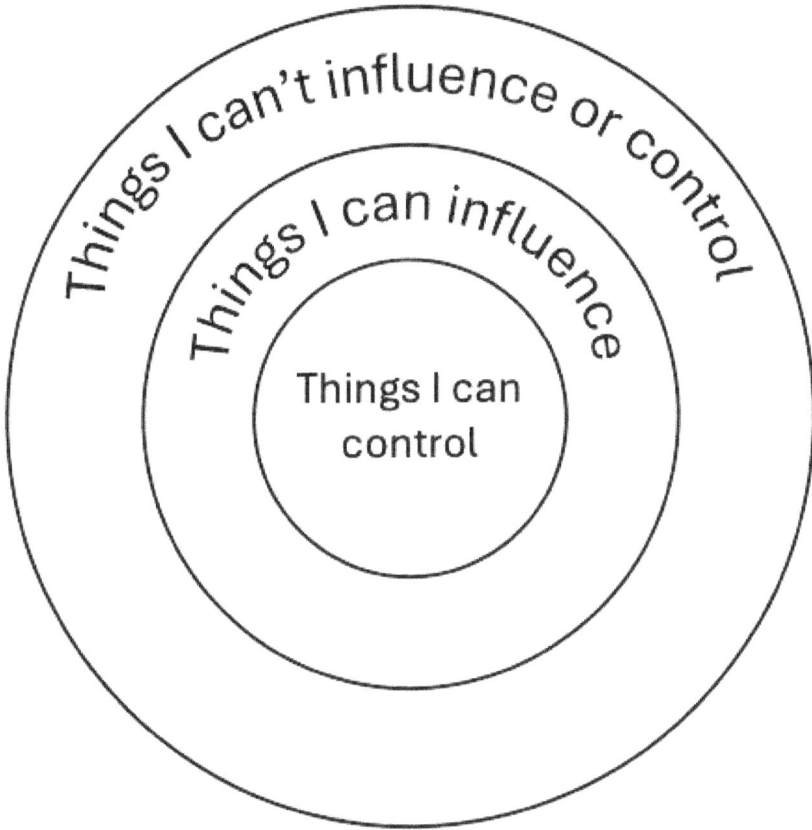

- <u>Things I can control:</u>
  The things that reside in the innermost circle are things you can absolutely and completely control: What you wear, what you say, what you choose to do. These are items you can and should take responsibility for. This is where personal accountability lives.

- <u>Things I can influence:</u>
  The things that reside in the next circle are things you may be able to influence but don't have direct control over: How your family treats the tube of toothpaste (roll from the bottom

or squeeze from the middle), whether family members complete their chores, decisions made at work by management. You can work hard to influence your manager's decision regarding the promotion you are seeking by delivering top performance, but you don't control that decision. At best, you can only influence it.

- <u>Things I can't influence nor control:</u>
  The outermost circle contains things that are totally beyond your control: The price of milk, the reduction in force your organization is going through, or the state of the economy. Strangely, these tend to be things people worry about most, yet are completely uncontrollable.

The way I use this chart is simple. I stand in front of it and ask myself questions, then force myself to answer by stating (or pointing) to the circle it resides in. I then redirect my response by backtracking to what I *can* control. I'm no longer allowed to focus on the worry if it is beyond my control. Here are two quick examples:

- *Question*: Will Frank like my presentation?
  - *Answer*: Outermost circle. It's none of my business if Frank likes or dislikes my presentation. My job is to be prepared and present the information in the best way I can. I am prepared, so I have nothing to worry about.
- *Question*: Will James want to go to the concert on Friday?
  - *Answer*: Middle circle. James probably won't want to go, but I may be able to influence his decision by compromising on the time we leave and where we sit.

Activity #3: Locus of Control Q&A

Take this opportunity to unpack some things from your overpacked luggage before you begin your journey into the Mobilize section. Try asking yourself a few questions about worries or concerns that are on your mind, and then answering them with the Locus of Control chart. Then, back up until you figure out what you can actually control and how you might take action to alleviate or lessen your concern. This can be a powerful tool to redirect your thinking back to a positive mindset while also letting go of unnecessary worry.

This chapter addressed three common areas we have difficulty letting go of: relationships, fears, and worries. By finding ways to shed these weights, we can lighten our load and get more mileage from the FUEL actions covered in the last three chapters (Fanning Your Flame, Unleashing Your Community, and Encouraging Input). I hope the examples and activities in this chapter gave you something to think about and will help you reframe and release unnecessary burdens.

HACK IT TIP:

I encourage you to use the activities in this chapter as an opportunity to form a partnership with a friend, mentor, or trusted colleague. Another way to lighten your load is by sharing it with someone who is willing to help you carry it. When you support each other, you will naturally find commonalities and can share perspectives, experiences, and additional tips.

Before we move onto the final step in the Breakthrough Formula, let's return to this chapter's breakthrough journey installment for part 2. This story isn't quite over. The intimidation breakthrough I achieved during the difficult meeting with Frank produced an interesting opportunity that I didn't anticipate.

My Real-Life Breakthrough Journey: *Installment 9 (Part 2)*

After my department and I started making progress in re-establishing ourselves as experts in the area of education and development and had re-introduced ourselves to neighboring departments, I received an invitation to meet with the Chief Nursing Administrator, Lena.

Lena was the head of all nursing activities in the health system. She reported to Frank and was considered one of the most powerful executives in the organization. She was responsible for the majority of the system's employees. Meeting with her was a privilege and an honor.

I was nervous, but she had been kind the few times I'd crossed paths with her. I just couldn't imagine why she would want to meet with me unless it was to express concern about the services my department provided to the nursing staff. It turned out to be something else altogether.

When I arrived at her office, she greeted me warmly and invited me to take a seat. "I bet you are wondering why I asked for this meeting," she said.

I agreed. "Yes, I am a bit curious. What can I do for you?" That's a safe opening, right? I was weighing every word and sitting on the edge of my seat, still uncertain about the cause of the meeting.

"Well, I want you to know that I was one of the people in your interview who encouraged Mack to hire you." She smiled.

That surprised me! "Thank you!" I responded, "Was there a specific reason you thought I'd be a good fit for the role?"

"Actually, yes. There was. It's what I want to talk with you about today." She went on to explain, "I think the hospital needs more emphasis on patient care, and I think you can help us with that."

What? I know nothing about patient care. I was at a total loss.

She continued, "There is a program that I think would benefit the hospital a great deal, and I think you are the person who can get the rest of the senior team onboard."

Wait a minute! She thinks I can do something she can't? Yes. That's exactly what she thought.

She went on to tell me that she appreciated my recent presentation and the way I demonstrated grace under fire when responding to Frank. She explained that she wanted to pursue a new culture change initiative that focused on the patient experience. She truly believed it would make a difference in the way the organization related to patients and had the power to change the core behaviors of every employee in the health system. She had a big vision but needed someone else to get it going. She had tried, but hadn't been able to get the traction it needed—and she was somewhat limited due to her reporting relationship to Frank. Lena had been observing me, the progress I was making with my team, and my handling of difficult situations and had decided I was capable of getting the program she wanted to sponsor off the ground.

I was astounded, shocked, and very flattered. Wow! She was willing to take a big bet on me and my team.

The good news was that my team and I were making progress, and we were making big improvements in our service quality. That fact was validated by Lena's request and her assertion that my team and I could tackle this huge culture change initiative.

But I was also wary. I had three concerns:

1) I had never attempted something this big in the arena of culture. I had in other areas, but nothing as difficult and complicated as this project.

2) The senior executive team wasn't fully on board. That was why she wanted me to tackle it. The factions among the senior team ensured that some would automatically vote down an idea from the "other side."

3) If Lena couldn't handle Frank on this matter, could I really handle it? Was Lena tossing me and my team to a pack of wolves?

I understood that from Lena's perspective, I was a somewhat neutral and nonthreatening choice. She identified that to get the project green-lighted, she needed to work around the politics and get the executive team to look at the merits of the program rather than focus on the person who was sponsoring it. That meant she couldn't sponsor it directly, or at least not alone. She needed my boss to co-sponsor it and me to lead it.

I listened intently to her logic and her heart for the work. She was very passionate about wanting to improve the experience for both patients and employees. I agreed to learn more about the program, visit with my boss about it, and get back to her.

I did just that. Mack and I weighed the pros and cons and decided that the benefits outweighed the possible risks. A few weeks later, my team and I were building a plan to present to the executive team for a new culture change initiative.

I'll fast-forward and share that we got the green light. Our team was given the opportunity to lead the biggest corporate culture initiative for the health system to date, which would take us over a year to roll out and several years beyond that to cement. I'll share glimpses into that portion of our journey as we work through our final step in the Breakthrough Formula: Mobilize.

Next Up: Launch Your Visibility Project with Mobilize MOVE Actions

We've completed the Energize section and the FUEL actions. In this section, you:

- Fanned your flames and created sustainable fuel by saturating your brain with positive energy, picking a word, and writing an affirmation.
- Unleashed your community by finding communities of shared commitment, sharing your vision, and inviting participation in your visibility project.
- Encouraged and welcomed specific input by exploring the difference between input and feedback, inviting your community to provide input, and cycling back to share how you incorporate their input.
- Lightened your load by letting go of work relationships, fears, and worries that are weighing you down.

Let's again pull out your personalized formula. Take a moment to revisit your plan and capture any activities, tools, or topics you want to remember from the Energize section. Then, decide which sections of the Mobilize step you want to pay particular attention to.

As we move into the final step of the Breakthrough Formula, Mobilize, I encourage you to start taking tangible action to MOVE your plan from paper to reality. To illustrate this, let's consider an example.

Have you ever "previewed" a workout video without participating in the workout? You know, just checking it out to see if you would like it and decide if it's right for you? I hate to admit that I have. On more than one occasion. Which makes no sense. How can you possibly evaluate whether a workout system actually works and delivers results if you don't get up and move? I'm sure you've heard the adage, "Workouts don't work unless you do!"

You see where I'm going with this. This book is all about achieving your next breakthrough—and that requires you to move into action. To help you MOVE forward, you are going to:

- Move Into Action
- Obtain Regular Feedback
- Verify Your Results
- Enjoy the Moment

When you Mobilize your plan by taking action, receiving regular feedback, and monitoring results, it's just a matter of time before you achieve your breakthrough victory. Think of this as the day you hit your fitness goal: you've lost the pounds, gained the muscle, the jeans fit, and you feel like a million bucks. So, let's MOVE into action and turn your visibility project into reality!

Let's Review:

1) To create lift, you also have to address drag by letting go of some of the weight you are carrying around.

2) We covered three categories of drag: relationships, fears, and worries that weigh you down.

3) Three tools were discussed to help you reduce your drag:
    ○ Use the anchors, tides, and wakes definitions to discern which of your professional and friend relationships you may need to set better boundaries around or let go of.
    ○ Identify your threat traps to regain control of your responses to threats and reframe them so you can create enough space to respond differently.

    ◦   Use the locus of control tool to correct your perceptions of what you can control, influence, or neither.

Think About It:

1) What relationships might you need to release or redirect? How can you do so with respect and kindness yet remain firm in the boundaries you need to be healthy?

2) Consider your FUEL journey. Are you ready to begin the execution phase of your visibility project? If not, what do you need to do to prepare for the work to come?

3) Consider what else may be weighing you down that wasn't included in this chapter. How might you address that weight and resolve it?

Take Action:

1) Complete the anchor, tides, and wakes exercise to right-size your relationships by investing in tides and positive wakes and addressing anchors and negative wakes.

2) Complete the exercise to identify your threat responses and triggers. Pick one trigger situation that you feel confident you can reframe and do it. Share it with a trusted friend so you have an accountability partner.

3) Complete the Locus of Control Q&A activity. What did you gain from this exercise? If you don't struggle with the concept of control, what else might you need to address?

Section 4

Mobilize!

Chapters in this section:

Chapter 12

Move into Action

My Real-Life Breakthrough Journey: *Installment 10*

The fastest way to alter your carefully crafted visibility project plan is to begin executing it. As soon as you "break the seal" and begin working to bring your plan to life, you will experience situations and realities you didn't anticipate, failed to consider, or simply changed between the time you planned and the time you began implementing.

Your resilience and commitment to your plan will likely be tested quickly and often. Your ability to overcome obstacles, pick your battles, and adjust or adapt your plans and actions will play a large role in your project's success. For that reason, I want to share an obstacle I encountered shortly after my team and I began working on the culture change project. It involves a workplace feud.

When I joined the education and development department, I unknowingly inherited a feud with the department across the hall. As I got to know my team and began learning about the department's history with our across-the-hall neighbors, I realized that there were many hard feelings on both sides that dated back several years. The dislike ran deep.

On top of that, my counterpart across the hall, Jan, and I didn't hit it off. Our personalities and styles were very different, and we seemed to rub each other the wrong way. This interpersonal conflict compounded the issues between the two departments and escalated the feud. It was high school all over again, complete with tattling and whispers in hallways. Not a fun work environment. And something I let linger for way too long. I didn't lead my team the way I should have by dealing with the issue. Instead, I let it fester.

After landing the corporate culture project, I realized that I couldn't lead a project about patient care and improving the culture if I was contributing to a senseless feud that was eroding the work environments of both teams. So I swallowed my pride, gathered my courage, and made the difficult trek across the hall to request a meeting with Jan to try to resolve our conflict and apologize for my part in perpetuating it.

That olive branch led to an uncomfortably frank and open discussion. You know, the kind where it starts something like, "You don't like me, and I don't like you, but we have to work together, so how about we ignore our mutual dislike and start over?"

To my surprise and relief, both Jan and I were tired of the feud, and we both agreed to let the past go. We committed to building a partnership and a future in which we didn't actively avoid each other. We talked through our mutual issues of mistrust and miscommunication and agreed to set a positive example for our teams. We mended our relationship and started publicly supporting one another.

Don't get me wrong, it didn't magically improve overnight. The relationship and our support of one another wasn't always easy, and it felt extremely unnatural, even phony, at first. Over several months, though, we were able to fully reconcile our differences. We even formed a tentative, if cautious, friendship and discovered that we had a few things in common. Jan was a fascinating person. She had a big heart and was fully committed to her work and her team. Before long, things between the departments improved, and we left high school drama behind. Good riddance!

What started as an obstacle and potential setback became one of the team's biggest and quickest wins. We lost an enemy and gained an unexpected partnership. Jan and her team became our allies in the culture change project. They provided help, support, and camaraderie we didn't realize we would need and would have never thought to request.

We quickly moved into execution mode after resolving the conflict with our neighbors. We spent months learning together and working crazy hours doing fun and meaningful work. I have incredibly fond memories of that time, even though it was part of my boot camp experience in healthcare. It was hard, but it was also a highlight of our careers. We knew we were making an impact, and our hard work was paying off every day.

I wish I could share a secret tip, a miraculous tool, or a shortcut that would get you to your breakthrough moment without hard work, setbacks, dips in motivation, or moments of discouragement that come with implementing your project. I can't. Execution requires good old elbow grease.

Short of doing the work, you've given yourself every advantage: you have your "what" and "why" locked into place, you have a solid but approachable plan to guide your actions, and you've fueled yourself with positivity-generating tools, a community that believes in you and will actively support you, and you've let go of the things that are holding you back. Your success is *almost* guaranteed. Now you just have to do the work.

Our Goals:

Our goal for this chapter is to kick your execution into high gear. We want to accumulate as many wins as quickly as possible. Wins lead to more wins. They prove you can do things you didn't think you could or would do. So, to accumulate wins, we are going to:

1) Identify your first set of quick wins and your quick win targets after that.
2) Create a tracker that keeps you accountable and your headspace clear, and can be shared with your community to communicate your progress and invite encouragement.
3) Discuss how you can overcome setbacks and keep going.

Magda's Situation

Do you remember Magda from Chapter 2? She is the last of the three leaders we met at the beginning of our journey together. We will use Magda for our examples in this chapter. For that reason, we need to understand where she is in her journey and some of the decisions she has made in preparation for the execution of her visibility project. An example of Magda's project documents are included in Appendix A.

Magda's Background

Magda has talents and skills in the areas of Strategize and Energize. Let's take a moment to refresh our memories about Magda's situation. Note the points that are emphasized.

Magda is an extremely talented and ambitious director with a strong desire for an executive role. She is universally liked, easy to talk with, and strategic. Her ideas are great. She is tuned into what is happening in the company and current events. People flock to her when they have problems, and she always makes time to visit with them.

Magda's issue is that while she always delivers for her external clients, she *cuts corners, procrastinates*, and *frustrates her colleagues* with *unmet promises*. Because she is so well-liked, no one wants to tell her that she drives them crazy by promising and then either *not delivering or delivering sub-par work* because she *waited until the last minute* to do the work. Because of this, she is *overlooked* for executive opportunities and key projects that would provide visibility despite her strengths and performance with external clients. She has so many great qualities but *can't be counted on to deliver quality work on time consistently*.

Magda is currently a Sales Director. Her ultimate *goal* is to become a *Regional VP of Sales*.

Magda's Word and Affirmation

To better understand where Magda is in her breakthrough journey, she has chosen her word and written her affirmation (with help from AI) from Chapter 8. Her word is "cultivate." Her affirmation is:

> I *cultivate* trust and reliability in all my relationships, delivering excellence to both external clients and internal colleagues with equal dedication and timeliness. Through consistent results and unwavering follow-through on my commitments, I build long-term relationships founded on dependability and mutual respect. (Perplexity.ai, 11/12/2024)

<u>Magda's Visibility Project</u>

Magda's visibility project is planning and organizing an off-site two-day internal sales conference for her region. It involves agenda development, speaker lineup, training activities, and social events. Her sponsor is her Regional VP of Sales, and she has been assigned a small team of colleagues to work with her on the event.

We'll use Magda's project for our examples in this chapter. Let's start by looking at the quick wins she has decided to tackle first.

Quick Wins

Nothing breeds success like making quick wins. When you move quickly into action by focusing on things you can complete in a short time frame, you generate momentum and create a rhythm of success that builds confidence. You can then leverage that momentum to tackle something a bit larger. This process kicks off a domino effect of action that turns plans into reality.

This is especially true when starting something unfamiliar, something that could be overwhelming or that you fear will fail - start small and accumulate wins. Few things prove your fears wrong faster than evidence you can succeed!

Let's put this principle to the test by planning out your quick wins.

<u>Activity #1: Identify, Prioritize, and Achieve Quick Wins:</u>

1) *Pull out your WBS task list*: This is the list of specific actions you created in Chapter 6 during the Strategize step and further refined in the Energize step based on the input you received from your community.

2) *Review your WBS task list:* Determine which of your activities qualify as possible quick wins that you can achieve in short order.

- Which activities do you have the time and ability to fully accomplish today? For example, research you need to do or something you need to write.
- Which activities could you initiate today that take longer to accomplish or that are dependent on others but must be started by you? For example, a call you need to make to initiate a conversation or meeting that will happen next week or an application you need to submit that requires outside resources to complete.

3) *Prioritize your list:* Challenge yourself to highlight three items on your activities list that you will accomplish first.
   - Which three activities would move you forward the most or be a huge relief once they are done?
   - If you can't do all three today, then commit to a timeframe in which you will complete them. Perhaps it's one that you will do today, one that you will do in the next two days, and one that you will do this week.

4) *Plan ahead:* Once you have highlighted your three quick win items, immediately find the next set of three things to tackle. Having three items in your "hopper" will push you forward and fix your focus on what's coming next.

5) *Do the work:* I'm sure you know several productivity tricks to help overcome procrastination, so use them now.

Keep up this cycle of systematically focusing on three items and getting them done. I know this seems simple, and it is. But it also works to keep procrastination and overwhelm at bay, feeds you positive energy from getting stuff done, contributes to your domino effect of wins, and ensures you make routine progress on your visibility project. Quick wins add up to executed projects and breakthrough opportunities!

Here is an example from Magda's project. After reviewing her WBS task list, she has picked the first three quick wins (noted as "1" in the Quick Win column) and the three she will work on next (noted as "2" in the Quick Win column).

WBS Task Outline	Quick Win
1. Project Initiation (Week 1)	
1.1. Define project objectives and scope (Day 1)	1
1.2. Identify key stakeholders (Day 2)	1
1.3. Assemble project team (Day 7)	
1.3.1. Identify list of possible team members	1
1.3.2. Present list to sponsor	2
1.3.3. Request team member assignments from dept heads	2
1.3.4. Prep agenda and meeting materials and send to team	2
1.3.5. Schedule Kick-Off Meeting & send invites	

Start developing a rhythm of consistently working on your visibility project every week. It needs to be something you are dedicated to and prioritize your time around.

If you need a boost of motivation, return to the work you did on your "what" and "why" worksheet in Chapter 3. Recall our discussion that your "why" has to be big enough to support your "what." And your "what" is what you are working on now.

Track and Communicate Your Progress

Let me return for a moment to my continuing breakthrough journey and our culture-shaping project. I shared that we received approval to proceed with the project. What I didn't share is that Mack and Lena teamed up to co-sponsor the project. The project had a sizable budget and large scope. It was important to keep both of them up to date without creating the additional burden of a cumbersome progress report.

I needed something easy to assemble, easy to update, easy to read, and that could be used for multiple purposes and audiences. I decided to create a very simple red, green, and yellow "stop light" report. The report was one-page long and listed the major milestones for the project (from the WBS task list), the items that were next up on the project plan, and the status of each item with a red circle (at risk), yellow circle (needs help), or a green circle (on track). The simple visual allowed our sponsor meetings to run smoothly. We spent most of our time talking through any red and yellow items, and then touched on the green if time allowed.

Here's another example from Magda's project. You can see that she added a few columns to her WBS task list that include her stoplight status, quick win priorities, estimated due dates, delegation assignments, and notes. (Also see Appendix A.)

Magda's Project: Regional Sales Conference Event

Due Date: 4 to 5 Months from assignment

Delegation Legend:

1=Project Manager (Magda), 2= Project Sponsor, 3=Communications Team Rep, 4=Sales Team Rep, 5=Administrative Support Rep, 6=IT Department Rep

Status	WBS Task Outline	Quick Win	Est. Due Date	Progress	Delegate	Notes
	1. Project Initiation (Week 1)		**Week 1**		1	
Green	1.1. Define project objectives and scope (Day 1)	1	Day 1	100	1	
Green	1.2. Identify key stakeholders (Day 2)	1	Day 2	80	1	
	1.3. Assemble project team (Day 7)				1	
Yellow	1.3.1. Identify list of possible team members	1	Day 2	50	1	Need help with IT team member
	1.3.2. Present list to sponsor	2	Day 3		1, 2	
	1.3.3. Request team member assignments from dept heads	2	Day 4		1, 2	
	1.3.4. Prep agenda and meeting materials and send to team	2	Day 4		1	
	1.3.5. Schedule Kick-Off Meeting & send invites		Day 7		1	

I've used the stoplight report for all my update meetings, whether I reported to a director or the CEO. Over the years, my managers have appreciated the simple, communicative report. It never fails to focus our attention and keep us moving forward.

Another even lower-maintenance option is below. If you fill this out each week, you will easily see your progress over time and will produce a ready-made accountability sheet you can share with your support community via a social post. Talk about accountability! I've also included some journaling prompts to help you stay focused on positive forward movement. Edit or add to this to make it your own. You can also easily turn this into a stoplight report with yellow, green, and pink highlighters.

Date:	Project:
My First 3 Quick Wins (And Due Dates): 1) 2) 3)	The Next 3 Quick Wins I'll Tackle: 1) 2) 3)
What I Accomplished This Week:	What I Want to Do Better or Improve on Next Week:
What I Feel Good About From This Week:	I will share this completed worksheet with _____ _____ (name) on _____ (date).

If this kind of report doesn't fit with your work style or need, there are so many other ways you can track your progress. There are apps, digital planners, paper planners and trackers, and other kinds of reports. Pick one and use it. Keep your tracking tool simple and easy. Consistency is the key. If it's not easy, you won't do it.

You need to have something in place so that when your head starts yelling that you aren't making progress, you can prove yourself wrong by pulling up past trackers and looking at your wins.

HACK IT TIP:

Consider whether you can add progress tracking to some part of your existing work routine. For instance, I set aside time every Sunday afternoon to plan and prepare for the week ahead. I call it my weekly date with myself. I do the same thing each month, with an after-action review of the prior month and a goal-setting session for the upcoming month. When I'm working on a project—which is most of the time—my project tracking is absorbed into my other tracking and planning activities, so I don't feel like I'm taking on something new. Instead, I'm attaching it to an existing process.

This works whether you are working on your project as part of your day job or after hours. I think the weekly review process is even more important if you are doing your project on your own time. It's harder to prioritize project work when you have less available time, so the benefits of efficiency, focus, and intention are even more necessary.

Keep Going!

When you start consistently executing your plan, you are going to run into setbacks, like the one in the opening story of this chapter. Obstacles are inevitable. James calls them "character-building moments." He's right!

A friend and I recently discussed this topic. We shared our struggles and our breakthroughs. I asked her, "Why do breakthroughs often feel like new setbacks?" We decided it's because breakthroughs come with a whole new set of requirements and new work to be done. Just when you think you are close to completion, you round the corner to see another challenge waiting for you. That's life, and the road is rarely straight and flat. Instead, the path curves, doubles back on itself, has hills and valleys, and then you look down to see you have a flat tire. That's the path of growth and development. There are no shortcuts. I don't think we would be better off if there were.

Imagine for a moment that you did find a shortcut that lets you cut across a cornfield and skip the winding road with the difficult uphill climbs. You would miss out on some rare and beautiful teaching moments. Teaching moments that help us close our gaps and grow in lasting and meaningful ways. Growth and development may be hard work, but it's worth it. No one can take the lessons, accomplishments, and wins away from you. Nor can anyone experience them for you. They are yours!

So when you are tempted to quit, don't. Take a break. Give yourself a moment of rest, focus on your "why," choose your attitude, and then go at it again. As I've been writing this book, I've had plenty of obstacles, brick walls, setbacks, and self-doubts. Through them all, James has patiently looked at me and said, "Keep going."

That simple encouragement has carried me through some tough times. So let me share it with you: Keep going! Those of us who achieve our career aspirations aren't the smartest and most talented. We are the most stubborn and consistent. We're the ones who keep showing up. I refuse to give up on my dream, and I refuse to stay quiet and let you give up on yours.

So, start taking action on the quick win items you identified in this chapter, track your progress in your tracker of choice, and keep going. Your next breakthrough is waiting.

In the next chapter, we will dive into obtaining feedback to support your ongoing growth and achievement. The execution phase is a fantastic time to lean into feedback. You have an audience who is cheering you on and paying attention to the new behaviors, skills, and experience you are gaining as you bring your visibility project to life. This is a great time to amplify your efforts and get extra credit from your advisors by asking for their support through feedback.

Let's Review:

1) Wins lead to more wins. They prove you can do things you didn't think you could or would do—to yourself and others. Quick wins help you accumulate wins and build momentum.

2) Use the task outline that you created in the Strategize step and updated in the Energize step to identify quick wins, map out priorities, and create a progress-tracking tool.

3) Setbacks are inevitable and happen to everyone. It's part of the growing process. Navigating through them teaches valuable lessons that become lasting wins. No matter what happens, keep going.

Think About It:

1) How do quick wins make you feel?

2) Consider a time when you overcame a setback. What did you learn? How has that lesson been applied to the way you work today?

3) What is one piece of advice you would give a younger version of yourself about facing setbacks?

Take Action:

1) Get moving on your project. This is the time for your execution ability to shine. Prioritize your task outline list and select your first three quick win activities and your next three quick win targets. As you accumulate quick wins, keep your hopper loaded with your next three action items.

2) Determine how you will track and record your progress. Keep it simple and update it regularly.

3) Keep going. Don't let setbacks hold you back. You've got this!

Chapter 13

Obtain Regular Feedback

My Real-Life Breakthrough Journey: *Installment 11*

Things with the team were finally grooving and falling into place. We were starting the slow turnaround of our department and making steady progress on our big culture change project. We even had more allies, like Jan and her team.

In the midst of all that, I reflected on my experience with Jan and realized that I needed to be more open to feedback. So, I signed up for a 360-degree feedback assessment. People who worked with me, for me, and above me were all asked to fill out a confidential survey rating my performance as a leader. Things were going well, so I thought the feedback would be relatively positive.

When I got the results report, I did what everyone does: I skipped over all the good stuff and zeroed in on the negative. The vast majority of the report was complimentary, but there was a negative comment about my age that flat-out made me angry.

The comment was that I was too young for the role, despite my experience. I was hurt. I couldn't do anything about my age, and the comment was just so unfair! My mind spun out of control with thoughts like, "I thought I was making good headway with the team." and "It's hopeless. Maybe I need to start looking for another job."

Let's pause for a moment. Based on what we know from previous chapters, we can confidently say that I allowed the negative comment to trigger my fight, flight, or freeze response. My RAS filter was set to focus on the negative, as demonstrated by my scan of the report, looking for the "improvements" I needed to make.

As all of this was spinning in my head, I called my dad for our regular mentoring chat. It became one of my most memorable coaching discussions. Before I share his wisdom with you, let me tell you a little about my dad and our conversations.

My dad is a retired manufacturing executive. For forty years, he worked his way up the ladder from a mechanic to the VP of Manufacturing for a natural gas engine company. His job required him to work with a wide range of skilled professionals, from engineers and accountants to mechanics. He loved leading people.

I remember walking through the mall with him as a teenager and being forced to wait while he chatted with one person after another. One day, I asked him who he had just spoken with. He replied, "Oh, that was Joe. I had to fire him last year."

When I expressed my shock that Joe would even talk to my dad, he chuckled and said, "He wasn't in the right job. He was stuck, so firing him was the push he needed to find the right job. I helped him find one that was a better fit. He's much happier now."

I repeatedly experienced this with my dad growing up. So, when I began my first paying job, it was natural to call my dad for advice. What developed was a weekly call on Friday evenings with my dad asking about my week, me spilling my guts, and him critiquing and gently correcting me. He then gave me "homework" to implement the following week. Now, back to the memorable coaching discussion.

I called my dad in a huff and vented my frustration with righteous indignation. I told my dad about the assessment report, the audacity of the written comment about my age, and my hurt feelings as I paced angrily around my backyard. I can only imagine what our neighbors thought. I finally stopped talking and waited in anticipation for him to tell me I was right, that my hurt feelings were justified, and to help me figure out how to set the record straight.

"Well," he said, "Is it true?"

I stopped pacing, and my jaw dropped. That wasn't at *all* what I expected.

I sharply replied, "What do you mean 'is it true'!? Of course, it's not true! How can you ask me that?" I was outraged and hurt. He was supposed to agree with me.

He accepted my harsh reply with a sigh and a chuckle. "Sweetheart, I care more about your *character* than I do about your *feelings*. So let me ask you again, is it true?"

The wind left my sails, and I deflated. My dad took my anger and redirected it smoothly back to what I could control: my response and my character.

We went on to discuss that while I couldn't change my age, I may be able to change my approach so my team didn't feel the separation of our ages quite so much. We discovered together that I had probably come across as having a chip on my shoulder in my zeal to prove myself.

I also needed to address the feedback with my team gracefully so we could continue to grow and move our culture project forward. I couldn't risk the team being afraid to share information with me. I clearly had some growing to do, and I wanted the team to continue sharing their thoughts with me.

When a project is in the execution phase, many things can arise that are outside the original plan. The team's ability to share information, *any information*, with me was vital to the health and successful completion of our work together.

That humbling conversation changed my approach and gave me the feedback and strategy I needed to further close the gap with my new team. To this day, I still ask myself, "Is it true?" and remind myself that my "character is more important than my feelings."

Feedback… It's everyone's least favorite subject. Do you cringe like I do when you hear the phrase, "We need to talk"? Or, "I have some feedback for you"? Even if your performance is fantastic and even when you are expecting a good conversation and positive feedback, just knowing that someone is going to weigh your work and potentially judge you naturally puts you on edge. And yet, feedback is critical for your growth and for the success of your visibility project.

One of my bosses and mentors often said, "Feedback is a necessary but insufficient ingredient for growth." And he was right. We need feedback, but feedback alone doesn't create growth. You grow when you receive feedback, learn from it, and apply it.

The execution phase of your visibility project will likely create many opportunities for you to receive feedback. I encourage you to seek as much feedback on your performance and progress as you can. You cannot achieve your breakthrough and attain a career you love and the future you want without feedback.

Our Goals:

In this chapter, we are going to work through the following:

1) Why you need feedback.
2) Creating opportunities for feedback by inviting your community to share their experiences with you.

3) How to manage your reaction and response to the feedback you receive so it is less threatening to both you and the people offering feedback.

By the end of the chapter, I hope you look at feedback a little differently and perhaps have some new ideas about how to ask for and respond to it. Let's begin by talking about how other people experience you with a discussion on blind spots.

Blind Spots Happen

We are all built with internal blinders that keep us from seeing things about ourselves that are obvious to other people. Think of them like blind spots when driving. Blind spots are spaces the driver has no way of seeing despite having windows, mirrors, and cameras. Because you can't see them or the potential obstacles they may contain, blind spots are hazardous.

Feedback helps us see our behavioral blind spots. We just can't trust ourselves to see certain things. We lack the perspective that distance provides. I once heard it said like this: "We judge others by their actions and ourselves by our intentions." That's why feedback from others is so important.

Feedback may not be a gift you always want, but it is a gift you need. A gift we should appreciate because someone cared about us enough to tell us that we have something on our face or that our zipper is undone. It's embarrassing for both people—the person providing the feedback and the person receiving it.

When we are unable to see something because of a personal blind spot, it's usually because we are looking at ourselves through the lens of our own intentions. That's why we must lean on other people to relate their experiences with us *to* us. Think of it as someone holding up a mirror for me and pointing out the ways my outfit is either flattering or unflattering. It's helpful, even when it's embarrassing.

The idea that people can "experience" you was a startling eye-opener, and it helped me truly appreciate and begin embracing the concept of feedback.

I was the leader of a small team and was in my dream job. I thought things were going well, but I was blind to an issue my behavior was creating and how it was impacting the team. Someone was kind enough to give me some really critical feedback that hurt me deeply. The essence of the feedback was that people were intimidated by me, felt I was unapproachable, and were basically afraid of me. That was the opposite of what I wanted. From my perspective, I cared deeply about the team and would do anything for them (filter = my intentions). In reality, they were experiencing me very differently (filter = my actions).

Here's how it looked from both perspectives:

My perspective: I was dealing with an issue that was intensely frustrating to me. To gain perspective, I stepped away from my desk and walked to the break room for a cup of coffee to clear my head. Internally, I was wrestling with the problem and trying to break loose the mental cogs that were preventing me from finding a solution. Since I was lost in my own thoughts, I wasn't aware of my facial expressions or what was happening around me. If I noticed others, I left them alone, thinking they were busy and going about their own business.

Their perspective: I passed people in the hall with a scowl on my face. I didn't greet them, wish them a good morning, or acknowledge their presence. I gave them the impression that I didn't care, didn't have time for them, and that they weren't worth the effort to greet. Because of that, they didn't greet me either and steered clear of me.

I didn't know I had a problem until someone was kind enough to clue me in and hold up a mirror. That realization jarred me into understanding how necessary feedback truly is and that I couldn't grow into the leader I wanted to be until I learned to seek, accept, and value feedback.

I wish I could tell you that I turned over a new leaf that day, and it never happened again. That would be a lie. I did improve, and I found ways to show my care, but I have and will struggle with this aspect of my personality forever. I'm an intense person with a poker face that needs work. I tend to wear my emotions openly, and I'm a hard charger on top of that. I have to use specific strategies to keep this aspect of my personality in check. And one of those strategies is… you guessed it: *feedback*!

For me, this behavioral tendency represents a blind spot that I will never be able to see fully without others' help and continual effort to increase my self-awareness. Here's the bad news: you have blind spots, too, and the only way to tackle them is with feedback.

Creating Opportunities for Feedback

Another interesting aspect of feedback is that people are just as hesitant to give feedback when asked for it as they are to receive feedback themselves. Why is this? I believe it is because we have all been stung by a sharp retort, a defensive comeback, or a rebuke we received after delivering feedback we've given with a sincere intent to help.

Have you ever metaphorically stepped on a land mine by introducing a topic that you didn't realize was off-limits to the person you were talking with? I have. And it is not always handled gracefully by the person you are conversing with. There is a reason for the phrase, "Don't shoot the messenger."

If we are to get the information we desperately need about our blind spots, we have to create an environment in which feedback is valued and messengers aren't shot. Whether this is feedback in a work setting or a personal setting, we have to create a sense of psychological safety so the people around us are willing to tell us what we need to hear.

We can best do that by creating multiple feedback collection methods and managing how we respond to the feedback we receive. Let's start with different collection methods.

How to Ask for Feedback

We've established the need for feedback, but other than random drive-by discussions that deliver feedback you weren't expecting, how can you collect it from more intentional sources and on a more frequent basis?

To answer that question, let's set ourselves up for success by examining three different sources of feedback and how we might build recurring feedback mechanisms with each one.

<u>1. Collecting Feedback from Team Members:</u>

The people you work with most closely are always the best sources of feedback. They have more experience being around you and seeing you in a variety of settings and situations. For that reason, these people are often the most hesitant to provide feedback. For the purposes of this discussion, "team members" refers to the group of people who work for you, with you, or around you. Here are a few ideas:

Proactive Feedback:

By its nature, feedback happens after the fact: a situation occurs, something happens that others want to share with you (positive or negative), and then feedback is provided. But you can flip the script by asking for feedback proactively.

When you start a new project or work with new people, you can set the tone for future interactions by asking how they prefer to work with others, what you should do to support their work style, and what you should avoid doing that triggers their pet peeves and aggravations. This creates an open invitation to share feedback, and you can avoid missteps by better understanding their needs and work preferences upfront.

Asking for specific feedback tied to a specific event:

People will usually be willing to share feedback with you on "safe" topics to test the water and see how you react before they share more meaningful feedback. For example:

- If you are going into a meeting, ask your team to pay attention to how you deliver the presentation and give them a few things to look for and evaluate.
- After the meeting, ask your team members to share their thoughts about how you performed in those specific areas.
- Then, ask them if they have any other feedback about the meeting that they are willing to share.

Creating a feedback process:

If you have a scheduled touch-base meeting with your team members, get into the habit of asking a general feedback question every time you meet. They may eventually take you up on your offer. And since you do it regularly, they are more likely to respond when they do have something to share. For example:

- Is there anything you can think of I need to keep doing, start doing, or stop doing?
- You can further qualify this question by adding "for this project," "for the team," or "to best support you."

Encouraging a culture of growth and sharing:

Consider how you can encourage everyone to share ideas about how the team, as a whole, can improve. Then, listen closely. Sometimes, the team's ideas are really things you may need to do differently. If the ideas are reasonable, do what you can to support them and incorporate them into your project work.

HACK IT TIP:

The process of routinely asking for feedback can feel awkward and unnatural, if this is something you aren't already doing. I'm more comfortable trying something new if I can offer something of value. It makes me feel less awkward and shifts the focus away from me and onto something *outside* of me that I'm offering. It also gives me and the person I'm engaging with something we can mutually focus on. Let me share an example.

When I was trying to drum up participants for my classes as a trainer, I would grab a basket and fill it with candy attached to small note cards with class information. Because almost everyone wanted candy, either for themselves or to take home to their kids, they wanted me to stop by their desks. The basket of candy broke the ice and eased us both into conversation. You can do the same trick with feedback. Here's how:

- Find an online personality assessment. I'm a fan of the PrinciplesYou assessment. ("PrinciplesYou From Ray Dalio," n.d.) It's free, backed by science, and extremely actionable.

- Absorb your results report. Then, identify one or two insights you are comfortable sharing with others, would like feedback about, and want to work on.

- Insert the candy basket trick. When you ask for feedback, pull out the portion of the report you want to share. If you don't want to share the whole report, share an excerpt. I highly recommend using a document you can both focus on rather than looking at each other. Then say something like, "I recently took this personality assessment. It pointed something out that I've been working on... and I think this happened in our meeting last week. I'd really appreciate your perspective."

Odds are good that you will get more feedback if you "confess" to a behavior, share how you became aware of the fact, and own up to an instance of it. By doing so, you take the potential sting and fear of conflict out of the conversation. This approach can work with any of the collection methods discussed in this section.

2. Collecting Feedback from Colleagues:

Colleagues refer to those who work in the same general area, department, or group but who don't work directly with you day in and day out. These are people who frequent some of the same meetings you do but have fewer opportunities to observe your day-to-day work.

Feedback Exchange:

Try swapping feedback with a colleague by asking them to help you grow by providing feedback on a specific trait you are working on. This works even better if you can give them very specific things to evaluate. The more specific you are, the better your feedback will likely be. Then, offer to do the same for them if they are interested in collecting feedback themselves. For example:

- I am trying to improve my accountability and follow-through. Would you check in with me next week on our action items from the meeting we just left?
- I'm working on speaking up more in meetings. Would you watch me today and let me know how well I performed?
- Would you be willing to come to one of my team meetings as a guest to observe how I interact with my team? I'm working on ensuring everyone is heard, but I don't always create enough space for that to happen. I'd appreciate your feedback on my performance after the meeting.

3. Collecting Feedback from Advisors:

Advisors are the coaches, mentors, and sponsors we discussed in Chapter 7. Since advisors have already demonstrated their interest in your growth by investing time in your development, they can be great feedback providers. They also aren't as timid as the other two in providing constructive criticism to help you grow.

Feedback Observations:

Let your advisor know the area you are working to improve, and ask for feedback based on their interactions and observations after working with you. They will either respond right away to share past observations, or they will begin to watch your performance more closely to give you feedback in the future.

Feedback Interviews:

Advisors are very helpful in collecting information about you from others under a banner of confidentiality that people would be hesitant to share directly with you. They can package up the feedback, remove the names and identifying circumstances, and deliver feedback to you for improvement. For example:

- You receive a report (like a 360-degree report) with feedback, but you don't understand the comments enough to develop an action plan. Your advisor can interview people who work with and around you to provide additional clarity.

- You want specific feedback on a topic that will be difficult to share directly with you. A feedback interview is a good way to get the feedback you need.

Now that you have some ideas about generating regular, recurring feedback, let's move on to managing how we respond to the feedback we receive, especially when we disagree with the feedback.

Managing Your Reactions to Constructive or Negative Feedback

Building a track record of responding well, especially when you are disappointed with the content of the feedback, will create a trust-building loop with your feedback providers. Over time, the feedback you receive will become more specific and helpful because your feedback providers can trust that you will handle the information well.

However, if you respond poorly, the opposite will happen. When feedback is involved, people are quick learners and intense observers. Challenging feedback is incredibly difficult not to take personally, and it's tempting to shift the focus to the person who is delivering the feedback when discussing this topic. I want to encourage you not to do that. Let's backtrack to the locus of control we discussed at the end of the previous chapter. We have zero control over the person who gave us feedback and their choice of what, when, where, why, or how they delivered the feedback. What we can and must focus on is how we respond to it.

Let me spare you the pain of regret with a word of caution: I've seen leaders with tremendous potential flatline their careers by making poor decisions after getting feedback they couldn't receive and handled poorly.

In most cases, the leaders chose to go "shopping for feedback" that agreed with their own assessments of their performance. Once they found a sympathetic perspective, they came back to the feedback provider to argue their case and present proof they were right by quoting the person they found who agreed with them. Their efforts would have been much better spent leaning into the feedback they had received to understand, learn, and grow from it. Even if they still disagreed with it, they needed to understand what was driving the feedback so they could make adjustments. By shopping around for a perspective that agreed with their own, they demonstrated a lack of maturity that eroded trust and stalled their career advancement.

I'm not saying you have to accept the feedback as truth. I'm saying you have to consider it without alienating the person who took a chance by sharing the feedback with you.

So, how do you realistically listen to feedback you disagree with or that feels like a personal attack and *not* respond strongly? I think it's a matter of perspective.

Perspectives on Feedback

In my experience, examining and receiving tough feedback is much easier if you focus on the reasons you should listen to and consider the feedback. Here are six helpful perspectives on feedback that have enabled me to absorb difficult feedback—whether I agreed with it or not.

1) The view shared with you through the feedback process exists whether you know about it or not. Personally, I would rather know what's being said and how others are experiencing me

than remain in the dark. By knowing, I put myself in the position of choosing what I will do with the knowledge.

2) There are times when you simply don't know what you don't know. Feedback can be helpful in instructing you about things you need to learn, understand, or improve.

3) I want to get better, constantly grow, and improve. Feedback is one of the fastest ways to do that. You can think of it as a learning shortcut.

4) I want to minimize or eliminate my blind spots and sincerely want to understand my impact on those around me. I need to understand how other people experience me so I can increase my effectiveness and better accomplish my mission of helping others grow. I can't do that if I stop growing myself.

5) I have a deep sense of appreciation and empathy for those who share feedback with me because I know it's not an easy thing to do. I'm grateful they care enough about me to do something as uncomfortable as sharing feedback.

6) I know that if I react poorly or make the person who is sharing the feedback uncomfortable, they will not share feedback with me again. I want to guard and protect the relationship that enabled them to share feedback with me in the first place.

If you can keep these objectives top of mind when you sense that feedback is heading your way, you will greatly improve your ability to handle the situation with grace, gratitude, and humility of spirit. Then, you can decide what to do with the feedback you've received.

Journaling Activity: Feedback Is a Gift

- Look at the list of feedback perspectives above. Which of these perspectives resonates with you? What other reasons can you add to the list?
- How can you put these perspectives to work the next time you seek or receive feedback? How can you position your view of the feedback so you react neutrally instead of negatively—whether you agree with the feedback or not?
- Think back to the last difficult piece of feedback you received. How did you respond? Would you change your response if you could? What did you learn from that experience?
- How could you use these perspectives the next time you deliver feedback? How might you approach the delivery of your feedback differently?

Now that you have begun executing your visibility project and you've set up regular feedback mechanisms, let's move on to the next chapter and verify that our projects are achieving their intended results. We'll also return to the story about the culture change initiative my team and I were implementing and revisit the vision statement we created as a team.

Let's Review:

1) We all have blind spots that we cannot detect without help from others. Feedback helps us better understand how other people experience us and increases our self-awareness.

2) Feedback can be just as hard to deliver as to receive. If you want to invite feedback that will help you grow, create a sense of psychological safety so the people around you are willing to tell you what you need to hear.

3) Six perspectives are shared to help you absorb and consider challenging feedback. Consider that the perspective shared with you through the feedback process exists, whether you know about it or not. So, use it as an opportunity to learn from it and improve.

Think About It:

1) What is the most challenging feedback you've received? How did you handle the situation? Are you proud of your response? How might you have handled the feedback differently?

2) What was the most beneficial, yet challenging, feedback you've received? What was different about it that made it so helpful? Was it your response to the feedback, your adoption of the feedback, or the way it was delivered? Analyze it.

3) If you could emulate one person who is a rock star at delivering all kinds of feedback, who would it be? What do they do that is so effective? How can you replicate that yourself?

Take Action:

1) Set up a few regular feedback mechanisms with the team members who work most closely with you, to help you grow in an area that will support your visibility project. How can you create a sense of psychological safety to ensure you are getting an unfiltered response?

2) Consider whether one of your advisors would be willing to conduct a feedback interview for you.

3) Complete the activity in this chapter by adding your own perspectives to the six presented. Consider taking an online personality assessment, like PrinciplesYou, to gain insight and have something you can share proactively with others.

Chapter 14

Verify your results

My Real-Life Breakthrough Journey: *Installment 12*

My team and I continued making changes and improvements to our plans, partnerships, and service levels. We ultimately created a leadership development program that brought together the top 400 leaders in the health system every three months over a year's time for a full-day training and engagement experience tied to the culture change initiative. We wrote the material, produced the event, and taught the entire program. It was a period of exciting growth for all of us. After two years of hard work, individual and team growth, successes, and lessons learned, we were able to see our collective efforts paying off in the way the organization responded to our services.

We were about to have another measure that would indicate whether we were truly meeting our improvement goals. Once again, it was time for the organization-wide engagement survey.

This time, our team reported the highest engagement levels of any department in the health system. We increased engagement in every area by 200 percent! Not only were we out of danger, but we had turned into the "cool kids" and the department that others wanted to join. We had built a reputation for being good partners who delivered quality work. We were all thrilled by our turnaround and by the impact we were having. We had materialized the vision we created in those first few weeks of our time together. Let's revisit the vision statement the team created in Chapter 9:

The Education and Development Department is a team of highly skilled professionals that create and curate award-winning leadership development content, provide expertise and consultation to health system educators, and lead enterprise-wide HR projects that improve the employee and patient experience. We are the top-performing corporate department in customer satisfaction, employee engagement, and budget management. Other people want to work in this department and with this team!

This period of my career and that team of people will always hold a very special place in my heart. We had some heartbreaking moments, including the unexpected passing of one of our teammates. It wasn't a bed of roses. But it was a dream we built together through hard work, honest conversations, joint accountability, and team growth. And perhaps that's why I want you to achieve your next breakthrough so badly. I want *you* to experience the life-changing growth that happens when you achieve breakthroughs, close skill and experience gaps, and achieve your career aspirations. I want you to experience a community of shared commitment. And I want you to build a career you love with stories you can tell others as you help them surprise themselves with their own growth.

Keep reading. We're not done yet! We have one more chapter to go and one final installment in this story.

Before we can wrap up, we need to pause and ask ourselves some tough questions.

Time for a tough question… Are you actually making progress with your visibility project? Are you closing your skill gaps?

Let's return to our workout metaphor. Like stepping on the scale each morning, we tend to approach viewing our results with one eye closed and a sense of dread. It can be tough to look at all of our efforts and not see the results we were hoping to see. Your muscles are sore, you're listening to the coaching you've received through feedback, and you are working your tail off. But are you getting results?

The process of growth and development involves learning, application, experimentation, and evaluation. When we begin, we don't really know what we are doing. Nor do we know what we may be missing. We are blind to the things we've not yet learned or experienced, so constant evaluation, review, and adjustment are critical to making forward progress.

So, we have to ask ourselves: Are we doing the right work required to achieve a breakthrough? And is it producing our desired results? That's what we're going to talk about in this chapter.

Let's take a close look at what is going right, what you need to tweak, and what you need to stop doing.

Our Goals:

In this chapter, we are going to verify that our visibility project is producing our desired results, and we're going to take corrective action if necessary. To do this, we'll focus on three things:

1) Honestly assess where you are in relation to where you need to be to achieve your next breakthrough.
2) Discuss the difference between effort and results.
3) Determine the appropriate actions to keep your plan moving.

Let's ask ourselves some hard questions and get clear on where we are right now so we can make decisions about where to go next. Our purpose is to achieve a breakthrough that leads to more income, impact, and joy at work. If that isn't happening (or starting to happen), let's be honest and pivot accordingly. Here's how you can go about this.

Kill a Senseless Rule

I used to work with an executive colleague who loved challenging the team to "kill a senseless rule." You can probably imagine how popular and well-received his challenge was. Everyone loved it because the statement was unapologetic in its rejection of unnecessary rules that waste time and energy for no good reason. Who hasn't come across a senseless rule they wanted to kill? And when that happens, don't we all wish we could kill it then and there? The truth is, we are bombarded with needless, nonsensical rules everywhere we go.

"Senseless rules" can be policies, practices, cultural norms, processes, and other restrictions that hinder us from moving forward by causing unnecessary and counterproductive friction. Think of them as speed bumps on a highway. They no longer serve their purpose, waste time, and may cause some harm.

I have a theory. I think most of those rules didn't start out being senseless. At one time, they were necessary for a good reason—like a "don't touch, wet paint" sign that is forgotten and never removed even though the paint is clearly dry. I think a reasonable, or even a good, rule can turn into a senseless rule when it has outlived its usefulness.

I've experienced this and even participated in it. I've written rules that turned into senseless rules because they didn't work the way I intended. I can admit that I really *wanted* them to work, so held onto hope and held onto a senseless rule. I've also killed senseless rules that I had a hand in creating, either partially or wholly (like an annual performance review process)! It's hard to admit when something you've put time and energy into creating isn't working the way you planned, expected, or believed it would.

I'm sharing this concept with you now because I want you to kill anything in your visibility project that isn't working for you. Your growth and success are too important to mess around with. We need to target the right actions to help you move closer to your goals. If there is something in your project that needs to be killed, I want you to do it quickly and then keep going! Even if it's something I encouraged you to do in an earlier chapter.

I think of this as failing *forward*. I failed, but as long as I learned something new from the failure, then it wasn't a complete loss. Yes, I failed. No getting around that. But the silver lining is that I now know more than I did before. I'm smarter and more experienced as a result. If I have to fail (and we all do), I want to fail *forward*!

Take Stock

Let's revisit your visibility project's one-page description. Is the overarching plan you put together working as you intended? Do you need to kill anything? Are you getting closer to achieving the "what" you identified in Section 1? Let's dig in to find out.

<u>Activity #1: Is It Working?</u>

1) Is your "why" (from Chapter 3) for wanting to achieve your breakthrough still valid? Does it still inspire you and support the work you are doing to accomplish it?

2) If so, continue to question 3. If not, go back to your plan and make changes to realign your plan with your needs. Then, return to Chapter 12, Move into Action, and get to work implementing the changes and executing your plan.

3) How are your project results helping you close the gap between where you are today and your career aspirations?

4) What do you need to do more of, less of, or differently?

5) In your honest estimation, how close are you to achieving your next breakthrough?

Now that we've ensured the plan you've built is the right plan to meet your needs, we'll turn our attention to the activities that should be producing results. We're going to zero in on what is working and what isn't. Use the insights you gained by asking the above questions as you move into assessing your effort and results.

Effort and/or Results

Have you ever seen a hamster running on a wheel? When I was a kid, we had a hamster named Angel. She had a tuft of hair that stuck up on her back. We thought it looked like an angel's wing. I remember seeing Angel run in the wheel she had in her cage. She would run and run, and I would watch her, wondering where she thought she was going.

I've often felt like Angel. I can work and work and get nowhere. I spin my wheels but have nothing to show for it except the passage of time. The sad truth is that effort is not the same as results. I wish it weren't so! You can expend a great deal of effort toward something without having anything tangible to show for it. It's quite possible to waste time without realizing it because you believe you are going to have a great result, only to realize later that it didn't turn out the way you believed it would.

Effort without results isn't totally pointless, however. If you are putting in effort to achieve a certain result and it falls short of the mark, consider it a test. You tested out an idea, and it didn't work. But you learned from it and can apply what you have learned to your next attempt.

Remember my pitch to Jack back in Chapter 7? It was turned down, but I was able to use much of that work in the healthcare organization. You never know how a failure today could turn into a game-changer in the future. Remember Thomas Edison's quote about the lightbulb: "I have not failed. I've just found 10,000 ways that won't work." ("Famous Quotes," n.d.) When we borrow Edison's perspective, we learn a lot and will eventually succeed.

At this point in your breakthrough journey, you don't have the time or energy to waste with activities that aren't working for you, that you aren't learning from, or that aren't producing a strong return on your investment. So, let's assess and pivot where needed.

Activity #2: Assessing Your Activities

Gather your tracking sheets from the last chapter or the app, journal, or other device you've been using to monitor your progress. You will need them to do this assessment. If your activities are clearly providing benefits, I still encourage you to take a few minutes to assess. You may be able to double down on something that is working well so it produces more results even faster. Similarly, if you are on the fence, or you know your efforts have been fruitful, but you can't pinpoint why they are working, then this methodical exercise may be helpful.

Grab your preferred beverage and sit down to critically review your tracking sheets. Then, answer the questions below. You can do this exercise for each individual activity you've tracked, or you can batch your activities into categories or groups of action and assess your progress in that manner. I don't recommend writing your answers to these questions out. Just walk through them and pay attention to insights—then capture your insights in writing so you can return to them later. Try to work through this quickly. Don't get bogged down in unnecessary detail. Keep moving! Our purpose is to get an idea of which activities are working (and why) and which activities aren't working (and why) so you can make necessary adjustments. Feel free to add your own questions to this list.

1) Are you doing the activity you said you were going to do?
2) Did you accomplish what you intended with the activity?
3) Can you clearly state what you learned, gained, or benefited from the activity?
4) Did the activity and the benefit it generated move you closer to achieving your goal (even if the movement was small)? In what ways?
5) Have you received any feedback about your performance on the activity from others? If not, how could you request feedback, and from whom would you request it?
6) If you had to do the activity again, would you? Why or why not?
7) Was the time and energy you expended worth the benefit you gained from doing the activity (i.e., did you get a positive return on your investment?)

After considering the above questions and your progress to date, summarize what you have learned from your journey so far. What activities do you need to change for your plan to be more effective? Consider what you could keep doing, stop doing, or start doing.

I recommend performing this evaluation periodically. You need enough time to make reasonable progress toward your plan, or this exercise will be more frustrating and arduous than helpful. This is also a great exercise to do with a supportive friend over coffee or on a walk. It will enable you to update your friend and get you talking about your plan and progress. Odds are good that your friend may be able to give you real-time feedback and ask additional questions neither you nor I thought of!

The Move Cycle: Rinse and Repeat

Your visibility project plan will probably take you more time to execute than it will take to read this book, so when you get to this stage of the Mobilize step, you will hang out here for a while as you implement your project and see your gap closing more with each day you work on it. You may also want to periodically revisit Chapter 3 and your "what" and "why", and Section 3, Energize, to get refueled as you continue to make progress on your project.

It's easy to become discouraged (or even bored) during your project implementation. To guard against that, intentionally engage with your community to stay present and focused. I also invite you to engage with me via social media and the communities I curate. I can be found most often on LinkedIn and YouTube with the handle @AskJennLandis or through my website, jennlandis.com. I post regularly on these channels to support the community of people who are working with and along-side me to achieve breakthrough success.

Once you've completed your visibility project, it's time to close out this project, assess where you are in your journey, rest up, and then jump back into the fray with your next breakthrough goal and a new visibility project. I'll see you in the next chapter, where we will do all of that and close out my breakthrough journey.

Let's Review:

1) Evaluate your progress often and critically. You need to know what is working and what isn't so you can swiftly and appropriately take corrective action.

2) Give yourself permission to "kill a senseless rule" and fail *forward*. Don't waste time chasing something that clearly isn't working. Kill it and move on.

3) Lean into your implementation period and fight off boredom and discouragement. You will cycle through the MOVE stages until you have successfully completed your visibility project. You may also want to periodically revisit Chapter 3 and your "what" and "why" and Section 3 to refuel your motivation and recharge your positivity.

Think About It:

1) Think of a time when you put a lot of effort into something, and it didn't turn out how you expected or hoped. What did you learn? How did you use that learning to be more successful on your next attempt?

2) Have you ever killed a senseless rule? Is there a senseless rule you could kill right now that would move you forward?

3) What is your favorite FUEL concept to keep you positive and moving forward? How will that concept come in handy during your MOVE cycles?

Take Action:

1) Take stock of your visibility project. Is the overarching plan you put together actually achieving your goal? Take action to either confirm your plan or to pivot it where necessary.

2) Assess your activities. Are the individual activities you are engaging in moving the needle and creating the results you want and need? If so, great job! How could you make them even more efficient and productive? If not, how can you learn from them and adjust your approach?

3) Consider how you can build refueling stops into your implementation journey. Everyone gets tired and bored, so build in your rest stops to refuel!

Chapter 15

Enjoy the Moment

Congratulations! You have one final chapter to go before our time together ends. If you are wondering where the final installment of my breakthrough journey is, keep reading. I share the conclusion of my story at the end of this chapter.

I'm so sincerely grateful for our time together. I trust that you have experienced moments of learning, growth, and breakthroughs as you've closed the distance between where you started and your career aspirations. I hope you've achieved your next breakthrough or are well on your way toward doing so.

While achieving one breakthrough doesn't usually transport us to the end of our journey, it does bring us one step closer. You have more knowledge, skills, experience, wisdom, self-awareness, and success today than you did when you started the journey. All of those can be leveraged as you continue to grow and break through new challenges to claim greater income, impact, and joy at work.

Before you are tempted to collapse onto the nearest couch and binge-watch all the episodes and social media posts you missed during your intense growth project, let's talk about how you can wind down and transition in a healthy way. We want to acknowledge and celebrate your hard work in a way that honors what you've done by holding onto what you've learned and accomplished but that also prepares you for the start of your next climb. How you choose to end this project will have a direct impact on your next project. Let's pull from our collective experiences.

Have you been part of an organizational project that ended with a last-minute sprint to the finish line where victory was claimed because the deadline was met, but the end product was less than stellar? I have, and it reminds me of one of my favorite childhood movie series.

As a child, I loved a series of movies from Disney about Herbie the Lovebug. (Stevenson 1969) The first one aired in the late 1960s. Herbie was a Volkswagen Beetle with a mind of its own and a penchant for winning races against all odds. He, (I always thought of Herbie as a "he"), and his driver always landed themselves in crazy situations that led to extreme measures and hilarious misadventures. By the end of the movie, Herbie was always battered and bruised, with a bumper or headlamp hanging on by a string. But he was also victorious.

While I loved Herbie as a kid, I don't want to emulate his success as an adult. And yet, if we go back to the example from a moment ago, I feel like a lot of corporate projects end that way. We race to the finish line with a broken windshield and a door torn off to claim victory. I've ended personal projects this way, too. My first degree was a lot like this. And I had a meltdown after it!

"But, Jenn," you say. "They made it to the finish line! That's what counts!" Umm... But does it? When we finish projects like those I've just described, we often miss elements of the final deliverables, and those projects don't tend to last. Thus, our collection of campaign t-shirts, like we've discussed several times. Worse, we often hop back in the car, rev what little engine remains, and speed off to start the next race. When we don't repair the damage that's been done by our mad dash to the finish line, refuel our engines, and restock our supplies, we cannot restart the journey with confidence that we won't break down.

In this chapter, I want us to focus on finishing our project well, managing the transition between this project and your next one, and then finding your next breakthrough opportunity to keep your growth going!

Our Goals:

In this chapter, we will wind down purposely and intentionally. We're going to spend time:

1) Wrapping up our visibility project fully so we retain what we've gained and benefit from it in the future.

2) Allowing ourselves the chance to rest and replenish our reserves before we recommit to our goals and rejoin the race. We will handle the transition from one project to another in an intentional, healthy, and sustainable way.

3) We will ramp back up and find a new breakthrough opportunity to pursue.

In addition to the above, I will also conclude the story we started in Chapter 1. You may be surprised at how it all ends. Let's wrap this project up!

Wrap it Up!

Before we start planning our post-project celebration (and you better believe there will be one), we need to clean up our mess. Just like a fantastic holiday meal, you sit down to eat when everything is hot and everyone is present. The pots and pans you used to prepare the meal are probably still dirty and sitting in the sink. You come back to clean up the dishes after the meal is over and before you call it a night. If you are very studious, you may even make notes on your recipes of what worked extremely well, which dishes were Mark's favorites, and what didn't pan out as well as you hoped with that last-minute ingredient substitution. We're going to take the same approach now.

Activity #1: Brain Dump Your Lessons Learned

Grab a quiet corner and your note-taking gear. This time, I really want you to write your answers to the questions below. This is how you will memorialize the lessons you've worked so hard to accumulate during your visibility project. These are things we don't want to forget. If the answers to these questions don't immediately come to mind, sit with them for a while. It will come to you. You worked hard for this moment, so enjoy the reflection process and the learning you are pulling from it.

1) As you reflect on the journey you are completing, what is your single most important takeaway or lesson?
2) Think through the Strategize, Energize, and Mobilize steps.
   - What did you learn from each step? (Whether the cause of the learning was the book content, your own reflection, something from your community, or the result of an aspect of your project.)
   - What did you do in each step that worked particularly well and that you would want to do again with your next project?
   - What didn't work?
3) What insights did you learn about yourself? If asked in an interview to describe your growth during this project and what you learned, how would you summarize it?

4) What activities do you need to close down or complete so you gain closure and move on?

   ◦ What administrative tasks do you need to wrap up? (File clean up, declutter your desk, organize paperwork, cancel recurring appointments associated with the project, etc.)

5) Who do you need to thank for their help and support? Make a list.

Be Grateful

As you close out your visibility project, think about how you want to thank those you listed above (which should include everyone who supported you). It's amazing to me how easy it can be for people to share their displeasure or disappointment, but sharing gratitude and appreciation is an afterthought.

A few months ago, I received a letter from a former employee. I had left the organization eight months earlier, and while we touched base a few times, I was totally surprised to receive a good old-fashioned card in the mail from her. The card was one of gratitude. She wrote in the card what she had learned from me during our working relationship and how grateful she was for our time together and my sponsorship of her. It blew me away. And it shamed me that I hadn't written more of those cards myself.

One of the mentors I've cited in this book ("Mack") passed away a few years ago. I deeply regret that I didn't reach out before he passed to share how much he meant to me. Including him in this book has been a personal way for me to memorialize him and to express my gratitude for his friendship and support, even though he isn't here to receive it. And that's my point. Gratitude isn't just for the receiver. It changes *you* when you express gratitude. Find a way that is authentic for you, and share your thoughts of gratitude with those who helped you get to this moment.

The 3 R's: Rest and Replenish, then Recommit

Once you've wrapped up the final housekeeping associated with your visibility project, it's time to smell the roses, hit the beach, enjoy a spa day or a round of golf, or whatever you do to recharge and rest. Only you know what that should be, but I encourage you to treat your rest as a form of celebration that is equal to your achievement.

To ensure we define rest and replenish the same way, here's what I mean.

- Rest gives us a chance to recover from the pace and demands we've put on ourselves while we worked to achieve our goals. The goal of rest is to stop the activities that drain us so we can begin the recovery process. Even if your work was fulfilling, it was probably still draining in some way. You need rest.

- Replenishing is the next step and involves activities that fill us up to our normal or natural levels of energy. Rest alone can provide some replenishment, but I believe there are times when just stopping something that drains us isn't enough to fill up our tanks. Sometimes, we need to take action to refuel. An example is an active gratitude practice, as discussed in Chapter 8. It takes some effort on our part to collect, process, and react to the things we are grateful for. Doing so replenishes our positivity reserves and balances our perspective.

Both are necessary to return us to our best selves. And both are needed constantly. I'm focusing on it here because, like Herbie, I think we often come screeching to a halt at the finish line with a few parts of ourselves missing. To avoid taking the Herbie approach of immediately revving up and rejoining the race, we need to intentionally rest and replenish.

According to Dr. Saundra Dalton-Smith, MD, there are seven types of rest. In her book *Sacred Rest*, she explains that rest is different from sleep and requires awareness and intention. (Dalton-Smith 2019) Achieving rest in each category centers on pulling back, evaluating our needs, and intentionally taking action to reduce the stress and strain we place on ourselves during periods of intense work. Let's briefly review the seven types of rest Dr. Dalton-Smith uncovered.

- Physical Rest: Tied to your physical body. Rest involves releasing tension from over (or under) used muscles and includes passive rest, like sleeping, and active rest, like stretching.
- Mental Rest: Tied to your mental capacity. Rest involves reducing cognitive demands by quieting your mind through breaks and mindfulness activities.
- Sensory Rest: Tied to your senses. Rest involves reducing stimulation by turning off devices and seeking calming spaces (quiet, low light, no strong smells or calming fragrances, soft surfaces, etc.)
- Creative Rest: Tied to an increase in positive mental stimulation. Rest involves seeking beauty and inspiration that rejuvenate the mind.
- Emotional Rest: Tied to emotional health. Rest involves seeking positive and balanced emotional states by processing emotions in a healthy way and exiting situations where negative emotions are strong.
- Spiritual Rest: Tied to spiritual beliefs. Rest involves seeking meaning and purpose through reflection and spiritual practices.

- Social Rest: Tied to stimulation from being in social situations. Rest involves solitude, limiting social interactions or engagements, and seeking support from trusted sources.

After reading the above, do you have a good understanding of the types of rest you need? After years of post-project detoxing, I know I need more spiritual, emotional, social, and mental rest than the others.

To help you think through how you can leverage the different types of rest, here are a few examples of how this plays out for me. Disclaimer—This is an area I struggle with and have to work on constantly. So, if you also struggle with this, we can work on it together!

- Physical Rest: Taking walks with James and Gracie (our Brittney spaniel), stretching and muscle tension release exercises, massage sessions, baths, and long hot showers, focusing on quality sleep and on what I eat to fuel my body.
- Mental Rest: Spending time alone by the fire or on the patio, taking short naps to clear my head and turn off my thoughts, taking breaks when I sense mental fatigue.
- Sensory Rest: Turning on my do not disturb, taking off my smartwatch, sitting in my closet (yep, that's not a typo - I have a stool in the corner of my closet where I go when I need a break from the world).
- Creative Rest: Reading books that make me think about things unrelated to my work, taking gratitude photos of nature, and engaging in creative hobbies in which I can create and play.
- Emotional Rest: Coffee dates with James, my sisters, or trusted friends, creating and opening pops of joy, listening to Christmas music, focusing on acts of gratitude.

- <u>Spiritual Rest</u>: Conversations with close friends who share my spiritual beliefs, reading my Bible, listening to devotions, and time spent in prayer.
- <u>Social Rest</u>: Quiet nights at home with James, management of my social calendar and obligations, scheduling purposeful quiet time after intense social engagements.

Replenishment Activities: I'm better at replenishing than resting. While I believe there is overlap between the two concepts, replenishing comes more naturally to me than resting, yet I understand why we need both. Here are some of my replenishment activities:

- I love to replenish my reserves by celebrating wins (big and small) with James. We have celebrated breakthroughs and career milestones with everything from a shared pizza on a Friday night to a Caribbean cruise, and just about everything you can imagine in between. We've celebrated quietly and loudly, with just us, and with my entire twenty-five-person family.
- I also enjoy replenishing with girlfriend trips, weekend adventures, thrift and antique store shopping with my mom, putting together an afternoon tea, and anything crafty.
- Closer to home, I enjoy replenishing with solo coffee shop trips and a good book, going to a movie by myself, long conference calls with my sisters to catch up, and spa days with a friend.

Now it's your turn. Use the activity below as a thought partner to plan out your rest and replenishment regimen.

Activity #2: Plan Your Rest & Replenish Activities

Using the table below, map out your rest. Which kinds of rest do you engage in regularly? Are there any kinds of rest that you don't engage in but would benefit from? What can you do to achieve the kind of rest you need?

Add any replenishing activities that you enjoy and that you know fill you up. What are your go-to refueling activities? What new ideas do you have for ways to replenish yourself?

Emotional Rest	
Physical Rest	
Spiritual Rest	
Mental Rest	
Social Rest	

Now that we are rested, replenished, and recharged, we can recommit and prepare to kick-start our next breakthrough journey.

Recommit: Find a New Breakthrough Opportunity

"Really, Jenn?!?" I can hear you groaning. "We *just* achieved our breakthrough and completed our visibility project. You're already telling us to start over?" Yes. I am doing exactly that. I'm thrilled that you completed your first visibility project. I couldn't be happier for you, and I hope you reach out and share your moment with me so I can celebrate you. But I'm a bit greedy on your behalf. I want more for you than a single breakthrough. I want you to have a lifetime of them. So, yes. Once you have rested and replenished, it's time to recommit.

Growth is a continual and lifelong process. If you repeatedly identify opportunity gaps with breakthrough potential, turn them into visibility projects, and leverage them to achieve your next breakthrough, you will continually grow and progress. Soon, you will be able to look back and see your life through a string of breakthrough experiences that shape you and lead you toward your aspirations.

My husband and I like to play a game about once a year. We spend an evening looking back at our lives and asking each other, "Did you ever imagine that we would…?" And "Did you think when [that] happened that it would lead to [this]?" We marvel at the connections we see woven between our stories and experiences. Soon, a string of adventures forms that we never saw coming but are so obvious when you look back.

Breakthrough moments have become a lifelong pursuit for us, and we won't ever give them up. Growth is a necessary ingredient for a healthy and full life, even though growth is hard and painful and causes grief and heartache—because it also brings joy, fellowship, community, and new opportunities.

Before we end our time together, I want to wrap up the story I've been sharing in each chapter. I think the end of this story may surprise you.

In Real Life: *The Last Installment*

"Ring, ring." I looked at my desk phone at work and tried to place the number displayed on my caller ID. I recognized the number but couldn't place it. I let the call go to voicemail as I continued working on my update report for Mack on the latest activity in our culture change project. A while later, I saw my voicemail light blinking and checked my messages.

"Hi, Jennifer. This is Jack from your previous company."

WHAT?!? Jack? Jack! The Jack I had pitched my idea to two years prior. The pitch that had led me to research my master's degree, and that led me to find the job opening for the dream job I was currently working in. That Jack!

I tuned back into his message, "I'm sure you've seen the acquisition we just closed in the news. I'd like to talk to you about that proposal you gave me before you left the company." He gave me his contact information and asked me to call him back.

I was stunned! I called him back and stumbled through the conversation. Long story short, he wanted me to consider returning to the company to implement the plan I had pitched to him and the CEO two years prior. I couldn't believe they still remembered my pitch and wanted to visit with me about it.

I went home that night and had a lengthy conversation with James. We decided to see where the conversation would lead, so I spent the next few weeks in conversations with Jack and several other executives at the company. They invited me to interview with them, and they offered me the job on the spot. I got the opportunity to go back to my former organization and start up the department I had dreamed of starting!

This was the third time this pitch had come into play in my career.

1) It created visibility and sponsorship when I made the original pitch.
2) It led me to find the director role at the health system and contributed to my successes there.
3) Now, it came full circle with an opportunity to create the department I had dreamed of two and half years earlier.

The kicker was that I really couldn't have done the job I pitched when I put the first proposal in front of Jack. I wasn't ready. I didn't know that at the time, but after the two years of boot camp growth with my team at the health system and the turnaround and culture work we did there, I can say with absolute certainty that I would have failed if I had tried it two years earlier. By the time the company was ready to implement my proposal, I had grown substantially and closed quite a few skill and experience gaps. I was now both capable and qualified to actually implement it.

It was a hard decision to leave my amazing team. We had been through so much together. In the end, I decided that I needed to make the move. I had accomplished what I set out to do with the health system team. They each went on to bigger and better roles.

As for me, I started over again with new skill and experience gaps to close, new opportunities to pursue, and new treks through the Strategize, Energize, and Mobilize system. After all, the company I was rejoining was growing, and I had a new department to initiate—which put me on the path to becoming the SVP and Chief HR Officer. Without my growth experiences and the triumphs and heartaches that came with them, I would never have been able to make that leap.

I also obtained greater income, impact, and joy. By the time I started the new role with Jack, I had increased my income by 2.5x, my impact had grown by 10x, and I learned that my joy could expand or shrink based on how I approached my work instead of being dependent on the work or the position. Learning that I could do hard things and not only achieve my own breakthroughs but support others in achieving theirs was perhaps the best reward and my biggest win.

So please join me in an adventure that never stops by growing, learning, engaging with others, and achieving your next breakthrough using the Breakthrough Formula. Grab a friend, colleague, or family member and get them to join you with their own breakthrough journey. I've found that getting to the finish line is way more fun when you have a crowd of community members and friends to celebrate with. I can't wait to see and hear all of your amazing breakthrough stories via social media. Together, we can create a community of support, growth, and lifelong learning!

Let's Review:

1) Wrap up your current visibility project by cleaning up your loose ends and capturing your lessons learned.

2) Consider rest and replenishment as part of your close-out activities. You need both to be healthy and able to recommit to your next breakthrough goal.

3) Growth is a lifetime journey, so keep going. Connect with me on social media so I can cheer you on.

Think About It:

1) Think about the five forms of rest. Which form do you need most often? Why do you think that is?

2) What is your favorite way to replenish and refill your energy? How can you make that happen in the next two weeks?

3) What is the next gap you are going to pursue? What will you take from your lessons this time around and apply to your next project?

Take Action:

1) Complete the Wrap-Up reflection activity. Close out any remaining tasks that are lingering.

2) Complete the Rest activity. Use your reflections to give yourself the rest you need. Then, replenish your energy stores.

3) Recommit and pick your next gap!

Keep going! You can break up, break in, and breakthrough!

You've got this!

Jenn

Give the Gift of Breakthroughs by Leaving a Review!

Thank You For Reading My Book!
I genuinely appreciate your feedback,
and I love hearing what you have to say.
Your comments help me improve and help spread the word that
career breakthroughs are possible!

I need your input to make the next version of this
book (and my future books) better.

Please take two minutes now to leave a helpful review on
Amazon letting me know what you thought of the book.

Thanks so much!
- Jenn

Bring The Breakthrough Formula to Your Organization

If you are looking for your next keynote speaker, executive coach, or want to bring the Breakthrough Formula to your organization as a workshop, let's connect! I'd love to support you and your team as you break up, break in, and break through!

JennLandis.com/speaking

Cheering you on!
Jenn

See Jenn's speaker's reel and contact her by visiting www.jennlandis.com

Appendix A
Example Documents

Section 2: Strategize Examples

Shawn's Story	<u>Talented in Energize and Mobilize but struggles with Strategize</u> Shawn is a bright, enthusiastic, extremely likable person who draws people with an innate charisma few possess. He is the first person to celebrate a team member's birthday. He arranges team bowling events, and he knows the names of everyone's family members and pets. He regularly volunteers for the company picnic, and the planning team breathes a sigh of relief when he's working on the project. He will make it fun and execute it incredibly well. Shawn's issue is that he is a great executor of other people's plans. He wants to lead a team, and the team loves him, but when given the chance to lead projects that require planning and forecasting, he stumbles and misses the mark. He is overlooked for bigger management roles because of his lack of long-range thinking and planning. He is viewed as a great team member and is well-regarded, but he isn't trusted with additional management responsibility. Shawn is currently an HR Director, working in the corporate services division of his company. He aspires to become a VP of HR.
Shawn's Selected Opportunity to Pursue:	The performance management process: After reviewing his work, Shawn believes there may be an opportunity for him to explore tackling the performance management process. It's a known pain point. Tom (the process owner) would likely be open to Shawn's interest in revisiting it, and it would require Shawn to develop new skills in areas he needs to develop while also leveraging his unique characteristics to give him an edge. Partnered with his strong Energize and Mobilize talents, this would be a good opportunity for him to grow *and* showcase skills that aren't well known.

Ch. 5,
Activity 1

Shawn's Mind Map

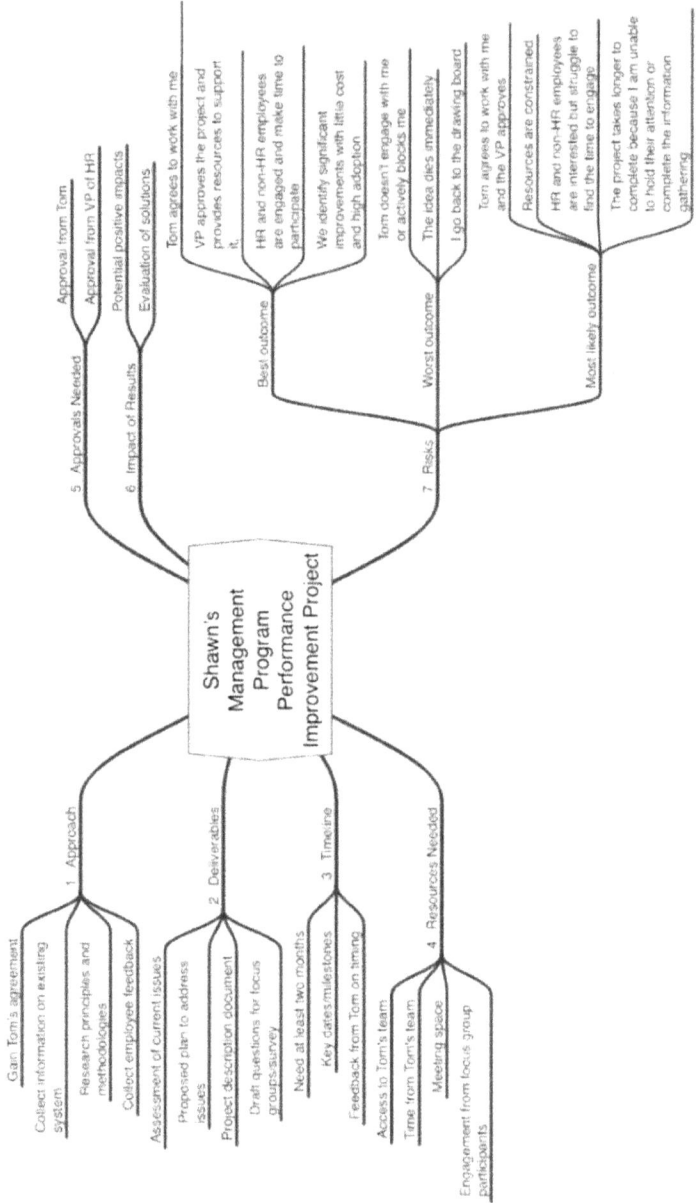

Shawn's Management Program Performance Improvement Project

1 Approach
- Gain Tom's agreement
- Collect information on existing system
- Research principles and methodologies
- Collect employee feedback
- Assessment of current issues

2 Deliverables
- Proposed plan to address issues
- Project description document
- Draft questions for focus groups/survey

3 Timeline
- Need at least two months
- Key dates/milestones
- Feedback from Tom on timing

4 Resources Needed
- Access to Tom's team
- Time from Tom's team
- Meeting space
- Engagement from focus group participants

5 Approvals Needed
- Approval from Tom
- Approval from VP of HR

6 Impact of Results
- Potential positive impacts
- Evaluation of solutions

7 Risks
- Best outcome
  - Tom agrees to work with me
  - VP approves the project and provides resources to support it.
  - HR and non-HR employees are engaged and make time to participate
  - We identify significant improvements with little cost and high adoption
- Worst outcome
  - Tom doesn't engage with me or actively blocks me
  - The idea dies immediately.
  - I go back to the drawing board
- Most likely outcome
  - Tom agrees to work with me and the VP approves
  - Resources are constrained
  - HR and non-HR employees are interested but struggle to find the time to engage
  - The project takes longer to complete because I am unable to hold their attention or complete the information gathering

Shawn's Project Description
Ch. 5, Activity 3

Project Name	Performance Management Program Improvement - Phase I
Project Purpose	Performance reviews impact every team member in our organization. While intended to be a valuable tool for employee development and organizational growth, the current annual performance review process has become a source of significant frustration for managers and team members alike. This frustration stems from several key issues, including time inefficiency, cumbersome systems, misalignment between performance measures and actual performance, and a lack of continuous feedback throughout the year. This project will attempt to better understand these issues and identify possible resolutions. **Project Goal:** Develop and present a comprehensive assessment of the current performance management system and provide a proposed improvement plan within 3 months by conducting research including: • Information about the existing performance management system and methodology • Performance management principles, methodologies, and systems • Feedback from at least 30% of HR staff and 10% of non-HR employees to understand the primary issues people are having with the current system
Project Scope	This project encompasses the evaluation of the existing performance management system, gathering feedback from HR and non-HR employees, and developing a proposed plan to address identified issues. It excludes the implementation of proposed solutions.
Deliverables	• Assessment report of issues identified with the current performance management system • Proposed plan to address the identified issues
Timeline / Target Dates	• Project duration: 2-3 months • Specific milestones to be determined in consultation with Tom, considering the annual performance management cycle

Shawn's Project Description Cont'd
Ch. 5, Activity 3

Required Resources	• Access to Tom and his team for report pulling and knowledge sharing • Meeting space (physical or virtual)for focus groups or interviews • Survey tool (if applicable) • Calendar assistance for scheduling meetings and focus groups • Time allocation from HR and non-HR employees for participation in feedback sessions

Sponsors & Key Stakeholders	• Shawn (Project Manager / Lead)
	• Tom (Project Sponsor)
	• VP of HR (Project Sponsor)
	• Key Stakeholders:
	    ○ HR team members
	    ○ Non-HR employees (participants in feedback sessions)

Shawn's WBS Task Outline
Ch. 6, Activity 2

Shawn's Work Breakdown Structure (WBS)	Performance Management Program Improvement - Phase I project

Performance Management Program Improvement - Phase I project

1.Project Initiation
  1.1. Define project charter
  1.2. Identify key stakeholders
  1.3. Establish project team
  1.4. Develop project schedule
  1.5. Secure necessary resources

2. Current System Assessment
  2.1. Gather existing documentation
  2.2. Review current performance management system
  2.3. Analyze current methodology
  2.4. Identify system limitations and pain points
  2.5. Document findings

3. Research Performance Management Best Practices
  3.1. Review industry standards
  3.2. Analyze modern performance management principles
  3.3. Explore alternative methodologies
  3.4. Investigate available performance management systems
  3.5. Compile research findings

4. Employee Feedback Collection
  4.1. Design feedback collection strategy
    4.1.1. Develop survey questions
    4.1.2. Plan focus group sessions
    4.1.3. Create interview guidelines
  4.2. Conduct HR staff feedback sessions
    4.2.1. Schedule sessions with at least 30% of HR staff
    4.2.2. Facilitate feedback sessions
    4.2.3. Document HR staff input

Shawn's WBS Task Outline Cont'd
Ch. 6, Activity 2

Shawn's Work Breakdown Structure (WBS)

4.3. Conduct non-HR employee feedback sessions
    4.3.1. Schedule sessions with at least 10% of non-HR employees
    4.3.2. Facilitate feedback sessions
    4.3.3. Document non-HR employee input
4.4. Analyze feedback data
4.5. Summarize key findings

5. Issue Identification and Analysis
5.1. Consolidate findings from system assessment and feedback
5.2. Categorize identified issues
5.3. Prioritize issues based on impact and frequency
5.4. Analyze root causes of major issues
5.5. Document comprehensive list of issues

6. Improvement Plan Development
6.1. Brainstorm potential solutions for each major issue
6.2. Evaluate feasibility of proposed solutions
6.3. Prioritize improvement initiatives
6.4. Develop high-level implementation roadmap
6.5. Estimate resource requirements and timelines
6.6. Draft improvement plan document

Shawn's WBS Task Outline Cont'd
Ch. 6, Activity 2

Shawn's Work Breakdown Structure (WBS)

7. Assessment Report Creation
7.1. Compile findings from all project phases
7.2. Develop report structure and outline
7.3. Write detailed assessment of current system
7.4. Summarize feedback results
7.5. Present identified issues and their impacts
7.6. Include proposed improvement plan
7.7. Review and refine report

8. Presentation Preparation
8.1. Design presentation slides
8.2. Develop key talking points
8.3. Prepare supporting materials
8.4. Conduct internal review and rehearsal

9. Project Closure
9.1. Present findings and improvement plan to sponsors
9.2. Gather feedback from key stakeholders
9.3. Finalize and submit all project deliverables
9.4. Conduct project retrospective
9.5. Archive project documentation

Emily's Word & Affirmation
Ch. 8, Activity 1

Emily's Situation	<u>Emily is talented in Mobilize and Strategize but struggles with Energize</u> Emily is a hard-charging, get-it-done professional who is technically brilliant and rarely (if ever)wrong. She knows her subject matter deeply. If Emily gives an answer, it is right. She is trusted to do the most complicated work and delivers it on time and with the highest quality. She is extremely valued for the consistency of her results and her unquestionable accuracy. Emily's issue is that she can be rude, impatient, and unintentionally unkind to others who do what she considers to be inferior work. People have quit after being assigned a project under her leadership. She has stated quite clearly that she expects to be promoted and has CEO aspirations. Because of her inability to effectively engage others, she is overlooked for executive positions, and her bid for CEO isn't treated seriously. She doesn't get the feedback she needs about her people skills because even her managers are unwilling to deal with the backlash they fear the feedback would produce. Emily is currently a senior operations manager and has a background in finance. Her ultimate goal is to become a CEO.
Emily's Word & Affirmation	Patience: Today, I will lead with patience and understanding, allowing each team member the space to grow and contribute, fostering a culture of respect and collaboration. I will also exercise **patience** with myself by recognizing that it takes time and practice to learn new skills.

Shawn's Word & Affirmation
Ch. 8, Activity 1

Shawn's Situation	Shawn is talented in Energize and Mobilize but struggles with Strategize Shawn is a bright, enthusiastic, extremely likable person who draws people with an innate charisma few possess. He is the first person to celebrate a team member's birthday. He arranges team bowling events, and he knows the names of everyone's family members and pets. He regularly volunteers for the company picnic, and the planning team breathes a sigh of relief when he's working on the project. He will make it fun and execute it incredibly well. Shawn's issue is that he is a great executor of other people's plans. He wants to lead a team, and the team loves him, but when given the chance to lead projects that require planning and forecasting, he stumbles and misses the mark. He is overlooked for bigger management roles because of his lack of long-range thinking and planning. He is viewed as a great team member and is well-regarded, but he isn't trusted with additional management responsibility. Shawn is currently an HR Director, working in the corporate services division of his company. He aspires to become a VP of HR.
Shawn's Word & Affirmation	Envision: I **envision** the future with clarity and purpose, transforming my execution skills into strategic insights that inspire and guide my team towards long-term success. I look around corners to anticipate needs, translating my strategic viewpoint into clear action plans and direction for myself and my team.

Magda's Word & Affirmation
Ch. 8, Activity 1

Magda's Situation	<u>Magda is talented in Energize and Strategize but struggles with Mobilize</u> Magda is an extremely talented and ambitious director with a strong desire for an executive role. She is universally liked, easy to talk with, and strategic. Her ideas are great. She is tuned into what is happening in the company and current events. People flock to her when they have problems and she always makes time to visit with them. Magda's issue is that while she always delivers for her external clients, she cuts corners, procrastinates, and frustrates her colleagues with unmet promises. Because she is so well-liked, no one wants to tell her that she drives them crazy by promising and either not delivering or delivering sub-par work because she waited until the last minute to do the work. Because of this, she is overlooked for executive opportunities and key projects that would provide visibility despite her strengths and performance with external clients. She has so many great qualities but can't be counted on to deliver quality work consistently nor on time. Magda is currently a Sales Director. Her ultimate goal is to become a Regional VP of Sales.
Magda's Word & Affirmation	Cultivate: I <u>cultivate</u> trust and reliability in all my relationships, delivering excellence to both external clients and internal colleagues with equal dedication and timeliness. Through consistent results and unwavering follow-through on my commitments, I build long-term relationships founded on dependability and mutual respect.

Magda's Project Examples

Magda's Story	**Talented in Energize and Strategize but struggles with Mobilize** Magda is an extremely talented and ambitious director with a strong desire for an executive role. She is universally liked, easy to talk with, and strategic. Her ideas are great. She is tuned into what is happening in the company and current events. People flock to her when they have problems and she always makes time to visit with them. Magda's issue is that while she always delivers for her external clients, she cuts corners, procrastinates, and frustrates her colleagues with unmet promises. Because she is so well-liked, no one wants to tell her that she drives them crazy by promising and either not delivering or delivering sub-par work because she waited until the last minute to do the work. Because of this, she is overlooked for executive opportunities and key projects that would provide visibility despite her strengths and performance with external clients. She has so many great qualities but can't be counted on to deliver quality work consistently nor on time. Magda is currently a Sales Director. Her ultimate goal is to become a Regional VP of Sales.
Magda's Word & Affirmation	To better understand where Magda is in her breakthrough journey, she has chosen her word and written her affirmation (with help from AI) from Chapter 8. Her word is "cultivate." Her affirmation is: I *cultivate* trust and reliability in all my relationships, delivering excellence to both external clients and internal colleagues with equal dedication and timeliness. Through consistent results and unwavering follow-through on my commitments, I build long-term relationships founded on dependability and mutual respect. (Perplexity.ai, 11/12/2024)
Magda's Visibility Project	Magda's visibility project is planning and organizing an off-site two-day internal sales conference for her region. It involves agenda development, speaker lineup, training activities, and social events. Her sponsor is her Regional VP of Sales, and she has been assigned a small team of colleagues to work with her on the event.

Magda's Project Description

Project Name	Regional Sales Conference Event
Project Purpose	To plan and organize a successful 2-day offsite internal sales conference for the regional team, featuring engaging agenda development, speaker lineup, training activities, and social events. Project Goal: To successfully plan and execute a high-quality, 2-day off-site sales conference for 75 regional team members in 3 months, by developing a compelling conference theme, securing engaging speakers, managing all event logistics, and staying within the approved budget, while leading the project team effectively and meeting all key milestones, including: • Venue selection within 4 weeks • Agenda finalization within 3 weeks • Speaker selection and confirmation within 6 weeks
Project Scope	The project encompasses the planning and execution of a 2-day off-site sales conference for 75 attendees, including venue selection, agenda development, speaker coordination, and social event planning. It excludes post-event evaluation and follow-up activities.
Deliverables	• Secured off-site venue with accommodations and meeting spaces • Comprehensive conference agenda • Confirmed speaker lineup • Organized training activities • Planned social events • Audio/Visual equipment and support, including Wi-Fi connection • Meals and snacks for all attendees
Timeline / Target Dates	• Project completion: 3 months (12 weeks) from start date • Project team assembly: 1 week from start date • Budget identification: 3 weeks from start date • Finalized agenda: 3 weeks from start date • Location and venue identification: 4 weeks • Speaker confirmation: 6 weeks from start date

Magda's Project Description Cont'd

Required Resources	• Budget allocation • Project team members from communications, sales, administrative support, and IT departments • Time allocation for project work during work hours • Audio/Visual equipment	• Catering services • Transportation arrangements (if necessary) • Conference management software or internal IT tools for agenda management and document sharing
Sponsors & Key Stakeholders	• Magda (Project Manager / Lead) • Regional VP of Sales (Project Sponsor) • Communications team representative • Sales team representative	• Administrative support representative • IT department representative • Regional Sales Team (75 attendees)

Magda's Mind Map

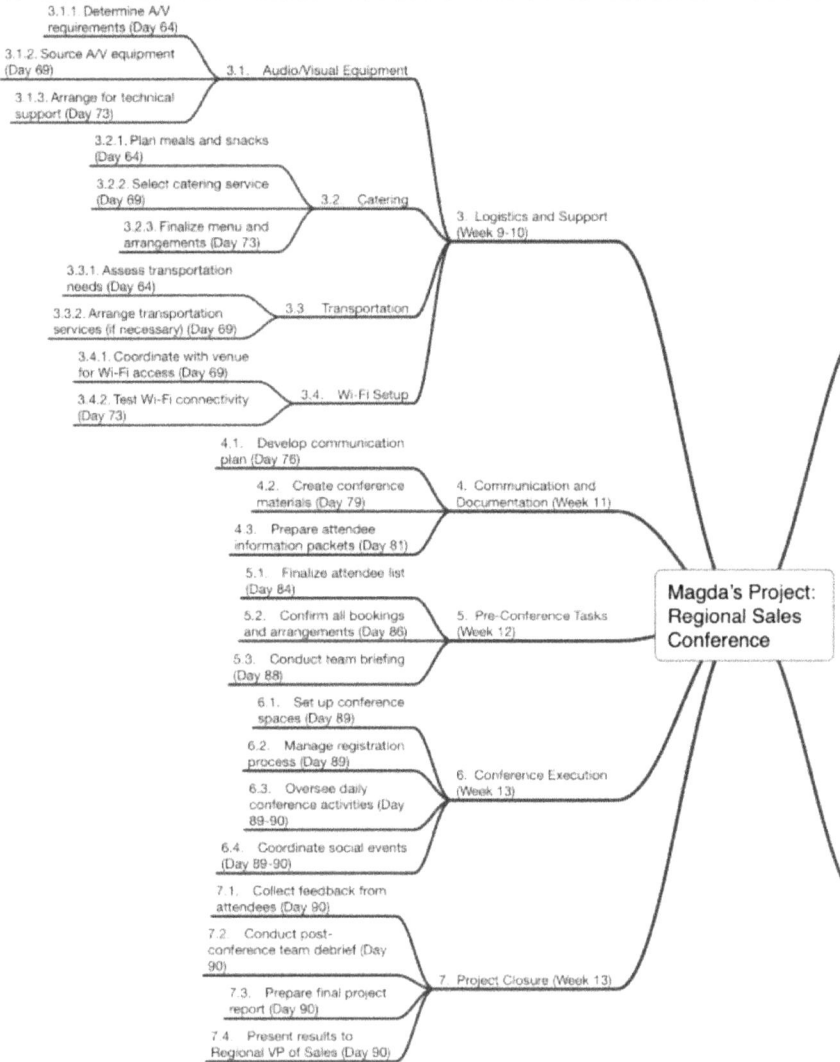

3.1.1. Determine A/V requirements (Day 64)

3.1.2. Source A/V equipment (Day 69)

3.1.3. Arrange for technical support (Day 73)

3.1. Audio/Visual Equipment

3.2.1. Plan meals and snacks (Day 64)

3.2.2. Select catering service (Day 69)

3.2.3. Finalize menu and arrangements (Day 73)

3.2. Catering

3.3.1. Assess transportation needs (Day 64)

3.3.2. Arrange transportation services (if necessary) (Day 69)

3.3. Transportation

3.4.1. Coordinate with venue for Wi-Fi access (Day 69)

3.4.2. Test Wi-Fi connectivity (Day 73)

3.4. Wi-Fi Setup

3. Logistics and Support (Week 9-10)

4.1. Develop communication plan (Day 76)

4.2. Create conference materials (Day 79)

4.3. Prepare attendee information packets (Day 81)

4. Communication and Documentation (Week 11)

5.1. Finalize attendee list (Day 84)

5.2. Confirm all bookings and arrangements (Day 86)

5.3. Conduct team briefing (Day 88)

5. Pre-Conference Tasks (Week 12)

6.1. Set up conference spaces (Day 89)

6.2. Manage registration process (Day 89)

6.3. Oversee daily conference activities (Day 89-90)

6.4. Coordinate social events (Day 89-90)

6. Conference Execution (Week 13)

7.1. Collect feedback from attendees (Day 90)

7.2. Conduct post-conference team debrief (Day 90)

7.3. Prepare final project report (Day 90)

7.4. Present results to Regional VP of Sales (Day 90)

7. Project Closure (Week 13)

Magda's Project: Regional Sales Conference

Magda's Mind Map Cont'd

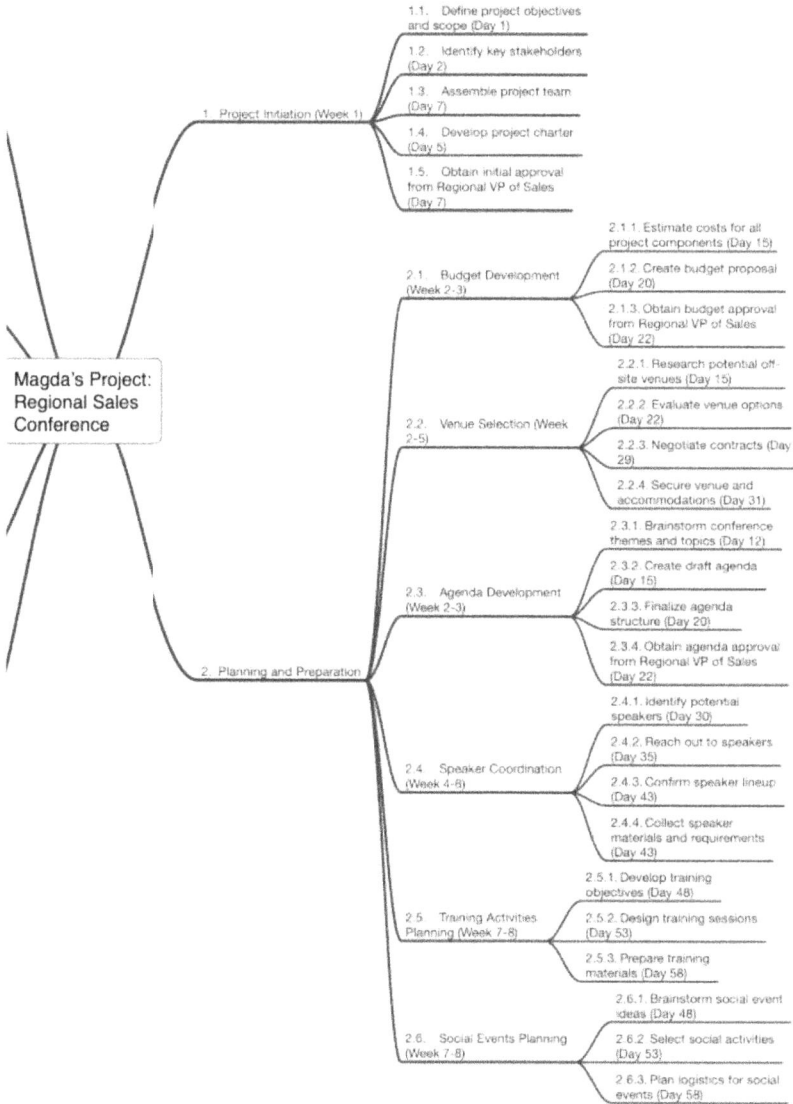

Magda's Project: Regional Sales Conference

1. Project Initiation (Week 1)

- 1.1. Define project objectives and scope (Day 1)
- 1.2. Identify key stakeholders (Day 2)
- 1.3. Assemble project team (Day 7)
- 1.4. Develop project charter (Day 5)
- 1.5. Obtain initial approval from Regional VP of Sales (Day 7)

2. Planning and Preparation

2.1. Budget Development (Week 2-3)
- 2.1.1. Estimate costs for all project components (Day 15)
- 2.1.2. Create budget proposal (Day 20)
- 2.1.3. Obtain budget approval from Regional VP of Sales (Day 22)

2.2. Venue Selection (Week 2-5)
- 2.2.1. Research potential off-site venues (Day 15)
- 2.2.2. Evaluate venue options (Day 22)
- 2.2.3. Negotiate contracts (Day 29)
- 2.2.4. Secure venue and accommodations (Day 31)

2.3. Agenda Development (Week 2-3)
- 2.3.1. Brainstorm conference themes and topics (Day 12)
- 2.3.2. Create draft agenda (Day 15)
- 2.3.3. Finalize agenda structure (Day 20)
- 2.3.4. Obtain agenda approval from Regional VP of Sales (Day 22)

2.4. Speaker Coordination (Week 4-6)
- 2.4.1. Identify potential speakers (Day 30)
- 2.4.2. Reach out to speakers (Day 35)
- 2.4.3. Confirm speaker lineup (Day 43)
- 2.4.4. Collect speaker materials and requirements (Day 43)

2.5. Training Activities Planning (Week 7-8)
- 2.5.1. Develop training objectives (Day 48)
- 2.5.2. Design training sessions (Day 53)
- 2.5.3. Prepare training materials (Day 58)

2.6. Social Events Planning (Week 7-8)
- 2.6.1. Brainstorm social event ideas (Day 48)
- 2.6.2. Select social activities (Day 53)
- 2.6.3. Plan logistics for social events (Day 58)

Magda's Task Outline & Stoplight Report

Ch. 12, Activity 1

Magda's Project: Regional Sales Conference Event

Due Date: 3 Months from assignment

Delegation Legend: 1=Project Manager (Magda), 2= Project Sponsor, 3=Communications Team Rep, 4=Sales Team Rep, 5=Administrative Support rRp, 6=IT Department Rep

Status	Category	Task	Sub-Task	Est. Due Date	Progress	Delegate
◐	**1. Project Initiation**			**Week 1**		**1**
		1.1. Define project objectives and scope		Day 1	100	1, 2
		1.2. Identify key stakeholders		Day 2	20	1
		1.3. Assemble project team		Day 7		1, 2
		1.4. Obtain initial approval from Regional VP of Sales		Day 7		1, 2
	2. Planning and Preparation			**Week 1**		**1**
		2.1. Budget Development		Week 2-3		1
			2.1.1. Estimate costs for all project components	Day 15		1, 4, 5
			2.1.2. Create budget proposal	Day 20		1, 5
			2.1.3. Obtain budget approval from Regional VP of Sales	Day 22		1, 2
		2.2. Venue Selection		Week 2-5		1
			2.2.1. Research potential off-site venues	Day 15		1, 5
			2.2.2. Evaluate venue options	Day 22		1, 4, 5
			2.2.3. Negotiate contracts	Day 29		1, 5
			2.2.4. Secure venue and accommodations	Day 31		1, 5
		2.3. Agenda Development		Week 2-3		1
			2.3.1. Brainstorm conference themes and topics	Day 12		1, 3, 4
			2.3.2. Create draft agenda	Day 15		1, 3, 4
			2.3.3. Finalize agenda structure	Day 20		1, 3, 4
			2.3.4. Obtain agenda approval from Regional VP of Sales	Day 22		1, 2
		2.4. Speaker Coordination		Week 4-6		1
			2.4.1. Identify potential speakers	Day 30		1, 3, 4
			2.4.2. Reach out to speakers	Day 35		1, 3
			2.4.3. Confirm speaker lineup	Day 43		1, 3
			2.4.4. Collect speaker materials and requirements	Day 43		1, 3, 5
		2.5. Training Activities Planning		Week 7-8		1

Appendix B
Bibliography

Alexandra Kredlow, M., Robert J. Fenster, Emma S. Laurent, Kerry J. Ressler, and Elizabeth A. Phelps. 2022. "Prefrontal Cortex, Amygdala, and Threat Processing: Implications for PTSD." *Neuropsychopharmacology: Official Publication of the American College of Neuropsychopharmacology* 47 (1): 247–59.

"Big Life Headquarters." n.d. Accessed August 30, 2024. https://biglifehq.com.

Bryner, Jeanna. 2009. "Why Kids Ask Why." Live Science. November 23, 2009. https://www.livescience.com/5892-kids.html.

Cascio, Christopher N., Matthew Brook O'Donnell, Francis J. Tinney, Matthew D. Lieberman, Shelley E. Taylor, Victor J. Strecher, and Emily B. Falk. 2016. "Self-Affirmation Activates Brain Systems Associated with Self-Related Processing and Reward and Is Reinforced by Future Orientation." *Social Cognitive and Affective Neuroscience* 11 (4): 621–29.

Cass, Betty. 1937. "Barn Raising in 1843." *Wausau Daily Record-Herald*, June 24, 1937.

Chouinard, Michael M. 2007. "Children's Questions: A Mechanism for Cognitive Development." *Monographs of the Society for Research in Child Development* 72 (1): vii – ix,1–112;discussion113–26.

Clips, Huberman Lab. 2022. "What to Do & Not Do When Setting Goals | Dr. Emily Balcetis & Dr. Andrew Huberman." Youtube. August 3, 2022. https://www.youtube.com/watch?v=H1bDIREguok.

Coles, Nicholas A., Jeff T. Larsen, and Heather C. Lench. 2019. "A Meta-Analysis of the Facial Feedback Literature: Effects of Facial Feedback on Emotional Experience Are Small and Variable." *Psychological Bulletin* 145 (6): 610–51.

Comninos, Andreas. 2017. "Emotion Regulation Essentials: Your Brain's Threat System." *Mindfulness & Clinical Psychology Solutions* (blog). July 28, 2017. https://mi-psych.com.au/your-brains-threat-system/.

Dalton-Smith, Saundra. 2019. *Sacred Rest*. New York, NY: FaithWords.

Diniz, Geyze, Ligia Korkes, Luca Schiliró Tristão, Rosangela Pelegrini, Patrícia Lacerda Bellodi, and Wanderley Marques Bernardo. 2023. "The Effects of Gratitude Interventions: A Systematic Review and Meta-Analysis." *Einstein (Sao Paulo, Brazil)* 21 (August):eRW0371.

DLD Conference. 2014. "Rethinking Positive Thinking (Gabriele Oettingen, New York University) | DLDwomen 14." Youtube. July 23, 2014. https://www.youtube.com/watch?v=7mobxikaYgU.

Doran, G. T. 1981. "There's S.M.A.R.T. Way Write Management's Goals Objectives." *Management Review* 70 (11): 35–36.

"Famous Quotes." n.d. Thomas Edison. Accessed December 29, 2024. https://www.thomasedison.org/edison-quotes.

Goleman, Daniel P. 2011. *Working with Emotional Intelligence*. Bantam.

Health Tips. 2022. "Dr. Andrew Huberman on Reticular Activating System (RAS)." Youtube. June 9, 2022. https://www.youtube.com/watch?v=ruBJYNKKKXY&t=88s.

Holland, Kimberly. 2019. "Amygdala Hijack: What It Is, Why It Happens & How to Make It Stop." Healthline. April 22, 2019. https://www.healthline.com/health/stress/amygdala-hijack.

"Julian B. Rotter." n.d. Accessed December 30, 2024. https://psych.fullerton.edu/jmearns/rotter.htm.

Kappes, Heather Barry, and Gabriele Oettingen. 2011. "Positive Fantasies about Idealized Futures Sap Energy." *Journal of Experimental Social Psychology* 47 (4): 719–29.

Kappes, Heather Barry, Elizabeth J. Stephens, and Gabriele Oettingen. 2011. "Implicit Theories Moderate the Relation of Positive Future Fantasies to Academic Outcomes." *Journal of Research in Personality* 45 (3): 269–78.

Kraft, Tara L., and Sarah D. Pressman. 2012. "Grin and Bear It: The Influence of Manipulated Facial Expression on the Stress Response: The Influence of Manipulated Facial Expression on the Stress Response." *Psychological Science* 23 (11): 1372–78.

LeMay Center for Doctrine. n.d. "US Air Force Definitions: Sponsor, Mentor, Coach." US Air Force. Accessed September 12, 2024. https://www.af.mil/Portals/1/documents/Mentoring/Sponsor_Mentor_Coach_Definitions.pdf.

Lopez-Garrido, Gabriel. 2022. "Locus of Control Theory In Psychology: Definition & Examples." *Simply Psychology*, November. https://www.simplypsychology.org/locus-of-control.html.

Mary McKone, Ed D. 2024. "The Reticular Activating System (RAS)." *BrainWorks* (blog). March 27, 2024. https://www.brain-works.org/post/the-reticular-activating-system-ras.

Oettingen, Gabriele, and Thomas A. Wadden. 1991. "Expectation, Fantasy, and Weight Loss: Is the Impact of Positive Thinking Always Positive?" *Cognitive Therapy and Research* 15 (2): 167–75.

Oettingen, Gabriele, Doris Mayer, Jennifer S. Thorpe, Hanna Janetzke, and Solvig Lorenz. 2005. "Turning Fantasies about Positive and Negative Futures into Self-Improvement Goals." *Motivation and Emotion* 29 (4): 236–66.

"PrinciplesYou From Ray Dalio." n.d. Accessed December 30, 2024. https://principlesyou.com.

Robbins, Mel. 2019. "Take Control of Your Life." Read by the author. Audible audio ed., 6 hr., 36 min.

Robbins, Mel. 2023. *The High 5 Habit*. Carlsbad, CA: Hay House.

Smyth, Joshua M., Jillian A. Johnson, Brandon J. Auer, Erik Lehman, Giampaolo Talamo, and Christopher N. Sciamanna. 2018. "Online Positive Affect Journaling in the Improvement of Mental Distress and Well-Being in General Medical Patients with Elevated Anxiety Symptoms: A Preliminary Randomized Controlled Trial." *JMIR Mental Health* 5 (4): e11290.

Stevenson, Robert. 1969. "The Love Bug." Burbank, CA: Walt Disney Productions.

Thoele, David G., Cemile Gunalp, Danielle Baran, Jamie Harris, Douglas Moss, Ramona Donovan, Yi Li, and Marjorie A. Getz. 2020. "Health Care Practitioners and Families Writing Together: The Three-Minute Mental Makeover." *The Permanente Journal* 24:19.056.

Thome, Janine, Maria Densmore, Georgia Koppe, Braeden Terpou, Jean Théberge, Margaret C. McKinnon, and Ruth A. Lanius. 2019. "Back to the Basics: Resting State Functional Connectivity of the Reticular Activation System in PTSD and Its Dissociative Subtype." *Chronic Stress (Thousand Oaks, Calif.)* 3 (January):2470547019873663.

Ullrich, Philip M., and Susan K. Lutgendorf. 2002. "Journaling about Stressful Events: Effects of Cognitive Processing and Emotional Expression." *Annals of Behavioral Medicine: A Publication of the Society of Behavioral Medicine* 24 (3): 244–50.

Wang, Yingying, Lu Luo, Guanpeng Chen, Guoming Luan, Xiongfei Wang, Qian Wang, and Fang Fang. 2023. "Rapid Processing of Invisible Fearful Faces in the Human Amygdala." *The Journal of Neuroscience: The Official Journal of the Society for Neuroscience* 43 (8): 1405–13.

Webster, F. M. 1994. "The WBS." *PM Network* 8 (12): 40–46.

White, Paul. n.d. "Barn Raising: A Pioneer Economic and Social Necessity." Accessed December 30, 2024. https://www.history-articles.com/barn-raising.html.

Wiswede, Daniel, Thomas F. Münte, Ulrike M. Krämer, and Jascha Rüsseler. 2009. "Embodied Emotion Modulates Neural Signature of Performance Monitoring." *PloS One* 4 (6): e5754.

Yang, Hongfei, and Huizhong Li. 2020. "Training Positive Rumination in Expressive Writing to Enhance Psychological Adjustment and Working Memory Updating for Maladaptive Ruminators." *Frontiers in Psychology* 11 (May):789.